# Meditations on
# African Literature

# Meditations on African Literature

Edited by Dubem Okafor

*Contributions in Afro-American and African Studies, Number 201*

Greenwood Press
*Westport, Connecticut* • *London*

**Library of Congress Cataloging-in-Publication Data**

Meditations on African Literature / edited by Dubem Okafor.
     p. cm. — (Contributions in Afro-American and African studies, ISSN 0069–9624 ; no. 201)
    Includes bibliographical references and index.
    ISBN 0–313–29866–1 (alk. paper)
    1. African literature (English)—History and criticism.  2. Africa—Intellectual life—20th
century.  I. Okafor, Dubem.  II. Series.
PR9340M44   2001
820.9′96—dc21        99–462059

British Library Cataloguing in Publication Data is available.

Library of Congress Catalog Card Number: 99–462059
ISBN: 0–313–29866–1
ISSN: 0069–9624

First published in 2001

Greenwood Press, 88 Post Road West, Westport, CT 06881
An imprint of Greenwood Publishing Group, Inc.
www.greenwood.com

Printed in the United States of America

∞™

The paper used in this book complies with the
Permanent Paper Standard issued by the National
Information Standards Organization (Z39.48–1984).

10  9  8  7  6  5  4  3  2  1

## Dedication

His literary-cultural-scholarly trajectory is coterminous with the literary-critical history of Africa, for which he remains a major motivation, which he continues to influence, and to which he continues to contribute prolifically. His selfless commitment to education and teaching has resulted in the production of generations of tried, tested, and worthy African scholars, who are committed to continue the meritorious race that Obiechina began at the London University College at Ibadan, and concluded at Cambridge University where, in 1967, he became the *first* black person to earn that university's Ph.D. in English. For his vast and unsurpassed contributions to literature, literary scholarship and criticism, cultural studies, popular culture, education, and humanism, we humbly and gratefully dedicate *Meditations on African Literature* to Professor Emmanuel Nwafor Obiechina, *Onye Nkuzi*.

# Contents

# Preface

*Femi Osofisan and Dubem Okafor*

It is not insignificant that this very opportune reflection on African Literature, *Meditations on African Literature,* should be appearing now, when our field appears to be most hotly debated and contested, and no less contentious. At the same time, it is equally significant that it is being produced from the United States of America, and not from the continent of Africa. For one thing, today, almost all our best writers live outside the continent, and most often in the North American subcontinent. Almost all our best critics speak from their new homes in North American universities. The most creative novels, plays, and poems; the most arresting forms of criticism ("arresting" at least in their loudness) come from presses located in America or in the old colonial metropoles. Meanwhile, apart from the possible exception of South Africa, almost all our countries in Africa have virtually declared war on literacy and literary activity, as they regularly maul their writers in gleeful cannibal rites presided over by a Philistine political leadership, often in the form of undisguised military totalitarianism. On campuses, abandoned libraries and laboratories accumulate dust, while poorly paid, derided, and frustrated scholars take to the Bottle or to the Book—that is, the Koran or the Bible, rather than to books of rational enlightenment. Hence it is not insignificant, within this extraordinary context, which is peculiar to us Africans, that only two contributors to this volume currently live or work on the continent itself. Given the hitherto fertilizing role of scholars in the literary life of their countries, what does this geographical displacement mean to the present phase of African literature and its criticism? How much does this factor of exile invalidate or enhance current critical observation and conclusions on the subject, based as they are so often on palpable fallacies and impudent assumptions? What telling prognostics—whatever the theologians of Chaos Theory may say about such exercises—what facts about the future of our literature does this phenomenon of exile foreordinate? And most crucially, what does it portend for the overall life of our people? These questions come up inevitably because we are dealing with the area of African literature that is insistently *engage,* and because our most important creators of literature and the criticism of it believe firmly in the ineluctable link between the imaginative order and the collective destiny. This belief in an almost mystical union is amply illustrated by the quotation from a seminal essay by Africa's most important critic and poet, "The Dilemma of the African Intellectual in the Modern World." In that essay, the author, Emmanuel Obiechina, reveals that our writers in Africa (together with the critics) see themselves as intellectuals, rather than just as entertainers. This means that they accept for themselves certain responsibilities and roles within the lives of their communities. This view of the humanistic role of literature, and of the critics to respect and preserve it is, of course, out of date now in the West, but not for us; and it can indeed germinate fruitfully in a number of directions, as the chapters here illustrate. The first consideration, if such a role is to be credible at all, must naturally bear on the writer's communicability, on his success or otherwise in reaching to his audience. Hence, the most contentious point about African literature has always been the problematic one of its language.

The debate over whether the "inherited"/imposed languages of the erstwhile colonial powers, which have been pragmatically adopted as *lingua franca* by the political leadership of various countries after "independence," should also be accepted by writers for their creative works is prolonged here, in the chapters by Ogundele and Okafor. Their reexamination of the longstanding controversy is both energetic and passionate, and testifies, if anything, to the unyielding persistence of the agonies and anxieties that African intellectuals continue to experience on this cultural site. Nevertheless, the disagreements between the two scholars in their proposed solutions to the problem also illustrate eloquently the difficulties and the elusiveness of a final solution. And the question will continue to resurface and haunt us, I believe, until we reconcile ourselves to the reality of our historical experience and of our situation in the contemporary world, and accept that, beyond our individual preferences, "African literature" will continue to be written in *all the languages* of Africa whose orthographies have been formally settled. This also means, to reverse that statement, that all literature written in *any* language spoken and used in Africa will qualify to be called African literature. Of course, the master, Chinua Achebe, has repeatedly maintained this position. These languages will include, whether we like it or not, our *localized or domesticated* versions of the inherited European languages, some of which are even more widely spoken than our indigenous languages, because of which they are now already being reclaimed in some quarters as African languages!, and which, in addition, give us the advantage of direct access to international forums. Thus the "cacophony" that Okafor's chapter identifies as characterizing the linguistic scene, and that, at present breeds so much needless anxiety, may then come to be welcome as a creative and enabling heterogeny, a fertile kernel of multiple possibilities, from which Mao's celebrated hundred flowers can bloom. And we need to note, in parenthesis to this conclusion, that even those who, like Ngugi wa Thiong'o, push a contrary view, still find it expedient to advance their arguments, not in the languages they themselves advocate, but in the very European language(s) they condemn.

The issue of the audience is, of course, pertinent to these concerns, and significantly, the chapters by Lindfors, Sugnet, and Ukala deal with this area. Lindfors seizes the opportunity to revisit his controversial exercise in literary statistics, a quantification of literary success, which he appropriately entitles FART (Famous Authors Reputation Test). Many writers were scandalized, when Lindfors first unveiled this project some years back; one hopes that this revised and updated version will dispel their displeasure. In any event, Lindfors should be commended for his dogged assiduity and undaunted courage. Very importantly, Lindfors' project invites us to examine and interrogate the silences and absences in, as well as the accuracy of, the relative positions, especially, of the lesser known and less popular writers of the Reputation Chart; it invites us to consider the fate and reputation of cultural workers whose labors are undertaken outside Europe and America in an environment where dramatic presentations are rarely reported or reviewed, and where academic journals are spasmodic and expensive to produce, resulting in the consignment of numerous papers, seminars, doctoral theses, masters' dissertations, and final-year, B.A. long essays to dusty files. Lindfors does not presume to possess all the answers, but his essay is very important in pointing us to these problems. FART remains a unique contribution to the sociological-quantitative analysis of African literature.

In his chapter, Sugnet focuses on Achebe, and lucidly analyzes the reasons for his (unintended) "double audience" against the premise of a "hidden" colonialist polemic, concluding that Achebe is "not just crossing a line between two fixed entities, inside and outside, or African and Western; he's continually negotiating a fluid boundary between cultures that are being constructed by the writing itself." And in his own chapter, Ukala is concerned with formalizing the defining parameters of drama in the indigenous tradition. His tool here is impersonation, for which he gives a somewhat controversial definition. But once this definition is accepted, the rest of his argument is persuasive. Ukala's nativistic concerns connect us with Okagbue's chapter, which discusses African revanchism in the Caribbean, by exploring the existing repertoire of theater in this Diaspora, with special reference to the works of the Nobel Laureate, Derek Walcott.

From Okagbue's, we move to the chapter by Egudu whose conventional approach echoes back to Socrates, in his presumption of an a priori ethical imperative to the literary genius. Hence his contribution here is a study of five Nigerian novels from the point of view, not of their hermeneutic structure or aesthetic achievement, but rather of their contribution to public morality, especially in the context of the Nigerian government's War Against Indiscipline (WAI). The underlying assumption here is the social-political function of the African writer-artist-intellectual, which imperative has defined African cultural productions. One could actually extend the Socratic logic of Egudu's argument to its ultimate conclusion by reading the constructed text of WAI against itself, thereby unmasking its inherent self-contradiction, and showing us where it is constrained because of itself to negate the very values it seeks to promote, which are the values of the novels and authors that Egudu studies here. In his own related study of Achebe's *A Man of the People*, Okafor marks the overdetermined contradiction inherent in the very "soul" of the superstructure of the Nigerian polity, which has been responsible for the tortuous and bedevilled ethical and political-historical trajectory of that country.

This book recognizes the importance, the place, and the contribution of women to our society and culture. Thus, though the many female scholars who were invited to do so did not find it very opportune to contribute to *this* volume, four chapters written by men focus on women and women's issues, from various angles. Nwankwo takes issues here with some feminist critics of Achebe, asserting rightly that Eve has never been the ancestral model of Igbo (African) womanhood, and hence Achebe could not be correctly faulted for not basing his women characters on this Judeo-Christian icon. It is not an accident, he avers, "that the world of all the female characters in [Achebe's] works has no room for those familiar dreadful personages who haunt the female consciousness in some [European] fiction and reality—the sexually depraved, the licentious wifebeaters, the evil seductresses, and other variations of the traitorous descendants of Eve. They are mostly absent [in Achebe] because they were likewise absent in traditional Igbo society. [Achebe's] is the expression of a consciousness in tune with Igbo history and culture, the hallmark of a storyteller whose craft is part of the story" (1993 vi).

This is a very powerful and eloquent defense, which reminds us of some earlier works, especially the one by Jeyifo, "Okonkwo and His Mother: *Things Fall Apart* and Issues of Gender in the Constitution of African Postcolonial Discourse" (*Callaloo* 1993), which transacts a more persuasive feminist reading. In any case, we do not forget that Achebe himself has returned to give a shattering response to the feminist assault in his latest novel, *Anthills of the Savannah*, and absolve himself of the earlier charges.

In a similar perspective, Echeruo refutes the argument that the colonial subject only passively receives and reproduces the colonial tropes of inferiorization. Through a lucid and perceptive reading of the newspapers of the colonial era in Lagos, and weaving his inquiry around the subject of "woman" as variously constructed by metropolitan papers and their Lagos counterparts, Echeruo discovers how Blyden was the first to give a "sophisticated" rereading of "woman" and the colonial subject, by redefining the problem essentially as an imperial and racial one. Echeruo very convincingly proves his thesis that the scholars are mistaken who imagine that the colonials merely accepted these prejudiced constructions of their own world and their persons.

The woman as author is Nazareth's theme, and specifically, the works of Grace Ogot, whom the prevailing books of criticism seem to have overlooked. Nazareth presents this author in his characteristically easy flowing prose, appropriately making use of copious quotations from works that are unfamiliar, convincing us that Ogot is an author who merits serious attention and rehabilitation.

The chapters by Jeyifo and Okpewho raise and discuss the crucial question: How will the fact of exile and physical relocation affect the products of our creativity and criticism? To answer this question, Jeyifo gives a symptomatic reading of Obiechina's essay referred to earlier, and notes his proto-Fanonist position, what Jeyifo defines as "a rationalist-nationalist orthodoxy, " because it valorizes the intellectual on the eighteenth-century ideal of reason. It is from this position that Obiechina comes to laud the achievement of our creative writers in reconnecting with our roots, while he berates the critics for having deviated and allowed themselves to be "intoxicated" and "trapped" by the inebriating resonances of Euromodernist discourses. But in response, Jeyifo gives a deconstructive reading of Obiechina himself, showing the silences that betray the fissures of his "totalizing vision" of an African "centeredness" and hence the weakness of his argument. The postmodernism that Obiechina rails against, Jeyifo points out, a la Jameson, is the inevitable "cultural dominant" of this stage of globalized, transnational late-capitalism, into which Africa has been long inducted by colonialism, and from which it can not at the moment be divorced. We are, therefore, just as vulnerable to the ascendancy of the "epistemologies of dispersion" as all the rest of the capitalist world, because our society's mental laborers are no longer, in Jeyifo's metonymic summary, typified by thinkers like Ogotommeli but rather by the Ireles, the Ogunyemis—and the Obiechinas! Furthermore, the separation of the professional "philosopher" from the community, which exile only makes more acute, is a factor that has always marked intellectual work (as in the town *versus* gown cliché), and because of this, Obiechina should not spontaneously see all re/dislocated intellectuals as tragically trapped schizophrenics.

If Jeyifo's deconstructive arguments sound complex, Okpewho's position is succinct, even if as equally underwritten by anguish. Okpewho surveys the entire Commonwealth region in order to answer the question—what will be the future direction of our literature? Appropriately tracing the cause of the present intellectual exodus to the failures of our societies and the viciousness of our governments, he observes that "the decay and the degradation that most of our writers have constantly decried have reached such proportions as to severely deter the growth of art in many countries. Writers are thrown into jail on the slightest pretext; increasingly fewer people can provide for themselves or their families; and the general frustration has given rise to social insecurity and political anomie. The effect of all this is to force many writers into exile." From this he predicts that "as long as the Commonwealth and its citizens continue to be subject to geopolitical forces that cause one kind of displacement or another, for so long will the genius of the writer try to find its range in the new environment." The reader is invited to discover the rest of his very interesting conclusions. It is proper that we pay tribute in the way that this book attests to our men of eminence.

It is a credit to Dr. Okafor that he has been able to assemble such thinkers to reflect on the present state of our literature in an age when our continent seems to be voraciously thirsty for the blood of those who insist on placing primal value on intellect and imaginative power, on integrity and spiritual adventurousness; an age in which our literary and cultural labors and products have not only not been adequately valorized, but continue to be seriously contested. The editor and contributors to this book have done us all proud, and we are both honored and delighted to present *Meditations on African Literature* to everyone interested in Africa and its literature.

# Chapter One

# The Cacophonous Terrain of Nigerian/African Literature

## *Dubem Okafor*

African Literature is not only a contested terrain, but the medium of its production and of its discussion is, to say the least, cacophonous. The situation can be likened to that in folk medicine, where the healer hired to exorcise the demons begins to run from the goblins. One can only speculate as to the fate of the possessed and troubled patient. One might also recall the other situation in folklore where people begin to chase after rats and lizards fleeing from the conflagrating house, rather than help to put out the flames. The same thing is happening in our field. Some of our creative writers agonize over the burden of linguistic expression, over which they have no choice, because colonialism had made that choice for them, and had made them more competent in an alien tongue; others are confronted by a situation where, were they even competent in their mother tongues, they would still need to communicate with their countrymen who speak several different languages; still, others attempt a lose-lose strategy that would have works first written in "native" languages translated into several hundred African languages and major European ones (where this latter strategy succeeds, the writers, of course, profit immensely from an almost global market!). In the meantime, critics and students of literature, whose job it is to make the creative labors of our writers accessible to their diverse readers, are themselves engaged primarily with the splitting of hairs and the spilling of ink—chasing after the rats and lizards!—over what languages the writers should use in addressing their readers. In the heat of academicist combat, the primary duties of both writers and critics are sidelined. To borrow a phrase from David Lloyd, the result is that, so far, African literature has failed to live up to the so-called "responsibility of literature, and other cultural forms" (1987 xi).

But one may ask: What is the present urgency of the stale debate? Indeed, the acrimony began way back in 1962. But it has become anything but stale. And it seems to me that the issue needs to be resolved one way or another, if writers and critics alike are ever to attend to their respective primary responsibilities. The immediate impetus for the present exercise is the Preface to a recent book of poems by the well known Nigerian novelist, Nkem Nwankwo. In that short preface to *A Song for Fela & Other Poems* (1993), Nwankwo declares his intention to "reopen the debate about decolonization of African literature," and asks quite pertinently, "how does one write poetry in a post-colonial situation addressing other colonials in the language and accents of the former colonial master?" (i). In this preface, which the author quickly declines to call a manifesto in the tradition of William Wordsworth's "Preface to the *Lyrical Ballads*," Nwankwo's anger appears to be driven by the same force that energizes Jamaica Kincaid when in *A Small Place*, she asks:

For isn't it odd that the only language I have in which to speak of this crime [the colonial depradation of her country, Antigua] is the language of the criminal who committed the crime? And what can that really mean? For the language of the criminal can contain only the goodness of the criminal's deed. The language of the criminal can explain and express the deed only from the criminal's point of view. (31–32)

Nwankwo is willing to dispense with Kincaid's questions and explanations, and would rather blast the head of Prospero with his dane-gun of discourse, which he has ingenuously called "cuss words," and which he endows with:

the virtue of clarity. There is no ambiguity, when these words are divested of selfconscious, learned, obfuscating energy. Cuss words not only bring robustness to speech, they are part of the long tradition of rebellion, lancing the boil of rage, helping to vent smoldering hatred, and liberating Caliban's creative powers. (*A Song for Fela* ii)

Nwankwo's strictures on Prospero do not end with his "cussing" him; he is ready to jettison Prospero's linguistic, political, and philosophical categories altogether, as well as "invent his own dialect, to bear the burden of his mongrel existence" (iii). An examination of Nwankwo's poetry to determine how far he has succeeded in dispensing with the linguistic bequest of his colonial master belongs in another discursive occasion. For now, it is enough that the preface reminds us, not only of the persistence of the linguistic-political-cultural problem, but also of its urgency. And underlying both the recalcitrance and urgency of the problem is the inescapable diagnosis: in the marketplace of tongues that designates the Nigerian (and African) cultural space, our creative-cultural labors are wont to be "null cacophony" as long as we lack community and "commonalty"; the kind of commonalty that David Lloyd talks about with reference to Irish literature: "In such a literature all Irishmen could trace a common origin in the very commonalty of the history of their difference" (3).

In Nigeria, for example, such dreaming of commonalty has continued to be elusive, rendered almost impossible because the very construction or constitution of the identity of nation was doomed, *ab initio*, by the structural craftsmanship of the colonial political engineers who made sure that difference rather than commonalty would continue to define the corporate political existence of Nigeria and its cultural articulations. Even though one knows that the metropole still exerts influence by remote control, direct colonial domination ended in Nigeria some forty years ago, and one should not spend the rest of eternity bemoaning that historic encounter. Generations of thinking women and men, including writers, have flourished, who have had, and still have, the opportunity to embark upon unselfish introspection, social analyses, and a course of treatment for Nigeria's bane. But not much has been done generally in that direction. Thus, it is ironic that what Lloyd says in discussing Matthew Arnold's ethnocentric and imperializing theorization applies so aptly to Nigeria, by reason of its negation in practice: "each writer's work, to a greater or lesser degree, prefigures the ultimate unity or synthesis of ethnic types in the production of which his works participate both as evidence and as influence. The aesthetic work . . . represents in itself a unity that is prior to it while at the same time, by drawing together disparate ethnic characteristics, it prefigures the future self-reflexive realization of that unity" (12).

No one seriously talks about "unity" or the "synthesis of ethnic types" in Nigeria, and I must make it clear, as I continue, that since my affiliation and loyalty is with "the quadrangle," my castigation throughout the discussion is of the comprador elite, the new-fangled bourgeoisie, the counterfeit, opportunistic, and self-serving intellectuals, and the political charlatans and rulers (never leaders) who have continued to misdirect the course of affairs in Nigeria. The quadrangle has always gotten along, and, even in the cacophonous linguistic situations in Nigeria, has either learnt the languages of the others or created a lingua franca of harmonious coexistence and inter-ethnic communication. But they have always been exploited by the wielders of economic and political powers who exacerbate ethnic rivalry and tension by always appealing to primordial, cultural, and linguistic differences. Thus, the dilemma that is the subject of this chapter is a problem, not of the people *as such*, but one that has been sustained by the elite and the intellectuals who, apparently, stand to benefit from the preservation of the cacophonous status quo.

So, while scholars and intellectuals elsewhere, like David Lloyd from Ireland, are interested in finding ways of resolving sociopolitical and cultural disarticulations in their societies, what we have in Nigeria can be best exemplified by the bickering exchange that took place not too long ago on the pages of the journal *Okike* (1982), [Okike = divine creation; creativity], a journal dedicated to creativity and scholarship in Africa, and edited (then) by Chinua Achebe, the father of African literature, between two accomplished Nigerian writers, critics, and university professors. One, Emeka Okeke-Ezigbo, an Igbo, and the other, Femi Osofisan, a Yoruba, both understand the multifarious problems of Nigeria, including the language problem which is partly the subject of Okeke-Ezigbo's article ("The Role of the Nigerian Writer in a Carthaginian Society," *Okike* XXI 28–37) that the editors saw fit to submit to Osofisan for a critique that would be printed alongside the article in the same number of the journal. While it is my conviction that, sitting face-to-face and parleying, these two critics would agree on most of the points and counterpoints of their respective articles, the trouble with Nigeria is such that even where, in matters of vital importance, like that of language, it is possible to come to an understanding and agreement, acrimonious debates which resolve nothing are the preferred route. Thus, Osofisan's critique, "Enter the Carthaginian Critic . . . ?" (*Okike* XXI 38–44), begins with a quick disclaimer of any "kinship," intellectual or otherwise, with Okeke-Ezigbo: "Okeke-Ezigbo's . . . tone is bold and acerbic. The editor must have thought of me spontaneously as a kindred spirit. It is promptly to refute this implied kinship that I have agreed to write this commentary" (38). Osofisan then goes on to respond, almost line by line, to Okeke-Ezigbo's essay. My concern here is not whether one scholar is right and the other wrong; my concern is with their refusal of consensus or agreement, which is both very possible and desirable, if their intentions are to contribute to the task of solving Nigeria's linguistic dilemma and of nation/community building in the bedevilled and distracted state of Nigeria.

In a country of "about 250 languages" (Barbag-Stoll 1983 102), and their 1001 dialects, if one jettisoned the colonial and neocolonial language, which made possible in the first place the exchange between these two scholars, what would one have in its place? There have been cries for the recuperation, development, and creative deployment of indigenous languages. But it seems to me that such cries are meant primarily to call attention to the criers, and not necessarily to the issue, because no serious-minded person really believes that that would facilitate interethnic communication among the many language and dialect groups. And no one has addressed the prospects of the epistemological nightmare and curricular disaster that will attend that linguistic free-for-all. If the miraculous happened—a rare dream in Nigeria—and everyone acquired literacy and competence in their indigenous languages, and writers sprouted overnight who created in these languages, would not the proliferation of such literatures still require translations to get to the larger audiences? Would that miracle then enable the cohesion of the cultural-linguistic sections or drive them further apart? Whose interests are actually being served by these nativistic surges of linguistic subnationalisms? The peoples who want to get along, or the mis-rulers and opportunists as well as their masters who profit from the politico-cultural cleavages? In the end are we helping to build a nation or finally to quicken the explosion of the dry and ready oil-bean pod of state? Okeke-Ezigbo's suggested adoption of Pidgin is dismissed swiftly and even derided, whereas it might well be that that linguistic salad bowl is what holds the secret of Nigeria's corporate being. But the trouble with Nigeria is that while everyone knows the solution to Nigeria's bane, everyone is busy, like the cowardly proverbial urchin, trying to capture the rats, even shrews, fleeing from conflagrating homesteads instead of helping first to put the fires out. Finally, regarding the contentious exchange between our exemplary scholars, one only needs to say that we have had enough of the divisiveness, and that vituperative name-calling and *ad-hominem* discursive bellicosity hardly belong in cultural criticism.

But this exchange, which took place in 1982, is important for pointing to the peculiar resilience and recalcitrance of problems in Nigeria. Some time ago, I had actually hoped, wishfully it has turned out, to have had the last word, and thus to end the fractious debate over the language question. I had then written, among other things:

Since some have argued that a writer cannot sincerely and meaningfully be engaged in cultural nativism who writes in an alien language, we wish, first of all to dismiss the language question and, hopefully, to end the debate that has been going on around it.

The argument has been raging for years around this question with undiminished vigour and rancour. The protraction of the debate raises a fundamental question as to the very sincerity and seriousness of the contestants' intentions. For, I believe, they all realize the futility of the exercise and are merely flaunting facile erudition. This is because all the points adduced for and against the use of a "colonial" language ignore a basic issue, which is the socio-historical inevitability of such usage. And the condescending advice to writers in a country like Nigeria where there are about two hundred languages—not dialects—to write in their different languages if they mean to address their countrymen, sounds puerile, to say the least. The point is that that historical "accident" which produced diffident Africans, which produced cultural apes, which produced politicians who are content to be agents of Westminster or Paris, which made it imperative for African countries to use English or French or Portuguese as their official languages, also created that situation which has compelled African writers to use the same languages that colonized them in addressing their audience. Whether the writers have their ears cocked to the West or have their eyes on the bigger slice of the gains of the publishing trade accruing from their mastery of the language of Prospero is beside the point. Like Caliban, they have been given the language of the master and they have learnt to curse in it as well. Until those factors are changed which colluded to bequeath to Caliban a strange tongue, all arguments are a futile exercise in sémantics and we can comfortably dispense with Obi Wali's prophecy which foresaw a dead end of African literature unless and until African "writers and their Western midwives accept the fact that any true African literature must be written in African languages." (Okafor 1980 45–46)

It was actually Obi Wali (murdered in 1993), who started off the debate with his controversial presentation at the 1962 African Writers' Conference titled "The Dead End of African Literature," later published in *Transition* IV: 10 (1963). Incidentally, Obi Wali taught me "Introduction to Literature" at the University of Nigeria, Nsukka, and it is interesting that during that one-year- long, nine-credit course, not only was no mention ever made of the literatures produced in indigenous Nigerian languages, but, apart from J.P. Clark's *Song of a Goat* (a play), and Ngugi's *Weep Not, Child,* not much else was talked about or taught that was African literature. Instead, we foraged among English, European (in English translation), and American literatures, relishing such texts as *The Great Gatsby*, *Room at the Top*, and *The Wild Duck*, and imbibing a sturdy dose of English metaphysical and romantic poetry.

But the controversy that he inaugurated has not only continued unabated, but has recently polarized into the Achebe and Ngugi polemical schools or camps: on one side are those who, like Ngugi, see "African languages and traditions as expressive of the collective essence of a pristine traditional community" and insist that true African independence requires a literature of one's own in one's own language (Appiah 1991 157). It does not occur to these followers of Obi Wali, apostles of essentialism, that they might, in fact, through a curious political/ideological irony, be preaching the same cultural relegation, marginalization, and, eventually, silence, through inferiorization and secondarization of African cultural productions, which imperialism once arranged, and which have in no wise abated. For we all know that even now "the usual attitude of Commonwealth-Literature scholars toward *Third World verbal art in vernacular languages* has been one, not merely of benign neglect, but rather of blissful, complacent ignorance" (Davis and Maes-Jelinek, 1990 95; my emphasis). Notice that even in this large-hearted and benevolent critique of the negligent attitude and unconcern of scholars, such cultural productions in indigenous languages do not get called "literature"; they belong, instead, in that undignified and nebulous category of "verbal art." One is not surprised by that relegation of third world "verbal arts" to the dustbin of inconsequence, which has nothing to do with the quantity or literary/aesthetic quality of such vernacular labors. The truth is that "no one will learn the language of a people without any economic or political power" (95). And economic and political disenfranchisement remains the fate of the laboring peoples of the third world.

On the other side of the polemical divide are those who are persuaded by the "fatalistic logic" that enables Achebe to see the use of the imperial language (or is it still that?) as a matter of prophetic inevitability, but that is amenable, at the same time, to creative manipulation that purges the language of its Eurocentric *sprachgeist*. Since Achebe, in his own creative practice, has shown this to be possible, his position becomes an eloquent and effective contestation and repudiation of the supremacist and imperialist concept of *sprachgeist* which assigns essentialistic attributes and spirit to a place and people whose language thus possesses a magic of meaning-making that no other people can access.

It is this belief in the mystique of *sprachgeist* that enables Thomas Davis to write, in his article on "Our National Language," that:

The language, which grows up with a people, is conformed to their organs, descriptive of their climate, constitution, and manners, mingled inseparably with their history and their soil, fitted beyond any other language to express their prevalent thoughts in the most natural and efficient way. To impose another language on such a people is to send their history adrift among the accidents of translation—'tis to tear their identity from all places—'tis to substitute arbitrary signs for picturesque and suggestive names—'tis to cut off the entail of feeling, and separate the people from their forefathers by a deep gulf—'tis to corrupt their very organs, and abridge their power of expression. (qtd. in Lloyd 66–67)

These are the effects that colonialism and colonial education, and with them the imposition of the English language, were supposed to have had on all colonized peoples. In Nigeria, it wasn't quite deleteriously the case. For English, had it succeeded in displacing indigenous languages, would, indeed, have given the people an alternative tongue with which to transact interethnic communicative acts and thus, if not completely, eliminated the consequences of multiethnicity and linguistic cacophony. But it did not quite do that, so that among the quadrangle, the indigenous languages, as well as the incipient lingua franca, are very much alive and well, while among the elite, including the writers, it is a case of serious bilingualism that cannot be simplistically addressed by the Ngugian either/or facility. In real life, including linguistic, situations, the "barbaric simple-minded-ness" of such either/or residue of Western philosophical tradition, which always bifurcates the world into a hierarchized evaluative binarity that recognizes only two terms: inside/outside, indigenous/alien, Western/traditional, black/white, is not always sustainable. In fact, as Achebe sees it, "I see no situation in which I will be presented with a Draconian choice . . . between English and Igbo. For me no either/or; I insist on both" (1989 61).

Moreover, one begins really to wonder, with Achebe, why English should continue to be called a colonial or imperial language. Does that language still belong to any one country, imperial or not? And with all the creative mutation and indigenization it has undergone in such resourceful places as Nigeria, can it still qualify as a non-African language? And so Achebe dilates on the question of language thus:

There has been an impassioned controversy about an African literature in non-African languages. But what is a non-African language? English and French certainly. But what about Arabic? What about Swahili even? Is it then a question of how long the language has been present on African soil? If so, how many years should constitute effective occupation? For me it is again a pragmatic matter. A language spoken by Africans on African soil, a language in which Africans write, justifies itself. (93)

So, for Achebe and the pragmatists, not only will English continue to be used, but they "intend to do unheard of things with it" (74). It is my belief that these "unheard of things" are the recipe for the long-elusive linguistic-ethnic harmony in Nigeria. For with the evolution of a lingua franca devoid of any derogating socioeconomic class implications, Nigerians of all "tribes and tongues" will have been given a common tongue with which they can begin the song of unity and community-building.

But these unheard-of things have not yet been given full chance. For the circus performers and academic/intellectual gladiators are still on the stage, unexhausted by a fractious debate that has now gone on without reprieve for forty-odd years. Thus special issues of *Research in African Literatures* were devoted completely to the old question of language (*RAL* volume XXI 1990).

But the remarkable thing about the continuing debate is that it designates our predilection for cyclicity and circularity, which are no longer restricted to the movement of the seasons and the reckoning of time in African societies, but extend to the general direction of affairs, be they economic, political, or academic-cultural.

This may, perhaps, very well account for the perpetual state of stagnation, lack of development and progress, and continuing dependency of Africa. For it is clear from reading the entries in *RAL* (1990) that none of them represents an advance on the points and counterpoints enunciated at the 1962 African Writers' Conference; they have simply restated, reformulated, disputed, contested, and not progressed beyond, those well-worn suggestions, first put forward in Kampala.

In his contribution to the debate, Biodun Jeyifo (*RAL* XXI.1 [Spring 1990] 33-48) gives a useful definition of culturalism as the sharing of an ethnic identity and a common "native" language between writer and reader who both live in the same culture and are "rooted in its customs, mores and codes" (38). It is not clear, however, how such a "rooted" writer can still connect the "freedom of artistic expression, experimentation, and innovation with a commitment to the task of constructing a socialist democracy in the conditions of underdevelopment" (43). It seems to me that this requirement of the writer must take cognizance of the multiplicity of cultures and native languages in Nigeria, and of the dilemma of many writers who, at best, are only bilingual (in English and in their own particular native languages), and, at worst, have lost their native tongues in a colonial/neocolonial condition, appropriately designated *glottophagia*, and must thus sing their anguish in the tongue which, in the first place, had colonized them.

If the writer is the sensitive point of the society; if he/she is the calibrated anemometer of that society; if the writer is indeed his/her society's teacher, who intends to show it where the rains began to beat it and where it dried itself, how can he/she afford not to communicate to the generality of that society? How can s/he write in a lingua, or, in fact, cultic lingo, which is inaccessible to the majority of the members of that society?

Chinua Achebe, who espouses this fundamental pedagogic and didactic role for the writer, has himself blazed the trail by writing in a style whose surface clarity cloaks the profundity and complexity of thought, and that some have called "translation" (see Okeke-Ezigbo 1984), but happens to be accessible and comprehensible to anyone averagely competent in the English language. And he is definitely not engaged in translation, even though his writings embody the Igbo world view, and even though the palimpsest is clearly Igbo (see Zabus 1991). Achebe's creative use of the English language is only an intimation of the "unheard of things." Unfortunately, while he has had a following, Achebe's footsteps have not generally been followed by many important writers whose texts, like those of Wole Soyinka (see *The Road*) and Kalu Uka (see *A Consummation of Fire*), remain linguistic acrobatics and teasers incapable of speaking to the many.

The need remains urgent, therefore, for a body of literature that can function as the center of articulation or cohesion or commonalty of the various cultural-linguistic sections. Such a literature cannot lack for those literary ingredients from the cultural doxa or repertoire of the various ethnicities that will make it not only meaningfully relevant, but importantly accessible, to them. Because these cultural sections are still largely oral, the task for the writers, as Abiola Irele summarizes it, is actively "to write an oral culture" (*RAL* XXI.1 61). Irele goes on to explain that:

Within the very form of expression of the modern African writer, the tensions and ambiguities that mark the African writer's situation are reproduced. The question that presents itself to the African writer then becomes how to create a formal harmony between expression and the objective reference of the expression. Formulated differently, the problem of the African writer employing a European language is: how to write an oral culture. (61)

Irele's position is important for my argument because it goes beyond diagnosis to a prescription or a solution. The futility of beating the expiring horses of native languages is recognized, and a case is being made for a creative practice that, by utilizing material from the fauna and flora of local languages and culture in a creative deployment of the domesticated English language, will both transcend the ethnolinguistic divide, and make English a homely tongue. According to Irele:

The fact of a direct progression from the oral literature is important here, since it is a question not merely of drawing upon material from the oral tradition, but essentially of re-presenting such material through the medium of print in order to give wider currency as well as new expressions to forms that are already structured within the languages themselves. This practice does not preclude a modification of the traditional forms within the new modes; indeed, such modification is inevitable . . . (given) the assimilation of modes and conventions of the Western literary culture. (57)

If Irele's position sounds both sensible and practicable, it still does not command the reasoned consideration of some critics, because the argument must continue *ad nauseam*. Whereas Irele has clearly identified the problem, "the situation of dual competence in an African and a European language [as] indicative of a fundamental issue of modern African expression raised by the situation of diaglossia" (57), a situation I have chosen to describe as cacophonous polyglossia, there are still many who would keep at that dead horse of language. Thus Mlana, in the same volume of *RAL*, is indignant:

How can an African writer today address the African masses without using their African languages? We are all aware that, even though our countries have maintained English, French, or Portuguese as national languages for over twenty years, these are not the languages of the people. The majority of all African countries' populations still communicate in the indigenous languages which are their mother-tongues. The writer, in a way, seems to have no choice but to write in these languages. Writers who use languages foreign to their audiences also place themselves outside the community and operate as outsiders, as people who can reach their audiences only through translation. (*RAL* XXI.4 10)

That is the point. The problems of Nigeria happen to be more intractable and complex than those of some other countries. And where no institution in Nigeria can be called truly national because languages and ethnicities continue to pull the country from/in 200 different directions, the need for unity and cohesion is more urgent, and we cannot afford the luxury of the examples of places like England, for example, where, after centuries of confusion, the Wessex dialect achieved ascendancy over the other dialects as the carrier of culture and means of national communication. Moreover, we are not talking of *dialects but languages* in Nigeria where, were I to write my poetry in Igbo for instance, I would be making sense only to those who have literacy and competence in the language. And were Soyinka to write his plays and poetry in Yoruba, he would make sense to me only after they had been translated into Igbo or English. And it makes no sense to suggest that people learn the others' languages, for one is hardly aware of any polyglot anywhere in the world who has demonstrated competence in 200 languages, as there are in Nigeria. This fact does not, however, deter Mlana who dismisses this problem as he goes on:

Writing in the mother-tongue for the African writer may require not only writing in the writer's mother-tongue but also in the mother-tongues of one's audience [what a task!]. There are many cases where writers are actually fluent in other African languages but refrain from using them on the grounds of political or ethnic prejudice. In situations where the writer is not competent in the audience's languages, the question of translation from the writer's mother-tongue to other African languages becomes important. . . . It is high time we emphasized the need for translations into the different languages of our linguistically diverse audiences. (13)

The whole ponderous impracticability of Mlana's "noble" and "modest" proposal strengthens the case for that medium of transethnic, translinguistic, and transdialectal communication that I have chosen to call *Nigerian language.* Indeed, I am happy to be making this bold suggestion now because, at long last, it would appear that that most militant advocate of linguistic nativism, Ngugi wa Thiong'o, has recognized the intractable dilemma confronting those writers and scholars who would follow in his trail, and especially those who, unlike him, have not achieved or attained the name and fame that ensure that publishers in every metropole will, like vultures, scramble to publish anything and everything issuing from his pen, in whatever language, even in languages yet unfabricated. So, in his Preface to the latest collection of his essays (1993), Ngugi clearly articulates the problem:

There are two [of my essays] that give me special satisfaction: "English, a Language for the World?" and "Many Years Walk to Freedom: Welcome Home Mandela! " because they are translations from the Gikuyu originals. The first piece was part of a BBC seminar on English as a possible language for the world held on 27 October 1988. The translation was later broadcast on the BBC World Service. The English version . . . and the Gikuyu original . . . were first published in the 1990 Fall issue of the *Yale Journal of Criticism.* The second piece, commissioned by EMERGE, . . . was the lead article in their March 1990 issue featuring the historic release of Nelson Mandela. But whereas the Gikuyu original of the piece on language has been published in the *Yale Journal,* the Gikuyu original of the Mandela piece is still in my drawer among a good number of others [WHY?]. In their different destinies, the two pieces illustrate the difficulties in the way of those writing theoretical, philosophical, political and journalistic prose in an African language. . . . The Gikuyu language community is for instance largely within Kenya. There are no journals or newspapers in the language inside or outside Kenya. This is true of all the other African languages in Kenya apart from the

All-Kenya national language, Kiswahili. This means that those who write in African languages are confronted with a dearth of outlets for publication and therefore platforms for critical debate among those using the languages. They can only publish in translation or else borrow space from European languages journals and both options are clearly not solutions. The situation does not help much in the development of conceptual vocabulary in these languages to cope with modern technology, the sciences and the arts. The growth of writing in African languages will need a community of scholars and readers in those very languages, who will bring into the languages the wealth of literature on modern technology, arts and sciences. For this they need platforms. It is a vicious circle. So while the two pieces mirror my current involvement in the struggle to move the centre of our literary engagements from European languages to a multiplicity of locations in our languages, they also illustrate the frustrations in the way of immediate and successful realisation. (xiii–xiv)

This excerpt speaks for itself and clearly demonstrates Ngugi's late recognition that the options to "publish in translation or else borrow space from European languages journals . . . are clearly not solutions" (xiv). One is, therefore, taken aback to read, a few pages after the Preface that for Ngugi:

Joseph Conrad had a certain amount of attraction. He was Polish, born in a country and a family that had known only the pleasures of domination and exile. He learnt English late in life and yet he had chosen to write in it, a borrowed language, despite his fluency in his native tongue and in French. And what is more he had made it to the great tradition of English literature. Was he not already an image of what we the new African writers, like the Irish writers before us, Yeats and others, could become? (5)

Ngugi's question deserves a reverberating "No." For Conrad can in no way be held up as a model for the new African writers. The suggestion itself is outrageous. Conrad was white, worked in the service of empire, and wrote (wittingly or no) to perpetuate racist stereotypes of the *other*, the savage and subhuman prowlers among beasts in the jungles of the Congo, Africa. More relevantly, however, Conrad's decision to write in English was his adult, deliberate *choice*, a luxury that colonialism and colonial education denied many an African who was literally forced to learn English and despise the "native tongue." Conrad was fluent in three languages while most African writers write fluently only in English, even though they also speak their native tongues. Many Africans are making a serious study of their native tongues quite late in life. Conrad made it to "the great tradition of English literature" not because he had written better novels than other writers in English whose native tongue like Conrad's is not English; he made it to that tradition because he was *white* and wrote major contributions to the monuments of imperialism and the orientalizing/Africanizing Eurocentric tradition. That is why Conrad is widely taught and studied in the English departments of universities all over the world, while, in some places, the name of even such a writer as Chinua Achebe may remain unheard of; that is why Wole Soyinka, winner of the 1986 Nobel Prize for Literature, could be Visiting Professor at Cambridge in the Anthropology, but not in the English or Comparative literature, Department. Ngugi's Marxian faith in the goodness of

man that anchors his unrepentant universalism should be tempered by the knowledge that the *Yale Journal of Criticism* does not go about soliciting essays written
in Gikuyu or Swahili or Igbo from just anybody. His call for frenzied cultural
productions in *all* languages in Africa seems to me, therefore, to be a prescription
for disaster and cultural Babel, a complication and exacerbation of the prevalent
cacophony. Being that I myself have been part of the formation of the text and
pretext of literatures from Nigeria and an active participant in the cacophonous
drama of its linguistic multiplicity, I wish to end this section on Ngugi by asking a
few questions: Were it not better that Nigerians, nay Africans, had a common
language, with which to talk to one another directly, rather than many, necessitating
translations? Why, for instance, should I write my poetry solely in Igbo? How many
Igbo read Igbo? How many non-Igbo would (if they could) read Igbo and my Igbo
poetry? If my colonial and neocolonial education and experiences have produced
for/in me a curious and complex cultural and linguistic braid, why should I deny a
part of my being by excluding from my poetry influences and matters that are both
exotic and indigenous?

It is this strong sense of history—of where and what we have been, of where and
what we are, and of where and what we aspire to be—as well as a sense of the
serious urgency of the situation that compels me to suggest *Nigerian Language* as
a transcendence of that country's cacophony and ethnicism. Only that literature
produced in that language accessible to the people, able to speak to the core of their
being, and capable of mobilizing them, as one, to social and political stance, if not
action, can assume the role of literature in "the political struggle to achieve
self-determination and to constitute a new nationality," in the construction of "a
cohesive future by laying bare the havoc wrought by 'civilization' and its agents on
traditional Africa, and by restoring to the African the dignity of his past" (Aizenberg
1990 85). Only such a literature will be able to represent the nation as such because
in such an imaginative recreation it will be possible to transcend divisive ethnic
polarities and boundaries. Only when such a language has been massively adopted
and continuously recreated and reinvigorated by the writers and elevated to national—and later, international—respectability, can we rejoice at the inauguration
of what can be truly called *Nigerian literature.* Apparently, my persistent reluctance
to designate the literatures that have so far issued from Nigeria "national" is lent
support by the acute observations made by Albert Gerard in his essay on the
"Historiography of Black Africa" published recently in the *ALA Bulletin* XIX.3
(Summer 1993). About the general situation in Africa Gerard speaks of, "Three
European languages, Arabic and about fifty African languages, and Afrikaans; three
scripts; numerous ethnic groups which are rarely coterminous with the frontiers of
the modern nation-state; an enormous geographical surface and a confounding
cultural diversity. A domain this vast and this heterogeneous (would hardly be
amenable to) our tradition of "national historiography" (26).

The halting phraseology of this excerpt is symptomatic and metonymic of the
truncation—cultural, linguistic, ethnic—of the situation in Africa. And Gerard goes
on to explain the cacophony: "Since decolonialization, the Third World . . . has

been divided into multiethnic and multilingual nations. . . . The national literatures of any of these African countries resemble more that of the entire European continent than the national literature of France, England, or Spain, if only from the point of view of linguistic diversity" (26).

My call for *Nigerian language literature* is enabled by the fact that that language already exists in Nigeria, and only needs creative and artistic fine-tuning, as well as the abandonment by the writers of the residue of colonial mentality which, because it regards everything that is not "Queen's English" as inferior and derivative (Barbag-Stoll 1983 37), has continued to assign that "dialect" mainly to lowly characters in their works. Once that mentality is jettisoned, and the fact recognized that this language, which is already spoken by millions across ethnic, socioeconomic, and even "national" boundaries, can be a vibrant, resourceful, and respectable medium of literary production, without the authorizing stamp or nod of Western critical approval, then the journey would have begun toward the imagined community and that national identity capable of subsuming and containing "the formidable heterogeneity of ethnic identities" (30). What I am calling for is, therefore, neither difficult nor far-fetched; it only demands of the writers to descend from their elitist towers and recognize that as long as we continue to refer to our pots and dishes as fragments, outsiders will continue to collect trash with them; it is time for the "respectable" and renowned writers to join ranks with writers of lesser stature and fame, who are already doing the necessary foundational work. As Gerard has also seen it:

One can observe the emergence of a popular literature all over black Africa. This literature caters for a local readership, and no longer for a European or Europeanized readership; its writers use European languages as they are spoken in Africa, creolize them without the slightest scruples. They are, thus, probably developing the future literary languages of Africa. (30)

On her part, Ann Barbag-Stoll (who devotes a book to the study of the social and linguistic history of Nigerian Pidgin English) talks of the "richness, vivacity and the unlimited resources of word-formation mechanisms of this medium" (101); of its ability to transcend linguistic barriers among Nigerians from different language groups (51); and of "its expressive function as a medium of artistic creativity" (101–118).

My call thus remains insistent because what Gerard observes is not a novel phenomenon. Even before his novel, *The Voice* (1964), made him both famous and (to some people) notorious for its radical linguistic experimentation, Gabriel Okara had articulated a similar position during that 1962 African Writers' Conference, at which Obi Wali had also made his controversial presentation, and which got published in the same issue of *Transition* IV.10 (September 1963) as Wali's own lecture. In his "African Speech . . . English Words," Okara discusses his creative craft, which I think is relevant to the present argument because the same technique of *calquing* or loan-translation or transliteration as well as direct/literal translation is operative in Okara's craft and in the so-called Pidgin. My panacea, which calls for resourceful eclecticism, thus recognizes the importance of Okara's contribution which he himself elaborates at length:

As a writer who believes in the utilization of African ideas, African philosophy and African folklore and imagery to the fullest extent possible, I am of the opinion the only way to use them effectively is to translate them almost literally from the African language native to the writer into whatever European language he is using as his medium of expression. I have endeavoured in my words to keep as close as possible to the vernacular expressions. For, from a word, a group of words, a sentence and even a name in any African language, one can glean the social norms, attitudes and values of a people.

In order to capture the vivid images of African speech I had to eschew the habit of expressing my thoughts first in English. . . . I had to study each Ijaw expression I used and to discover the probable situation in which it was used in order to bring out the nearest meaning in English. I found it a fascinating exercise. . . . Take the expression "he is timid" for example. The equivalent in Ijaw is "he has no chest" or "he has no shadow." Now a person without a chest in the physical sense can only mean a human that does not exist. . . . A person who does not cast a shadow of course does not exist. All this means is that a timid person is not fit to live. Here, perhaps, we are hearing the echoes of the battles in those days when the strong and the brave lived. But is this not true of the world today? In parting with a friend at night a true Ijaw would say, "May we live to see ourselves tomorrow." . . . On the other hand, how could an Ijaw born and bred in England, France or the United States write, "May we live to see ourselves tomorrow" instead of "Goodnight"? And if he wrote "Goodnight," would he be expressing an Ijaw thought? Is it only the colour of one's skin that makes one an African?

Why should I not use the poetic and beautiful "May we live to see ourselves tomorrow" or "May it dawn" (Igbo), instead of "Goodnight"?

What emerges from the examples I have given is that a writer can use the idioms of his own language in a way that is understandable in English. If he uses their English equivalents, he would not be expressing African ideas and thoughts, but English ones. Some may regard this way of writing in English as a desecration of the language. This is of course not true. Living languages grow like living things, and English is far from a dead language. There are . . . versions of English. All of them add life and vigour to the language while reflecting their own respective cultures. Why shouldn't there be a Nigerian or West African English which we can use to express our own ideas, thinking and philosophy in our own way? (15–16)

I have quoted this passage extensively in order to mark its present cogency, even though the presentation was made by Okara more than thirty years ago. In fact, in a recent theoretical redressing, Ashcroft et al. (1989) have elegantly described the v hole process at work:

The crucial function of language as a medium of power demands that postcolonial writing define itself by seizing the language of the centre and replacing it in a discourse fully adapted to the colonized place. There are two distinct processes by which it does this. The first, the abrogating or denial of the privilege of "English" involves a rejection of the metropolitan power over the means of communication. The second, the appropriation and reconstitution of the language of the centre, the process of capturing and remoulding the language to new usages, marks a separation from the site of colonial privilege.

Abrogation is a refusal of the categories of the imperial culture, its aesthetic, its illusory standard of normative or "correct" usage, and its assumption of a traditional and fixed meaning "inscribed" in the words.

Appropriation is the process by which the language is taken and made to "bear the burden" of one's own cultural experiences . . . to "convey in a language that is not one's own the spirit that is one's own." [The literature produced in such a language through] the simultaneous processes of abrogation and appropriation . . . is therefore always written out of the tension between the abrogation of the received English which speaks from the centre, and the act of appropriation which brings it under the influence of the vernacular tongue. (38–39)

Even though I refuse to designate, like Ashcroft et al., the variants of English used in the ex-colonies in the lower case (english), I agree with them that the linguistic experimentation executed by Okara in his novel illustrates "the creative potential of intersecting languages when the syntactic and grammatical rules of one language are overlaid on another" (44). It is the same creative potential that I have seen taking root, especially in postwar Nigerian literary productions, which encourages me to sustain the call for Nigerian language. Moreover, the perennity of the ethnolinguistic rivalry and tensions and the very cloud of political uncertainty and confusion hovering over Nigeria, make the need urgent for a transethnic, transvernacular language of national consciousness and solidarity. This language, the "supreme vehicle of culture" (Okafor 1979 12), together with what Fanon calls "a common life, common experiences and memories, common aims" (175), will produce in time a Nigerian literature, and a Nigerian nation. Already, as is evidenced by its, presently unsystematized, prevalence in literary works produced by Nigerians this language, so metaphorically rich and nuanced, is capable of adequately embodying indigenous Nigerian experience and drowning out the cacophony.

## WORKS CITED

Achebe, Chinua. *Hopes and Impediments: Selected Essays.* New York: Doubleday, 1989.

Aizenberg, Edna. "The Untruths of the Nation: *Petals of Blood* and Fuentes's *The Death of Artemio Cruz. Research in African Literatures* XXX.I (Winter 1990): 58–103.

Appiah, Kwame Anthony. "Is the Post- in Postmodernism the Post- in Postcolonial?" *Critical Inquiry* XVII (Winter 1991): 336–57.

Ashcroft, Bill et al. *The Empire Writes Back: Theory and Practice in Post-Colonial Literature.* London: Routledge, 1989.

Barbag-Stoll, Ann. *Social and Linguistic History of Nigerian Pidgin English.* Tubingen: Stalfenberg-Verlag, 1983.

Davis, Geoffrey and Hena Maes-Jelinek, eds. *Crisis and Creativity in the New Literatures in English..* Amsterdam: Rodopi, 1990.

Fanon, Frantz. *A Dying Colonialism.* Trans. Haakon Chevalier. New York: Grove Weidenfeld, 1965.

Gerard, Albert. "Historiography of Black Africa: A Personal Testimony." *African Literature Association Bulletin* XIX.3 (Summer 1993): 24–32.

Irele, Abiola. "The African Imagination." *Research in African Literatures* XXI.1 (Spring 1990): 47–67.

Jeyifo, Biodun. "The Nature of Things: Arrested Decolonization and Critical Theory." *Research in African Literatures* XXI.1 (Spring 1990): 33–48.

Kincaid, Jamaica. *A Small Place.* New York: Farrar, Straus, Giroux, 1988.

Lloyd, David. *Nationalism and Minor Literature. James Clarence Mangan and the Emergence of Irish Cultural Nationalism.* Berkeley: University of California Press, 1987.

Mlana, Penina Muhando. "Creating in the Mother-Tongue: The Challenges to the African Writer Today." *Research in African Literatures* XXI.4 (Winter 1990): 5–14.

Ngugi, wa Thiong'o. *Moving the Centre: The Struggle for Cultural Freedoms.* London: Heinemann, 1993.

Nwankwo, Nkem. *A Song for Fela & Other Poems.* Nashville, TN: Nigerhouse, 1993.

Okafor, Dubem. "The Cultural Validity of Soyinka's Plays." *Nsukka Studies in African Literature* I.2 (March 1979): 12–29.

––––––. *Nationalism in Okigbo's Poetry.* Enugu, Nigeria: Fourth Dimension Publishers, 1980.

Okara, Gabriel. "African Speech . . . English Words." *Transition* IV. 10 (September 1963): 15–16.

Okeke-Ezigbo, Emeka. "The Role of the Nigerian Writer in a Carthaginian Society." *Okike* XXI (July 1982): 28–37.

––––––. "What Is a National Literature?" *Nigeria Magazine* 149 (1984): 1–13 .

Osofisan, Femi. "Enter the Carthaginian Critic . . . ? A Comment on Okeke-Ezigbo's 'the Role of the Writer in a Carthaginian Okike Society.' " XXI (July 1982): 38–44.

Wali, Obi. "The Dead End of African Literature." *Transition* IV.10 (September 1963): 13–15.

Zabus, Chantal. *The African Palimpsest: Indigenization of Language in the West African Europhone Novel.* Amsterdam: Rodopi, 1991.

Chapter Two

# Language, Theory, and Modern African Literature: Some More Questions

## Wole Ogundele

The original project of modern African literature, in both its Anglophone and Francophone developmental phases, was cultural retrieval and assertion. Its early formulation by Chinua Achebe (1975) is still worth quoting: "Here then is an adequate revolution for me to espouse—to help my society regain belief in itself and put away the complexes of the years of denigration and self-abasement. I would be quite satisfied if my novels (especially the ones I set in the past) did no more than teach my readers that their past—with all its imperfections—was not one long night of savagery from which the first Europeans acting on God's behalf delivered them" (44–45).

But inextricably linked with the cultural was the political project and, in good time, much of Africa south of the Sahara was politically decolonized. Looking at the present state of this literature, however, one cannot but be struck by a sense of monumental historical irony: through the banner of cultural nationalism it contributed much to the success of political nationalism, only to have itself trapped in the latter's success. One can, of course, point to some cultural successes: international recognition and serious study of African arts, oral traditions, and religious systems; possibly even greater recognition and respect for the new literature itself, through which many non-African scholars learn about the richness of the continent's societies and traditions. But especially in their relationship, there is an irreducible, irremediable disparity between the picture the cultures portrayed in the literature, and their state in reality. When considered in conjunction with the fact that these cultures are portrayed in a literature written in the first languages of other societies and cultures, the victory begins to look pyrrhic indeed.

This sense of pyrrhic victory is especially evident in the two controversies that have dogged the literature from the 1960s: the language and hermeneutics-aesthetics controversies. Both have more or less run parallel, but it is clear that they are but two different "symptoms" of the same political and cultural contradictions that have their source in the language question.

In this chapter I look at the controversies again, taking as my points of departure (but not exclusively) the arguments of the two novelists Chinua Achebe and Ngugi wa Thiong'o, and of the critic Abiola Irele. Basically, I extend Ngugi's arguments as follows: that both the choice of European languages for modern African literature and the arguments supporting it have "sacrificed" cultural aspirations to the political; that this literature, contrary to the norm, is not in a dialogic relationship with African languages, cultures, and peoples; and that it will be extremely difficult for truly indigenous hermeneutic-aesthetic theories/paradigms to emerge and displace foreign ones in their reading, in spite of their being strongly marked by "the African imagination." Collapsing the controversies into the single one of culture versus politics that they really are, I finally focus on certain neglected cultural aspects of the linguistic choice, to show that in overlooking such aspects, the agenda of true political liberation of African peoples was hobbled from the start. In all that follows, I take my cue from Claude Levi-Strauss's idea that "language can be said to be a condition of culture because the material out of which language is built is of the same type as the material out of which the whole culture is built" (1967 67).

## THE AFRICAN INTELLECTUAL AND HIS COMMITMENTS

Modern Anglophone African literature was just getting into its stride (for which the 1962 Kampala conference was a celebration) when Obi Wali published his spoilsport essay prophesying its dead end. Wali condemned many contemporary intellectual ideas, but his sharpest barb was reserved for the literature: African literature "as now understood and practiced is merely a minor appendage in the main stream of European literature," he said. And "until [African] writers and their Western midwives accept the fact that any true African literature must be written in African languages, they would be merely pursuing a dead end, which can only lead to sterility, uncreativity, and frustration" (14). Given the socially, culturally, politically (and also economically) privileged status of this literature in relation to African language literatures then, Obi Wali might have worried more about that dire fate befalling the latter rather than the former; that is to say, his concern was basically a cultural one.

Not so cultural, or even literary, however, were the responses to his argument; none less so than Achebe's pragmatic rebuttal, delivered as a lecture in 1964 on "The African Writer and the English Language." Looking at "the reality of present-day Africa" then, Achebe saw that the colonial language brought together "small, scattered" polities and unified them into the present large ones that hold out great prospects (57). These new nations needed one language and literature, both of which only the colonial language could supply.

Furthermore, in Achebe's arguments the privileging of the colonial language as national language and the language of national literature meant the marginalization of African languages and their literatures as ethnic (56). Looked at again from this distance in time, even the subsidiary call to the African writer to (like himself) "aim at fashioning out an English which is at once universal and able to carry his peculiar experience" (61) is a more political than literary argument—a mere extension of the main one. Delivered with the authority that he had already acquired by then, and supported authoritatively with a perfect example from his own work, Achebe's points in the lecture clinched the argument in favor of the colonial languages, and returned the literature written in them to the first lane. However, the language controversy was only silenced, not resolved, precisely because it was conducted and carried on in unlike terms.

It flared up again, twenty years later when Ngugi wa Thiong'o delivered the 1984 Robb lectures in New Zealand and subsequently published them under the title *Decolonising the Mind: The Politics of Language in African Literature* in 1986. This time around, the political and literary circumstances are vastly different. Obi Wali's dire predictions have come true, but only for the larger political units that Achebe (and every African then) was so optimistic about. The literature instead has grown bigger and stronger. It has also weaned itself from European literatures—or so it seems. Furthermore, the cultural-literary and general relationships of Africa to Europe have modified somewhat, and Ngugi makes his arguments within the cultural contexts of global capitalism and new, skeptical cultural discourses that theorize these contexts. We must not, of course, neglect the stature of Ngugi himself: a major African writer who has achieved fame and success by writing in English, and is as politically committed as anybody could possibly be.

Ngugi made his arguments in his characteristic combination of trenchant ideological polemics and praxis, with first-hand literary knowledge. He then backed up his case with renunciation of English as his language of imaginative expression. The minor political significance of this gesture is not only in its elimination of the binaries of ethnic/national languages and literatures, but in its challenge to other African writers to, at least, rethink the linguistic choice made at the 1962 conference. Moreover, by premising his political arguments on language and culture, Ngugi reconnects what in African literary practice has been implicitly separated; he also shows that in the retrieval and revitalization of African cultures (for which African language literatures are a metonymy) lies the path out of the continent's present political malaise.

In expatiating on this basic argument, Ngugi starts by reviewing the 1962–64 controversy and questioning Achebe's solutions (which at that time seemed so reasonable and right):

Why, we may ask, should an African writer, or any writer, become so obsessed by taking his mother tongue to enrich other tongues? Why should he see it as his particular mission? We never asked ourselves: how can we enrich our languages? (1986 8)

Ngugi makes the finer details of his argument along the lines of recent psychosocial theories of language, culture, and environment, to end on a grand, visionary note: "So I would like to contribute towards the restoration of the harmony between all the aspects and divisions of language so as to restore the Kenyan child to his environment, understand it fully so as to be in a position to change it for the collective good" (28).

This visionary flight is anchored, however, in a concrete, historical sense of the inseparability of literature from language: "We African writers are bound by our calling to do for our languages what Spencer, Milton and Shakespeare did for English" (29). This is no simple-minded nativism, but a recalling of the original cultural nationalism from which modern African literature arose. It is also an envisioning of the reconnection among language, literature, and political culture, and of the writer as one primarily at the service of his (inherited) language. In this Ngugi is also challenging certain corollaries implicit in the modern African writer's choice of European languages: that even literary language is functional and the writer *on top* of it, rather than *within* it; that when he chooses to write in the colonial language, the African writer can empty that language of its cultural content and fill it with his own, without contamination from the other; and that the African audience's response to a second language literature will be as visceral and total as his response to his first.

This is the dark side of the alienation condition that Ngugi seeks to reverse through the language perspective. Hence his point about the restoration of harmony among the Kenyan child, his language, and his environment. In transferring the alienation theme from the artist to the Kenyan child, Ngugi relocates this African condition from the realm of fiction where it has more or less resided to the plain of reality: the separation (conflict, reality) between knowledge learnt in school in a foreign language and knowledge imbibed at home, in the mother tongue. Following Ngugi's line of thought enables us to ask, of the great project of reshaping the colonial language to carry the African's experience: Can it ever be done successfully *outside* literature so as to achieve that restoration of harmony? Until that happens, African literature, culture, and life are condemned to translation. This point was made a long time ago by Martin Esslin in a review of Wole Soyinka's and J.P. Clark's plays:

We are here presented with African peasants, African fishermen, African labourers express-ing themselves in impeccable English. Of course in reality they speak their own languages equally impeccably and the playwrights have merely translated what they would have said in those languages into the equivalent English. Precisely! Which is to say that these original plays labour under the universal handicap of all translated drama. (qtd. in Irele, 1981 44)

I have copied this statement from Abiola Irele, who quotes it in his very reflective essay on "African Literature and the Language Question." Irele uses it in recogni-tion of the "translation'"bind. However, he tries to resolve it, not by seeking a way out, but by further condemnation (to translation): The African writer should seek to be so *competent* in the European language and use it with such *credibility* that it would accommodate to an African reality, *as if it were an African language*" (53;

Irele's emphasis). Implicit here, again, is the disconnection of literature from reality at the aetiological and existential levels, which parallels the separation of language from literature spoken of earlier in this chapter. What Irele's position reveals is a general and often acute awareness of the language dilemma on one hand, but, on the other, a readiness to seek compromise rather than consider a way out. This state of affairs is quite typical in African literary criticism: recognition of the problem, various formulas of evasion or accommodation; but all still within the political bind. The language problem, then, is not the writer's alone; it is also that of the literary scholar's, whether as humble critic or grand theorist.

## THE CRITICISM-THEORY CONTROVERSIES

The hermeneutic-aesthetic controversy attending modern African literature has had three phases now, all running into and implying each other. The first, almost simultaneous with the rise of modern Anglophone African literature, is what Achebe labeled "Colonialist Criticism." In this quarrel, foreign critics were (rightly) seen as having a paternalistic, proprietorial attitude toward the newly emerging African literature. The second is the quarrel about "universal aesthetic criteria" and "universal human experience," when Western (and some eminent African) critics sought to impose Eurocentric aesthetics and values on the literature, under the guise of "universal standards of excellence and truth." The third is the current phase, in which the territory of African literary discourse is being defended against real or imagined threats of appropriation by current Euro-American theories and movements. These controversies merely show that criticism of African literature, like the literature itself, has continually suffered its own autonomy and identity crises and has yet to find either. As with the literature itself, the problem here too stems from the same source: the language question. But whereas the literature has at least identified the source, the criticism has not at all, because of various false leads and diversions.

The "universal aesthetic criteria" arguments, which raged from the late 1960s to the middle 1970s, illustrate both the crises and the search for false solutions. The idea of universal aesthetic criteria was seen by African critics as yet another attempt to impose specifically Eurocentric literary conventions and critical norms on modern African literature and criticism. Such norms were resented on the grounds that they were reminiscent of the racial-cultural arrogance at the root of colonialism, and also that they were in any case incompatible with the inherent aims, functions and nature of African literature. Furthermore, there really were no "universal" aesthetics as such, criteria of excellence in the arts being to a large extent culture-bound and always changing. The controversy spurred African and Africanist critics to search for African aesthetic practices, conventions, and social values, in oral literatures and in other art forms, by which the new literature could be interpreted and judged. Hence, ideas of the public-orientedness and functionality of African literature became stressed, along with the search for its roots and origins in indigenous traditions. "Commitment" became a recurrent term of critical praise;

writers who were deemed to be individualistic or not practicing functional (or, as used by Achebe, "applied") art were dismissed as indulging in decadent (Western) art for art's sake.

But there were still problems of textual interpretation and exegesis, and of determining whether one novel was better than another and why, especially in the classroom. In tackling these problems, African critics inevitably resorted to a contextualized type of New Criticism from the beginning to the present; the late 1970s to the middle of the 1980s, however, witnessed the triumph of Marxist criticism. In other words, while African criticism embarked, on the one hand, on a search for indigenous aesthetic and critical standards, it, on the other, engaged in Western ones eclectically, but vigorously. It is not only Western critical practices that were freely applied to African literature, but Western epistemological and generic categories too. Joseph Okpaku's edited *New African Literature and the Arts: I* (1970) illustrates quite well the brave attempt to derive hermeneutic-aesthetic parameters from oral tradition for application to the new literature, and also its severe handicaps. After disposing of the idea of a universal aesthetic in the chapter "African Literary Standards for African Literature and the Arts," Okpaku moves on to seek out those standards "in the area of those common aspects of life most frequently dramatized in the arts" (19), and in audience response. Having found that musical accompaniment is central and vital in oral traditions, he erects "rhythmical language" as one indispensable criterion. And since the language of novels, being prose, is often preponderantly not rhythmical, Okpaku finds, against overwhelming evidence, that "the very form of the novel (is) inadequate for the fullest expression of African literary talent" (19). Another criterion Okpaku sets up is African attitudes to birth, death, love, and so on, though he does not say how this sociological-anthropological one is to be applied. The underlying difficulty of the problem Okpaku's efforts embody is perhaps best manifested in the fuzziness of his "Philosophy of the New African Literature" constituted of "one, the change from the provincial to the universal; two, the freeing of the African writer to develop a multithematic literature—that is, a literature with a multiplicity of various and diverse themes; and three, the emphasis on philosophical depth in African literature and art" (5).

It is not essential here to multiply examples from other would-be critical legislators. What needs to be said, rather, is that the prospects of a successful transfer of critical paradigms from oral tradition to the written literature hinge on at least one indispensable condition: the writing to which they are to be applied must in the first place have followed the conventions of the oral genre from which those paradigms are abstracted. Even in writers as closely influenced by the oral tradition as Masizi Kunene and Okot p'Bitek, this is both physically and mentally impossible (if it were, they would not be writers but oral performers). There will always be gaps in execution and totality of work (including the material medium of transmission) that such criteria cannot deal with. The relationships between oral and written literatures are often quite complex for, as Walter J. Ong has shown, what is involved is more than a mere change in the technological medium of transmission. When the transition from orality to literacy is overlaid by a linguistic transference (translation), those relationships cannot be as simple and direct as is often assumed by the advocates of traditional critical standards. The critical factor here is language, which Irele gives central recognition in his essay "The Criticism of Modern African Literature." As he frames it, the discontinuity almost amounts to incompatibility between the new literature and the aesthetic conventions or criteria of the old: "I personally take the view that the African is being transformed not into something or somebody else, but into something or somebody new, and similarly I tend to look upon our literature as tending towards the transposition of an old scale of feelings and attitudes into a new key of expression" (1981 32).

From Marxism through to feminism and postcolonial discourse, all the new literary theories are also theories of culture and politics. They are new ways of reading literature, of questioning its supposed ontological identity on one hand; of insisting on the social and political determination of writing and reading on the other; and of empowering the powerless and interrogating the old bases of power. Feminism and postcoloniality in particular would seem to give intellectual ammunition and moral support to all that modern African literary discourse has stood for all along. One would, therefore, have expected African scholars to warmly embrace them. This has not been the case. Instead, the theories are held at arm's length, and considered by those African scholars sufficiently interested in them to be in need of drastic remodeling if they are to be meaningful to Africa. The reasons for the suspicion and reluctance are not far to seek, and some of them have been cogently framed by Biodun Jeyifo: "What gives a particular critical discourse its decisive effectivity . . . is the combination of historical, institutional and ideological factors that make the discourse a "master" discourse which translates the avowed will-to-truth of all discourse into a consummated, if secret, will-to-power. In other words, this "master" discourse becomes the discourse of the "master," in its effects and consequences at least, if not in its conscious intentions" (34).

This speaks for others like Kwame Anthony Appiah, the African-American critic Henry Louis Gates, Jr. and the poet Niyi Osundare. Osundare's vehement rejection of these theories is worth quoting in part for its embedded doubleness (that is perhaps not intended): "Either as a result of the politics of their provenance or an inherent crisis in their modes and methods of analysis and application (or both), "mainstream" Western post-structuralist theories have demonstrated little or no adequacy in the apprehension, analysis, and articulation of African writing and its long and troubled context" (1993 18).

What Osundare quarrels with is not the theories themselves but their inadequacy "in the apprehension, analysis, and articulation of African writing and its long and troubled context" (18). Would these theories be welcome if they recognized Africa's peculiar case, despite their source in "foreign, historically imperialist perspectives and institutions?" (18). This is a minor point, surely, but it is indicative of, on one hand, the real difficulty of getting away from what is rejected and, on the other, the even more difficult task of evolving African alternatives. This situation will persist as long as African literature and its criticism remain, in Abiola Irele's adaptation of

Soyinka's symbol, "a half-child." If this "indeterminate" literature presents a problem for criticism, theorizing it is a more formidable endeavor. In its choice of European languages over African ones, the literature is not only a half-child, but also a prodigal and exile—to appropriate Okigbo, another Nigerian poet's adapted symbol. The literature is truly new in its hybridity, for even its relationship with African oral traditions is a new kind of relationship. As such, it still lacks both archaeological and genealogical depths—attributes that facilitate theorization. In the absence of both, all that can be done, and is being done, is to talk about the desirability (or otherwise), problems and prospects of theorizing it.

## A CULTURAL AND POLITICAL CRITIQUE OF THE LANGUAGE CHOICE

This chapter has so far reviewed only the linguistic and critical controversies that have been part of new African literature especially from the 1960s to the present. It has also tried to show that though both have run parallel, they are connected in that they both have a common origin in the language choice. In this section, I wish to return to the major reasons for that choice: the national unity and "Africanization" of English (or French) reasons. Even the second reason, as hinted earlier, is more political than literary. It is, therefore, necessary to dwell at some length on the omissions and negative cultural as well as political implications of the one, and the fallacy of the other. In the process, I will be drawing on some points already made by writers and scholars who argue for a return to African languages.

This new literature started, let us remember, as part of the dual historical imperatives of cultural nationalism and political decolonization. (Although this public aim does not fully account for all the motivations for writing, it was important.) Perhaps at that historical stage the need to write in the language of the colonialist was inescapable, for various reasons. One of them was to turn the colonial state, created as much by language as by the Gatling gun, into a unified political front from which to push off its creators. This positive irony in turn created its own cultural irony, this time less positive: so successful was the political agenda that the cultural one became identified with it in all ways, but most especially in the language question. Projecting African cultures in texts written in European languages became a substitute for retrieving and revitalizing those cultures in reality, and through African languages. Both were left to their own devices, so to speak. But in neglecting the cultural retrieval program, the postcolonial political agenda of nation building was also being poorly served. In this regard, the effects of the language choice on both national politics and literary nationalism in Africa have never been fully confronted.

Achebe's defense of English as the right language for national literature in Anglophone Africa was made in a tone and mood of buoyant political sanguinity. As one after the other, African countries became independent, even the most sober realists could not but be infected. This mood of universal, infectious optimism pervades all of the lectures Achebe gave in 1964, but it is especially noticeable in the prediction that " the single most important fact in Africa in the second half of the twentieth century will appear to be the rise of individual nation-states" (1975 56). That was 1964, but in 1990 Achebe more or less repeated this nationalistic argument (8). Yet, in the intervening years, not one single African country has risen; all have sunk instead, some to the point of total collapse. The new literature, for its own part, has gone from strength to strength; many of its producers have turned their back on the nations, both imaginatively and physically—especially physically. The fact that there are probably as many, if not more, African writers living abroad now (in the countries where the language they write in is the first language) as in their countries underlines the tenuous connection between the two. What all this leads to is that, at this point in time, the political justifications for the language choice need to be reexamined rather than reaffirmed.

The colonial language as national language in independent Africa may have brought together the thin, literate, and professional upper crust in each of the nation-states; it certainly silences the vast majority of Africans. It denies them any meaningful participation in any form of political process. The language barrier means that the doctrine of liberalism, central to nationalism, never percolated down to these vast majorities. It continues to make the political process of "reaching the people" a process of interpretations, and therefore a perfect hostage to abuse, misrepresentation, and manipulation—very much the way the colonial governance, also dependent on interpretation, was manipulated by the "interpreters," as narrated in *Arrow of God* and *The Fortunes of Wangrin*, for example. This in turn made possible and facilitated the replacement of the ideal of liberal, democratic politics as a marketplace of ideas by practice of the politics of charisma and pathetic fallacy. Surely, the retention of colonial languages as national languages is not alone responsible for all of the continent's political woes, but the fact that the majority of the citizens of any given African country are politically inactive simply because they cannot speak the *national* language is a crucial factor. These vast majorities cannot participate effectively and meaningfully in the culture of debate and dialogue that is so vital to any democratic process. This situation is reflected in many African novels: the "noneducated" African as merely a passive witness when it comes to national political matters. Thus, all the centuries-old political traditions, experience, and wisdom embedded in the languages are marginalized and repressed.

Literatures are, of course, being produced in African languages, but this does not stop those languages from being deprived for, after all, languages are not for general daily interpersonal communication and literary expression alone. African languages are deprived because very few discourses in other areas of human activity (science, technology, history, literary theory, criticism, etc.) are carried on in them. The "educated" African's participation in all these other fields far outstrips the growth and expansion of African languages. This surely is bound to have effects on even the literatures written in them.

In the recent phase of the language controversy, Ngugi and others (see especially D.P. Kunene, Akinwumi Ishola, M. Kunene, Kofi Anyidoho, Alamin Mazrui, Gabriel Ruhumbika, and Oyekan Owomoyela in *Research in African Literatures*

XXIII.1) have hinted at some of the points being made here. I may end this section by saying that the intention has not been to blame African writers for not being (un-)acknowledged legislators on the language issue in independent Africa. Rather, the point being stressed is that African writers at the beginning considered it a more or less barely political issue, and in a very narrowly political sense at that. Secondly, nobody, least of all the critic, can deny any writer the right to make his/her own choices. That being so, what I am attempting in this chapter is merely to set the corporate losses against both corporate and individual gains in an account that is as cultural as it is political. We may now return to the more specifically literary aspects of the issue.

The "Africanization of English" argument has, over the years, grown into something of a critical doctrine. Repeated and elaborated upon often, it has now been raised to the level of theory by other critics, more recently by the authors of *The Empire Writes Back*, by African writers like Gabriel Okara and Saro Wiwa, and by individual critics like Desai and Robson. But the dogma has been challenged, on valid grounds. First, whatever conscious (Achebe, Okara) or unconscious (Tutuola) experiments are done with English in the creative pursuit of its Africanization, the ultimate beneficiary is the English language and its literary traditions. It is these that grow and proliferate and show more possibilities, at the expense of whichever African language and its oral traditions are transliterated. Indeed, given the context of global capitalism that accompanied (and replaced) colonialism, and that has been facilitated by the arrival of a "world language" such as English, it is not too extravagant to apply the term "commodification" as an economic metaphor to this cultural process. African linguistic and other cultural resources are just another category of raw materials processed in the plant of a world language. The analogy can be taken a step further: as physical raw materials are taken out of the physical soil, so are these linguistic and other symbolic resources taken out of their cultural soil. And like minerals, they too can be depleted if they feed literatures in other languages more than they are replenished by literatures in their own. Chantal Zabus calls this depletion of linguistic resources "glottophagia or neoglottophagia in West African Europhone literature" (19). After a detailed examination of its instance in Achebe's use of proverbs in his novels, Zabus concludes darkly as follows:

The gradual extinction of a discursive species such as Igbo *ilu* and other orature-based devices recuperative of the ethnotext could signify the gradual death of Igbo and all African oral-formulaic tradition. In a chirographic context, discursive glottophagia replaces the manducation of the word. What is being eaten here is the *logos* or *verbum* of the proverbum or proverb. Achebe *qua* proverbalizer voices nonsounded words. The present-day proverbalizer is thus textually bound to be a logos-eater. (1990 28; Zabus' emphasis)

Languages do, of course, change; in the process, some old things are lost, while some new ones are gained. This is especially so when a society moves from orality to literacy. But in order for there to be a chance for the gains to more than adequately compensate for the losses, the bulk of intellectual production must be done in the language so that it can expand with the new vistas and avenues of experiences opened up. Since this has not exactly been the case so far in sub-Saharan Africa, it is difficult to share Irele's optimism (quoted earlier) concerning the relationship between traditional and new African literatures.

The failure of the cultural retrieval project is also political. I make this connection not just in the sense that the act of renewing an inherited tradition and passing it on in a usable form is a very political act. I make it also in reference to W.H. Auden's statement that:

As a poet—not as a citizen—there is only one political duty, and that is to defend one's language from corruption. And that is particularly serious now. It's being so quickly corrupted. When it is corrupted people lose faith in what they hear, and this leads to violence. (qtd. in Achebe 1975 55)

If we make the slight substitution of "deprived" for Auden's "corrupted," his perceived political duty of the poet becomes an urgent one for African writers.

The arguments being pursued here may perhaps be best focused with an example. In the language and critical problems, and discontinuity with tradition, facing African literature in European languages, no text better illustrates the issues more than Amos Tutuola's *The Palmwine Drinkard*. Tutuola's fellow countrymen may have been wrong in turning up their nose on his "embarrassing" English and not appreciating the "grandmother imagination" that his narrative represents, while his Western admirers may have been right in being charmed by both. The former's argument, however, was quite simple: Literature is a synthesis of language and vision, and by language is meant something like "the best words in the best order." Tutuola's compatriots did not need any Western poet to tell them this: all their oral traditions practice and say it. It is clear, also, that if Tutuola had had a better command of English he would have used it. But, thrilled by his exotic vision and language, his Western admirers were only cooperating in the split among language, vision, and tradition already implicit in the cultural disempowerment of colonized Africa. A simpler perspective of these issues might be gained if we ask: Would Tutuola's Yoruba readers (for whom he presumably wrote) have appreciated his efforts that much if he had written that novel in as exotic a Yoruba as he actually did in English? In the instant and enduring popularity of his Yoruba mentor, D.O. Fagunwa, we have sufficient evidence that Yoruba readers know and appreciate mastery of their language when they see it.

The second point about discontinuity is also related. Tutuola follows Fagunwa phonologically as well as in drawing upon the Yoruba mythico-magical narrative tradition and cosmology. But whereas Christian influence intruded on the latter's vision to make his novels sometimes tediously didactic, Tutuola's imagination remains wholly secular and ludic. He therefore could have represented an important stage in the transition of the Yoruba narrative tradition from the oral to the written, and from the confinement of religious and moralistic conservatism to the open space of the secular and empirical, reflecting subtle attitudinal changes in society. But Tutuola writes in English and the loss is Yoruba literature's, for which his novels will always constitute a rupture.

Thirdly, Tutuola's case highlights the problems inherent in any attempt to use poetics from oral tradition to evaluate the new, written literature. Under what prose narrative genre are we to put his stories? Again, Irele puts his finger on it when he says, "orality invites us to a revision of notions about genre and generic conventions" (1990 55). However, the reverse case can be made too: might not the poetics of foreign (written) genres, given their current prestige, have also induced us to revise our notions of oral genres, especially in the hermeneutic effort to realign them with the new literature? Moreover, we know that genres generally are flexible, oral genres famously so. The line of "direct progression from oral literature" to written literature in African languages becomes a meandering, problematic one when we try to trace it in the new literature in European languages. Are ritual performances proto-drama or full-scale drama in their own rights? Are there forms of (prose) narrative that make the novel not a truly foreign import to Africa, as is sometimes claimed? Does tragedy exist in traditional theatrical forms? The point is not to answer these questions here one way or another. What is to be stressed is that the critical and theoretical efforts so far spent expanding these European terms to accommodate their African approximates or rough equivalents might have been more fruitfully invested in asserting their autonomous, different, and uniquely African existence. It is, therefore, small wonder that a substantial portion of African literary criticism is protest criticism. Not just in the sense of protest against the incursions of Western criticism into a terrain that it is sometimes not quite familiar with. It is protest also in the sense that, even when it fully embraces contemporary Western theoretical and analytical tools, it uses them to protest against Western cultural and intellectual imperialism. The case of African-American literary discourse is in this regard only slightly similar to Africa's, but Henry Louis Gates' position illustrates the entire ironic enterprise. After questioning the adequacy of Western criticism in dealing with the black literary idiom and admitting the impossibility of inventing a black alternative, Gates has to be content with the compromise that black critical voices infiltrate white theoretical discourse in order to subvert its domination (1–24). But Africans are less implicated in white culture than African-Americans, and they still have their own traditions to fall back on. Yet James Comas welcomes the application of Western theories and critical practice (especially Derrida's deconstruction) to African literature because it can reveal such African works to be challenging "the traditional values underlying Western thought . . . for example, the British crisis of imperialism" (1990 28). If it thus proves itself to be relevant as a tool of African protest, another Eurocentric theory will have become "universalized." Meanwhile, African criticism remains condemned to a hermeneutic politics and morality of protest. This is a heroic occupation, no doubt, but one that does not answer to the needs of the continent—except in its external relations. But more importantly, it is surely no substitute for the production of original, home grown theories and conceptual and analytic methods.

One may imagine that Achebe was responding partly to this generalized role of perpetual protest assigned to both modern African literature and African literary criticism in his 1990 lecture. He seized the opportunity then to remind his London audience that Africans also use their arts and literature to celebrate. "The new literature in Africa," he said, "is aware of the possibilities available to it for celebrating humanity in our continent" (10). Celebration also includes making possible the conditions that can facilitate the growth of indigenous theories and paradigms.

## POSTCOLONIALITY AND AFRICAN LITERATURE

One of the cultural-political discourses that have arisen in recent years, post-coloniality, claims the new African literature as part of its field for theorizing. This claim rests on three arguments, more or less: made up of different "national literatures," this new literature is produced in a common, international language; within this language, these national literatures share a complex of related tropes, rhetorical strategies, and themes deployed for more or less identical politico-cultural aims; and, being products of the same imperialism, they have as much in common with one another culturally as with the nations (or continents) by which they have been named.

This is a logical development of both the history and the character of the nation-narration relationship in colonial and postcolonial Africa. Colonialism created the nation-state; in the process of consolidating its hold on these irrational polities, it incidentally put in place conditions that would coalesce in time and facilitate the production of the new literature soon to be called *national* literatures. Thus, the nation came before the narration that would seek to normalize it retroactively. But the full-blown rebellion that the literature was supposed to represent, in companionship to the political one, never took place. In consequence, the postcolonial nation-state and postcolonial African literature started drifting apart almost from the start. The result now, as Irele has pointed out, is its increasing marginalization (1990 49–50). It has not, in other words, played the hoped-for catalytic role of precipitating the emergence of nationness and nationhood. Ngugi's repudiation of English as the language of his literary expression has to be understood as both a symptom of, and a reaction to, the failure, and the nation-narration separation. But it also has to be comprehended in the context of postcoloniality and other contemporary discourses whose predominant skeptical temper is that of interrogating and deconstructing all received truths and orthodoxies, colonial ones especially.

The questioning of the "master-narrative" was, of course, effectively done by the new literature. However, in focusing its attack on the ideological foundations of colonialism, Postcoloniality also indirectly chips away at the most visible, concrete structure erected on that foundation: the post-colonial nation-state. Post-colonial discourse also undermines the ideology of nationalism and national unity in its theoretical stress on decentring, heterogeneity, and difference. Ngugi may not be a self-declared follower of the discourse, but this statement of his puts him right in its center: "Moving the center in the two senses—between nations and within nations—will contribute to the freeing of the world cultures from the restrictive walls of nationalism, class, race and gender" (1993 xvii).

Thus, from the irresistible emancipatory force that it was barely five decades ago, nationalism and nation-ness in Africa now has become a wall of restrictions. Ngugi no doubt characterizes it as such within the universalist vision of socialism, but the epithet resonates most evidentially against the background of postindependence traumas on the continent. The "inchoate dreams" (1993 128) that Anderson found to be at the foundation of colonial nationalism in Africa have more or less been realized as structured nightmares. In the language aspect of the inchoate dreams, the impossibility of "vernacularization" led to the political compromise of bilingualism, in which the colonial language, the second language, became privileged over the first: the one in which to imagine the new polity and forge a larger, unified nation out of precolonial *nations*.

But neither in the areas of politics nor of culture has this had much success. In many an African country, "narrating the nation" has never appreciably risen above narrating the history and culture of specific ethnic groups. While the intention behind this has been to use such narratives as metonymies and allegories, the result has been a strengthening of ethnic identity and awareness. Not surprisingly, therefore, the idea of categorizing the new literature according to national boundaries has always proved awkward and inoperative. Thus, with all his readiness to concede the corporate existence of many African countries because of the "territorial imperative," Irele still doubts the nation-ness of African "national literatures":

the European-language literatures in Africa (for which a national status is being canvassed) are not yet generally experienced as having attained such a status, largely because the languages in which they are expressed have at best only an official acceptance; they are neither indigenous to the societies and cultures on which they have been imposed, nor are they national in any real sense of the word. (1990 52)

The language-nation-literature triad in postcolonial Africa is full of contradictions and ironies, some of which I have tried to bring to the foreground in this chapter. There is a last one to be considered, in which both the linguistic and hermeneutic-aesthetic controversies finally meet. This has to do with the status of English especially as a world language, and the "internationalism" of the literatures, criticisms, and theorizations carried on in it. When Wole Soyinka won the Nobel Prize for Literature in 1986, there were, inevitably, those who saw the hand of politics in it. A commentator from India took up issues with *The Economist* and *The Daily Telegraph* of the U.K. for saying so, defending the laureate on the "meritorious" ground that he is not a third world writer because he writes in English:

Literary discourse is language-specific. English is not a third world language. It is the first and the second world language. African states have adopted it . . . because that is the only solution to the language problem of multi-tribal and multi-linguistic states. To be a third world writer can only mean to be a writer in a third world language, because the discourse of literature is language-specific. (qtd. in "GPD" 2022)

Thus, according to this polemicist, the language a writer uses is the whole determinant of his identity (as a writer); the political and cultural backgrounds from and for which he writes come a far second. Always latent and implicit in postcolonial discourse, the erasure of "national literature" category and cultural differences in all postcolonial states that use a common language is now being openly canvassed. Bill Ashcroft, one of the authors of the pioneering book *The Empire Writes Back*, in a recent essay can, for instance, find much in common between Africa and Australia because both continents "exist in contemporary consciousness (as) specifically colonial constructions" (1994 161). Defining PostColoniality as "the discourse of opposition to colonialism which begins from the first moment of colonization" (162), Ashcroft in this technicist vein goes on to identify the use of English as one of the three areas the two postcolonial spaces (Africa and Australia) share in common: "in both regions the development of literatures in English has given birth to some of the most resonant imaginings of cultural experience" (163). From this large claim for English in Africa, Ashcroft asserts its centrality in the African writer's contemporary imagination: it is "one of the most powerful ways of communicating cultural difference as well as re-imagining a social future" (164). Thus, while the use of English by African writers may emphasize Africa's cultural difference from the imperial center's, it makes all the ex-colonial margins one undifferentiated creative response to colonialism, and one undifferentiated *post*colonial culture.

It is but one more step from this to bracketing out the problem word "national" from "national literatures." This, in fact, is what Christopher Clausen does in his essay " 'National Literatures' in English: Toward a New Paradigm." Clausen starts from the premise that all literatures in English are now thoroughly hybridized, and proceeds to argue that this "strain . . . has mutated so profusely (as to produce) the new phenomenon of a worldwide literature that is the product of no single culture yet exhibits inescapable family resemblances, reciprocal borrowings and influences too intimate for the claim of separateness to be really possible" (61–62).

He questions the idea of the nation itself, and asserts that "With the arguable exception of countries with long non-English literary traditions, such as India, any 'national literature' in English has a closer relation to any other than it has to any non-English literature" (63). Clausen's new critical paradigm, not surprisingly, would comprise "literary relations among authors, literary movements, societies, and periods" (61). In the case of African literature for example, this will displace social, political, and cultural (the use of traditional elements) particularities. One may heartily disagree with Clausen's proposed critical paradigm, but not so easily dismissed is his conclusion: "There is no distinct national character or essence for literature to express. . . . Instead there is something better: a nearly inexhaustible complex of changing cultures and polities that influence each other constantly through a common medium of communication." (71).

Thus having become a "rhizome" (Ashcroft's metaphor), English language that, it was hoped, would give national unity, character, and cultural identity to the literatures produced in it by Anglophone African writers, is in the process of denying all.

## CONCLUSION: REIMAGINING THE "NATION"

In their present states, African literature in European languages and its criticism have taken up political and intellectual lives of their own, exist in a relationship of mutual reinforcement (rather than reinforcement from realities of the African situation), and are a part of the cultural by-products of global capitalism. In other words, this literature bears out Bakhtin's premise, but in an ironic manner:

The literary structure, like every ideological structure, refracts the generating socioeconomic reality, and does so in its own way. But, at the same time, in its "content," literature reflects and refracts the reflections and refractions of other ideological spheres (ethics, epistemology, political doctrines, religion, etc.). That is, in its "content" literature reflects the whole of the ideological horizon of which it is itself a part. (1989 16–17)

That is, the structure and totality of African literature in European languages reflect and refract the literature's postcolonial or neocolonial condition. We might say that, in following the politicians in the choice of European languages over indigenous ones, African writers chose to consolidate the political and cultural legacies of colonialism, in the hope of turning such legacies around, rather than envisioning new, *post*colonial beginnings. At any rate, the linguistic choice meant that the political cart was put before the cultural horse—to use an old cliché. In this, writers have collaborated in a subject that has been taboo in Africa since independence. Perhaps what is required now is to put the horse and the cart in their proper order—to commit an act of linguistic transgression that is also political; but is only a return to what is after all the norm, the original vision and motivation: cultural and political commitments to the peoples of the continent, minus the restrictive walls. This in itself is no magic wand, but it can begin that process of restoration of harmony between the African child and his/her human and physical environments, the thoughts of which propelled Ngugi's own personal transgressive act. More and more in the contemporary intellectual world, the gap between literature and the other human sciences, never separated in traditional African societies, are closing. This fact alone means that literature can no longer be separated from the languages and cultures of the peoples it is meant to serve, and that African literature must take the lead. My thesis in this chapter has been quite straightforward: that modern African literature and criticism must get out of the language trap into which both have fallen since the days of nationalism. In this regard, it is useful to recall those two fictional characters who have become characterological archetypes in Africa's colonial experience: Okonkwo and Obierika in Achebe's *Things Fall Apart*. Okonkwo, we remember, has a linguistic handicap that makes him a permanent source of danger to himself, his family, and his community. As his inarticulateness increases, he becomes more alienated from all three until, finally, he comes to grief. Obierika, on the other hand, is a master of eloquence, a thinker, and a cultural critic. He is able to conceptualize what the foreign intrusion in the community truly means and absorb it into the terms of that community's philosophic-symbolic system, *in its own language.* Maybe the gap between Achebe and Ngugi is not so wide after all.

## WORKS CITED

Achebe, Chinua. "African Literature as Restoration of Celebration." *Chinua Achebe: A Celebration.* Eds. Kirsten Holst and Anna Rutherford. Portsmouth, NH: H.E.B., 1990: 1–10.

——. "The African Writer and the English Language." *Morning Yet on Creation Day:* London: H.E.B., 1975: 55–62.

——. "The Novelist as Teacher." *Morning Yet on Creation Day.* London: H.E.B., 1975: 42–45.

——. *Things Fall Apart.* London: H.E.B., 1958.

Adeeko, Adeleke. "The Language of Head-Calling: A Review Essay on Yoruba Metalanguage: Ed. Iperi Yoruba." *Research In African Literatures* XXIII (Spring 1992): 197–201.

Anderson, Benedict. *Imagined Communities: Reflections on the Origin and Spread of Nationalism.* London: Verso, 1983.

Appiah, Kwame Anthony. "The Postcolonial and the Postmodern." *In My Father's House: Africa in the Philosophy of Culture.* Oxford: Oxford University Press, 1992: 137–57.

Ashcroft, Bill, Gareth Griffiths, and Helen Tiffin. *The Empire Writes Back: Theory and Practice in Post-Colonial Literatures.* London: Routledge, 1989.

Bakhtin, M. M. & P. M. Medvedev. *The Formal Method in Literary Scholarship: A Critical Introduction to Sociological Poetics.* Trans. Albert J. Wehrle. Cambridge, MA: Harvard University Press, 1989.

Bamgbose, Ayo. "Deprived, Endangered, and Dying Languages." *Diogenes 161*, 41.1: 19–25.

Clausen, Christopher. " 'National Literatures' in English: Toward a New Paradigm." *New Literary History* XXV.1 (Winter 1994): 61–72.

Comas, James. "The Presence of Theory / Theorizing the Present." *Research in African Literatures* XXI.1 (Spring 1990): 5–31.

Desai, Gaurav. "English as an African Language." *English Today* XXXIV.9 (April 1993): 4–11.

Emenyonu, Ernest. *The Rise of the Igbo Novel.* Ibadan: Oxford University Press, 1978.

Gates, Henry Louis, Jr. "Criticism in the Jungle." Ed. *Black Literature and Literary Theory.* New York: Methuen, 1984: 1–24.

"GPD." "Who's a Third World Writer?" *The Economic & Political Weekly.* Bombay, India. (November 22, 1986): 2022.

Greenblatt, Stephen. "Culture." *Critical Terms for Literary Study.* Eds. Frank Lentricchia and Thomas McLaughlin. Chicago: University of Chicago Press, 1990: 225–32.

Irele, Abiola. "African Literature and the Language Question." *The African Experience in Literature and Ideology* (1981): 43–65.

———. "The African Imagination." *Research in African Literatures* XXI.1 (Spring 1990): 47–67

———. "The Criticism of Modern African Literature." *The African Experience in Literature and Ideology.* Ibadan: H.E.B., 1981: 27–42.

Jeyifo, Biodun, "The Nature of Things: Arrested Decolonization and Critical Theory." *Research in African Literatures* XXI.1 (Spring 1990): 133–48.

Levi-Strauss, Claude. *Structural Anthropology.* Trans. Claire Jacobs and Brooke Grundfest. New York: Doubleday, 1967.

Ngugi, wa Thiong'o. *Decolonising the Mind: The Politics of Language in African Literature.* London: James Currey Ltd., 1986.

———. *Moving the Centre: The Struggle for Cultural Freedoms.* London: James Currey Ltd., 1993.

Okara, Gabriel. "Towards the Evolution of an African Language for African Literature." *Chinua Achebe: A Celebration* (1990): 11–18.

Okpaku, Joseph, ed. *New African Literature and the Arts: I.* New York: Thomas Crowell Co., 1970.

Ong, Walter J. *Orality and Literacy: The Technologizing of the Word.* London: Methuen, 1982.

Osundare, Niyi. "African Literature and the Crisis of Post-Structuralist Theorizing." *Dialogue in African Philosophy Monograph Series.* Ibadan: Options Books and Information Services, 1993.

*Research in African Literatures* XXIII.1 (Spring 1992 ) Special Issue: The Language Question.

Robson, Andrew E. "The Use of English in Achebe's *Anthills of the Savannah.*" *CLA Journal* 4 37.4 (June 1994): 365–76.

Soyinka, Wole. "The Writer in a Modern African State." *Art, Dialogue, and Outrage: Essays.* New York: Pantheon Books, 1993: 15–20.

Tutuola, Amos. *The Palmwine Drinkard.* London: Faber and Faber, 1952.

Zabus, Chantal. "The Logos-Eaters: The Igbo Ethno-Text." *Chinua Achebe: A Celebration* (1990): 19–30.

Chapter Three

# On the Concept:
# "Commonwealth Literature"

## Isidore Okpewho

The geographic classification of any literature may be considered a healthy exercise, to the extent, that is, that it represents an honest desire to identify the enabling context and thus the defining cultural outlook of that literature. But we can hardly deny that such an exercise begs a political question, and indeed introduces a certain cultural chauvinism whether or not this may have been intended. The regional bias of Emmanuel Obiechina's epoch-making *Culture, Tradition, and Society in the West African Novel* may be defended at least by the consideration that the bulk of the work done in this genre by African writers came, as they no doubt still do, from the western portion of the continent. But even such a delimitation carries with it an underlying query that Obiechina was evidently aware of: Is there anything in the intrinsic qualities of those novels that may be considered peculiar to western as distinct from, say, eastern Africa and thus provides further justification for the regional analysis pursued by Obiechina?

The question becomes less tractable as we set such a study within a more clearly defined political geography, whether on a small or a large scale. In a lecture I delivered at the University of Calabar in 1990, I explored certain considerations that might make it easier to speak of an *African* than a *Nigerian* literature: the color black, or shades of it; existence within a natural rather than an artificial geographic entity; common historical experiences such as enslavement and colonization; and a world view and mores bred by a combination of history and geography.

I had a slightly different problem dealing with such an issue when, at the award ceremonies for the Commonwealth Writers Prize held in Singapore in November 1993, I was asked to predict the direction in which the fiction written by citizens of that august union called the Commonwealth of Nations was heading. Although the question appears to concern itself with matters artistic, there is at least a general sense in which, even in the terms defined by the question, the artistic future of the union may not be considered independently of its political future. In other words, the identification of the art with a recognized political formation (Commonwealth) implies some level of stress between the fate of the art and the political realities within which it is located. We may thus reconstruct our question in the following way: Will the art of the novel in the Commonwealth always follow the political fortunes of the union?

Let us begin our prognosis by looking at the story so far in Africa. Of the African writers who mark the beginnings of the contemporary novel on the continent, two names are worth special mention because of the classic merit of their works. I speak here of the Sotho Thomas Mofolo and the Yoruba Daniel Fagunwa. These two men were in fundamental ways representative of the colonial order that defined life and thought in their respective nations on the southern and western parts of the continent. Trained by and attached to the Christian missions that were very much part of the colonial machine, these writers used their skills to justify the doctrines and ideologies that sustained the machine, even as they paid homage—in medium (both wrote in their native languages) and material—to the traditions out of which they had grown.

Mofolo's heroic romance, *Chaka*, illustrates the point in a unique way. Arguably, Mofolo was driven by honest nationalist pride to tell the story of a great African leader, borrowing the mythical resources of the oral tradition to project a figure who might be seen as a counterweight to the dominant colonial power of the time. Or he may well have tried to use the image of Chaka to demonstrate why Africa failed in its confrontation with forces outside itself. That the latter is the case may be explained by the portraiture given to the Zulu leader in that story: a man superbly endowed with physical and mystical powers, but one who allowed an uncontrollable urge for power to get the better of good sense and basic humanity, thus setting himself on an irredeemable course toward damnation. So, in a spirit somewhat contrary to the style of the oral tradition, the Christian-trained Mofolo portrays the heroic leader as really somewhat of a villain, a victim of the sin of pride which goeth before a fall.

Fagunwa—like Amos Tutuola after him—plumbed the Yoruba oral tradition of hunter tales for the five novels which he wrote from the late 1930s to the early 1960s. In content and imaginative texture, these novels faithfully mirror a folktale world in which human beings mingle with both natural and spiritual elements of the environment in a complex fantasy where all the sensations known to man are given the most vivid representation. Fagunwa also follows the oral tradition in concluding his stories with lessons in proper conduct and the ways of the world; and here the colonial-missionary establishment made its influence felt. For in these novels, written primarily for use in the mission schools as a complement to doctrinal education, Fagunwa often adorns his lessons not with indigenous Yoruba images but with those borrowed from Christian dogma ("God on High helps only those who help themselves"). On the whole the stories, composed under the superintending nod of the educational establishment, have been designed less to inspire the imagination than to indoctrinate the mind of the youth in a colonial system.

These biases merit our attention because they partially explain what happened to the works in question at the hands of African writers of a later day who had reason to revisit them. In his *Emperor Shaka the Great*, the Zulu poet and scholar Mazisi Kunene presents a considerably different portrait of the heroic leader from the one we find in Mofolo. Here Shaka emerges not as a bloodthirsty megalomaniac but as a skilled military tactician and a consummate administrator who paid a heavy price for the complex organization he had put in place. It may well be that the differences between Mofolo and Kunene have nationalistic undertones: the Chaka of Sotho oral tradition could hardly be identical to the Shaka as his Zulu compatriots hailed him. But evidently also Mofolo had taken his mandate from a system that Kunene, a political exile from it, had little reason to respect.

The Nigerian writer Wole Soyinka was to translate the first of Fagunwa's tales, *Ogboju Ode ninu Igbo Irunmale* (1938) into *The Forest of a Thousand Demons* (1968). Like every Yoruba pupil who read Fagunwa's works in school, Soyinka had tremendous empathy for the master and was to find him a dependable imaginative guide in his own creative exploitation of Yoruba mythology. Yet he was all too conscious of the climate of relationships wherein Fagunwa worked; so that, although in his "Translator's Note" to *Forest* he laments "the inhibitions of strange tongues and bashful idioms" that he may be imposing on the masterpiece before him, Soyinka goes ahead nonetheless to provide a free translation of the text that succeeds somewhat in liberating him from the doctrinal and ideological commitments of Fagunwa's creativity. The text may be Fagunwa's, but the tone is eminently Soyinka's.

It may be said in defense of Mofolo and Fagunwa that, in their day, the weight of the colonial machine was too heavy for the African writer's independent genius. In opting to write in their indigenous languages, they were being encouraged to aid in the evangelical work of missions trying to press their doctrines into the hearts of the subject cultures. But the corollary of colonial power was that the subject peoples saw the tools of domination, not the least of which was language, as a useful source of empowerment in their efforts to deal with the colonial machine. We will recall how, in Chinua Achebe's earlier novels, some leaders of the people guardedly encouraged their children (especially the males) to join the new dispensation so as to derive whatever benefits of empowerment were available therefrom.

When these native sons gained adequate confidence in the new language of empowerment, the first task they set themselves was to find out how their people got into the colonial predicament in the first place—in Achebe's words, "where the rain began to beat us"—and how much to recover of what had been compromised. The generation of African novelists after Mofolo and Fagunwa thus found themselves charged with contributing to the contemporary political effort to rid the land of foreign domination and reassert their cultures. They used the language of the imperial power because they needed to address the adversary in the medium of his own devising, but even here they endeavored to find room for the indigenous sensibility.

The earlier works of writers like Achebe and Ngugi bear ample marks of this dual responsibility. Take *Things Fall Apart*. Achebe's portrait of the conflict between the foreign presence and the indigenous traditions no doubt exposes the arrogance of the intruder, seeking refuge in military and other material means of coercion when it becomes clear that the argument of culture offers no justification for his claims. But we are equally invited to examine the logic of indigenous conventions as well as the credentials of those who took responsibility for the defense of the land: Were they altogether blameless? But perhaps Achebe's major effort here was to initiate a tradition in the African novel whereby the indigenous language was recognized within the context of the language of empowerment.

Why did Achebe do this? Although the British colonial administration in Africa did not go so far as the French in enunciating a policy of *assimilation* that consciously sought to make Europeans out of Africans, it is no secret—and I believe I suggested this in my point above about the quest for the tools of empowerment—that even in Anglophone Africa the cultivation of European culture guaranteed one key advantage. Indeed, as Achebe himself in one of his essays has lamented, the African youth were on the whole made to feel embarrassed about identifying with the indigenous culture. In the colonial culture, therefore, the indigenous speech suffered a certain absence, and Achebe's copious use of Igbo words in his earlier fiction—even in places where there are perfectly usable English equivalents—was a deliberate effort to reinvest his culture with a presence and place it on equal terms with the dominant one.

Ngugi has gone further than Achebe in this dual program. In a novel like *A Grain of Wheat*, the shortcomings of the key players in the struggle between the forces of imperialism and the freedom fighters are more than suggested. The arrogance and the cruelty of colonialism are, of course, roundly denounced in the Thomas Robsons and the John Thompson of the novel. But the psychoanalytic lights are trained just as intensely on the Mugos, the Karanjas, the Gikonyos of the Mau Mau movement, and other African characters to reveal Ngugi's, and the Kenyans', serious fears about the quality of the emergent African leadership.

In the matter of language, Ngugi is just as uncompromising. In *Things Fall Apart* Achebe at least provides editorial guides to the Igbo words he has used in the predominantly English text: highlighting them in italics and explaining them in a glossary at the end of the story. But in *A Grain of Wheat* Ngugi transcribes a proverb or a whole song in the original Kikuyu without a translation and with only the slightest hint, as the narrative proceeds, as to what the text is all about. And throughout the story, Ngugi uses the Kikuyu words for various objects (agricultural tools, plants, dress styles, etc.) not in italics but in the normal roman fount, no doubt because he considers them the natural words for those things and therefore endowed with as much referential value as all the rest of the text around them.

The creativity of the first two generations of African novelists in Anglophone Africa—as, arguably, in the rest of Africa as well—may thus be seen largely as a programmatic contestation, in varying degrees, of the imperial presence and the superior claims of its culture. With the attainment of political independence by their nations in the 1960s, the writers set about articulating their cultures with an eloquence that more than matched the silence into which these had been effectively consigned by the colonial machine. The "conflict of cultures" novel, as the tradition inaugurated by Achebe has been rightly called, had a particularly fertile run in his part of Nigeria in the 1960s, celebrating the indigenous selfhood with a vengeance. Novelists like John Munonye, Flora Nwapa, and Elechi Amadi followed Achebe so dutifully in documenting (in an almost ethnographic sense) the culture, and exploiting the indigenous speech, as to appear little more than Achebe clones; even a 1993 novel like Phanuel Egejuru's *The Seed Yams Have Been Eaten* has a surfeit of Igbo words in the text and a glossary at the end. The epitome of this cultural assertion may be seen in Gabriel Okara's *The Voice*, which subjects the English of the novel to the syntactical structure of Okara's native Ijo.

It took less than a decade for the novel in these independent nations to turn its attention elsewhere. The fears expressed by Achebe and Ngugi—about the propensities of Africans poised to inherit power from the colonial administration—were justified after all. Consequently, the next generation of novelists found themselves grappling with the postindependence evils of corruption, decay (moral and environmental), nepotism, and the general misdirection of power practiced by native African rulers. Achebe himself ushered this trend with *No Longer at Ease* (1977), but it was in the hands of Wole Soyinka (*The Interpreters*, 1965) and Ayi Kwei Armah (*The Beautyful Ones Are Not Yet Born*, 1969) that it hit its most imaginative form.

A decade, therefore, that celebrated the transfer of power from Britain and a liberation (however partial) from her cultural control now ended up denouncing the record of controls by the native African leadership. The shift of attention in the novels dealing with these things is significant. Whatever may be the terms of withdrawal of the African nations from British political control, some writers, at least, showed considerable independence in training their lenses on local problems without necessarily setting them—although they sometimes chose to do so—against the background of foreign influences.

With the continued deterioration of the social, political, and economic scene in Africa, the need to subsume the links with Britain has become increasingly less urgent for the writers—again, even when Britain may be considered partially responsible for these problems. Take a novel like Festus Iyayi's *Heroes*, which won the Commonwealth Writers Prize in 1987. The strident proletarian concern of the story may be attributed to the Marxist leanings of the writer, but the responsibility for the sociopolitical tragedy of the Nigerian civil war is placed squarely on the shoulders of various segments of the indigenous Nigerian leadership—the soldiers, the church, the businessmen, the professors, and so on—who have kept alive and exploited the social inequities and the ethnic cleavages among the people.

Iyayi must know of the fundamental problems created by the colonial infrastructure on which Nigerian society continues to exist. But he also knows, as most fellow

Nigerians do, that roughly four decades after political independence from Britain Nigerians should be smart enough to know how to put their house in proper order. And I believe one could safely say that the prominent mark of the Commonwealth novel in Africa is as follows: While it perceives the subtleties of foreign influence on local political fortunes, it is somewhat more committed to castigating those indigenous forces within the present dispensation that continue to frustrate the people's pursuit of peace and the basic needs of life.

Now, where is such a novel going? Lest I be thought naive in underplaying the role of foreign influences in African life, perhaps I should begin my prognosis by recognizing Ngugi's recent analyses of our cultural dilemma that have led him to advocate the use first of the indigenous language (*Decolonising the Mind*) and, more recently, of a regional patois like Swahili (*Moving the Centre*). It is, of course, foolish to condemn the nationalist inspiration for Ngugi's declarations on the issue of language. But I think his shift in allegiance indicates that he himself realized the inherent risks in his program, not the least of which is the potential rivalry between one cultural chauvinism and another within the continent. Ngugi must know, of course, that a lot of fiction is written today in various African countries—as in various other countries of the world—in indigenous languages. But I suspect that he is not quite aware how little practical chance its authors have, perhaps due to no fault of theirs, of influencing the world by the force either of their genius or of their vision.

I am more interested, however, in why Ngugi shifted his support from his native Kikuyu to the more widely used Swahili. Could it be that further reflection on the matter broadened his mind and gave him a wider regional rather than a narrow ethnic outlook? Or could it be, rather, that the experience of exile provided him a vantage point from which to look at the world beyond the limited boundaries of his native Kenya? For the recognition of Swahili as only one among many linguistic or cultural centers available for the location of global power clearly argues a more ecumenical outlook than the more jealous embrace of Kikuyu may have done.

Whatever the implications of Ngugi's change of position, this latter possibility certainly draws attention to the tragic reality of present-day African society: the decay and degradation that most of our writers have constantly decried have reached such proportions as to severely deter the growth of the art in many countries. Writers are thrown into jail on the slightest pretext; increasingly fewer people can provide for themselves or their families; and the general frustration has given rise to social insecurity and political anomie. The effect of all this is to force many writers into exile.

Several things are likely to happen to such writers. They may be so thoroughly disoriented, socially and culturally, that they lose the will to write. Or they may be driven by a feeling of nostalgia that expresses itself in one of two ways: (1) the more skillful ones keep faith with their roots by continually exploiting the indigenous traditions for symbolic or stylistic essences; (2) the less endowed ones are so eager to touch base with home, but so out of tune with the subtle dynamics of daily life within it, that their writing descends to a romantic evocation of stages of cultural awareness that their societies have left fairly behind.

Let me stress that there will continue to be novelists who live in their native African countries, although the present economic conditions of such countries leave little room for the sustained growth of the creative imagination. In the two possibilities that I raised above, I had in mind writers who continue to take their subjects entirely from Africa. Now a third possibility leads me back to what I said earlier about Ngugi's new-found ecumenical outlook. This is that, since the creative imagination is more viably nourished by the environment in which it abides, there will be increasingly more African novelists in exile dealing with subjects that transcend their native lands.

The mildest form of this imagination—which we should perhaps call not so much exile as peregrine—may be seen in Ama Ata Aidoo's *Our Sister Killjoy.* The radical concerns raised by its protagonist, Sissie—about the obsequious cultivation by African politicians of their European mentors rather than their native constituents, the uncritical taste for foreign culture among intellectuals and socialites alike, the naive faith in an easy racial rapprochement in southern Africa, and especially the marginalization of women that goes against the grain of our indigenous traditions—may well have been influenced by Aidoo's experience of these realities in her native Ghana. But these realities equally exist in a wider geographical swath of the African continent than the areas defined by the so-called Commonwealth. Besides, the fact that Sissie's critique has been inspired by her travels across the Western world demonstrates that the novel's enabling genius may be sought beyond the limited confines of the Commonwealth even though its author is still *technically* a citizen of it.

A more revealing prospect is contained in recent works by two non-African citizens who are now technically exiles. The Indian-born writer Bharati Mukherjee, who now lives in America, has said that the inspiration for her recent novel, *The Holder of the World*, was a seventeenth century Indian miniature she saw at a pre-auction show at Sotheby's in New York, in the form of a blond Caucasian woman in ornate Mogul court dress, holding a lotus blossom. The novel itself tells the story of an American woman, Beigh Masters, who recreates the experiences of a seventeenth century jewel owner through the three regions of the world where Mukherjee herself has lived—India, Britain, and America—in a tale that impressively demonstrates the interrelatedness of their cultures. But in his novel, *Coming Through Slaughter*, the Sri Lankan-born Michael Ondaatje has moved away altogether from the Commonwealth as we know it, to New Orleans in the American South, recreating the colorful but tormented career of Charles "Buddy" Bolden in a syncopated format that brilliantly captures the artistry of the jazz form created by Bolden and his contemporaries at the turn of the century. If we find the novel torn between the contending claims of American and Commonwealth literary history, then we may understand why, for some time now, critics have had trouble deciding in whose cultural territory Joyce Cary's Nigerian-set novels really belong.

Clearly, Mukherjee and Ondaatje demonstrate which way the Commonwealth novel is going as the citizens of the union move out of their original homelands, for whatever reasons, and become citizens of a wider world. The Commonwealth novel, that is, may be leaving the Commonwealth even when her citizens continue to live in some part of the union; no doubt, the fact that Bharati Mukherjee has recently taken an American citizenship stretches the argument considerably further. The answer, therefore, to the question: Will the art of the novel in the Commonwealth always follow the political fortunes of the union?—may thus be a qualified Yes. For as long as the Commonwealth and its citizens continue to be subject to geopolitical forces that cause one kind of displacement or another, for so long will the genius of the writer try to find its range in the new environment. However, unless we can identify such a thing as a Commonwealth mind, then we may find that in many cases the political union will lay fewer claims to the products of the writer's peregrine genius. In other words, if geopolitical forces continue their present trend, what kind of Commonwealth novel will there be when all of its enabling genius has been forced to flee the political union and seek life elsewhere?

No doubt the same question can be asked of the overall field termed "Commonwealth literature." Whether or not we accept the term as a viable definition of an activity within a recognized political union—and, despite the disclaimer issued by the authors of *The Empire Writes Back* (22–24  180), the concept is still very much alive—we can hardly evade the political burden that this recognition bears and that this chapter has intended to highlight: what good *is* the Commonwealth to the literature? Even more directly, what good is this august body called the Commonwealth to its citizens?

It is sufficiently clear, from our survey above of the growth of the Anglophone African novel, that the trend has consistently been toward an affirmation of a way of life that the colonial presence may have tried to suppress, and a disavowal of the unhealthy propensities of the postindependence polity. But it is hardly clear that the custodians of the august union we call the Commonwealth share the interests that its writers have sought to defend. For its political leaders have continued to look conveniently aside, indeed, have tended to smile with approval,while the writers are thrown into jail and kept there for interminable periods without formal charges (let alone a trial), and would seem to sigh with some relief while several others are forced to flee their countries and settle down in places where they would hardly have chosen to spend the rest of their active lives. If the Commonwealth and the literature which it presumes to shelter are to continue to mean anything, then its political leadership must rethink the union's charter of existence so as to take practical steps, even military ones, if need be, to restrain those who make life untenable for those others who would continue to practice the art in their native lands. Enough is enough.

## WORKS CITED

Achebe, Chinua. *No Longer at Ease*. London: Heinemann, 1977.

————. *Things Fall Apart*. London: Heinemann, 1958.

Armah, Ayi Kwei. *The Beautyful Ones Are Not Yet Born*. London: Heinemann, 1969.

Ashcroft, Bill, Gareth Griffiths, and Helen Tiffin. *The Empire Writes Back: Theory and Practice in Post-Colonial Literatures*. London: Routledge, 1989.

Egejuru, Phanuel. *The Seed Yams Have Been Eaten*. Ibadan: Heinemann (Nigeria), 1993.

Fagunwa, D.O. *Ogboju Ode ninu Igbo Irunmale*. Edinburgh: Nelson, 1938. Trans. Wole Soyinka as *The Forest of a Thousand Demons*. London: Nelson, 1968.

Iyayi, Festus. *Heroes*. Harlow: Longman, 1986.

Kunene, Mazisi. *Emperor Shaka the Great*. London: Heinemann, 1979.

Mofolo, Thomas. *Chaka*. Trans. D.P. Kunene. Oxford: Heinemann, 1981.

Mukherjee, Bharati. *The Holder of the World*. New York: Knopf, 1993.

Ngugi, wa Thiong'o. *Decolonising the Mind*. London: Currey, 1986.

————. *A Grain of Wheat*. London: Heinemann, 1967.

————. *Moving the Centre*. London: James Currey, 1993.

Obiechina, Emmanuel. *Culture, Tradition, and Society in the West African Novel*. Cambridge: Cambridge University Press, 1975.

Okara, Gabriel. *The Voice*. London: Deutsch, 1964.

Okpewho, Isidore. "Is There a Nigerian Literature?" *The Guardian* (Lagos) 6 October 1990: 18.

Ondaatje, Michael. *Coming Through Slaughter*. New York: Penguin, 1976.

Soyinka, Wole. *The Interpreters*. London: Deutsch, 1965.

# Chapter Four

---

# Who Counts?
# De-Ciphering the Canon

## *Bernth Lindfors*

In 1985, I introduced a simple arithmetical scheme for measuring, both compara-
tively and diachronically, the literary stature of writers from anglophone Africa.
Since this elegant blunt instrument is not yet widely known, and since I now intend
to extend its scope up to the end of 1991, it may be well for me to rehearse once
again the ground rules governing the reduction of fine literary distinctions to the
less subtle certainties of round numbers.

My objective was to provide verifiable answers to several looming but unresolved questions: Who are the major authors in anglophone Africa today? How can
the reputation of one be measured against the reputation of another in an objective
manner so that the relative importance of each can be ascertained quickly, accurately, and dispassionately, without the least trace of subjective bias? How, in other
words, can we determine scientifically who stands where in the pecking order
established by the preferences and prejudices of public opinion? How can we
quantify qualitative discriminations?

As one approach to these problems, I devised a Famous Authors' Reputation
Test that records the frequency with which an author and his works are discussed
in detail in print by literary scholars and critics. A score is thus arrived at that can
be compared to the scores achieved by other authors from the same data base. Those
who score highest can be said to have gained wider recognition than those who
register a lower number of substantive citations. The Famous Authors' Reputation
Test ensures that an author's fame will be assessed not intuitively or ecstatically but
purely mathematically. Plain numbers will determine the final ranking.

The data base from which statistical information has been taken in this quest for
objective analysis is the most comprehensive one I could lay my hands on—namely,
my own bibliography, *Black African Literature in English: A Guide to Information*

*Sources* (Detroit: Gale, 1979), and its two five-year supplements, *Black African Literature in English, 1977–1981* (New York: Africana, 1986) and *Black African Literature in English, 1982–1986* (Oxford: Zell, 1989), to which I will now add the data from the latest five-year compilation, *Black African Literature in English, 1987–1991* (Oxford: Zell, 1995)—volumes, which together attempt to list all the important critical books and articles (in whatever language) published on anglophone black African literature from 1936 to 1991. The first volume (hereafter cited as BALE I), covering the earliest forty years of academic productivity, contains 3,305 entries; the second (BALE II), covering five additional years, contains 2,831 entries; the third (BALE III), covering another five years, contains 5,689 entries; and the most recent five-year supplement (BALE IV) contains an impressive 8,772 entries—a proportional increase testifying to the tremendous growth of critical interest in this literature in recent times. The expanded data base now consists of 20,734 books and articles produced over a fifty-five year period. This is not a small or inconsequential corpus of criticism.

But while these four volumes seek to be as comprehensive as possible, they remain to a degree selective: certain materials of marginal interest are deliberately omitted. For instance, brief reviews of books and of stage performances, political biographies of statesmen, and newspaper reports on some of the nonliterary activities of famous authors are excluded, but not review articles, biographical materials and newspaper items possessing some literary significance. No creative works—novels, stories, plays, poems, anthologies—are recorded unless prefaced by a critical introduction. The intention throughout is to provide thorough coverage of major scholarly books and periodicals as well as selective coverage of other relevant sources of informed commentary.

In each volume, the bibliographical corpus is divided into two parts, the first organized by genre or topic, the second by individual author. Annotations are appended to some entries, mostly to identify the authors with whom the article or book is primarily concerned. The general rule of thumb is to note all authors who receive at least a page or two of commentary. If many authors are mentioned but none is discussed at length, the annotation indicates that the work is a survey. "Et al." (and others) is used whenever a work briefly treats additional authors.

A concerted effort has been made to list each item in the cumulative bibliography only once and to provide numbered cross-references to it in all other sections to which the item belongs. For example, an article on Nigerian drama discussing J.P. Clark, Ola Rotimi, and Wole Soyinka in some detail (i.e., devoting at least a page to examination of each writer) but treating other Nigerian dramatists in a cursory fashion (i.e., discussing them in less than a page each) would appear in the drama section in Part One with an annotation reading "Clark, Rotimi, Soyinka, et al." The number of that entry would then be included among the cross-references following the individual sections in Part Two listing books and articles devoted exclusively to Clark, Rotimi, and Soyinka, respectively. On the other hand, a specialized article on only one author (e.g., "Pidgin English in Soyinka's Plays") would be recorded under Soyinka in Part Two with numbered cross-references appearing in the topical sections on "Drama" and "Language and Style" in Part One. So each author treated in the bibliography has a special niche in Part Two where all the books and articles dealing with him or her alone are listed, after which numbered cross-references provide leads to all other items in the bibliography that offer substantive commentary on his or her work. A good many of these cross-references may yield no more than a few pages of sustained criticism, but certain of them—book chapters, lengthy monographs, or doctoral dissertations focusing on only two or three writers, for instance—may provide much more exhaustive treatment of specific texts than do some of the individual articles.

Nonetheless, in devising a scoring system for my Famous Authors' Reputation Test, I have decided to award three points for every discrete entry on an individual author and one point for every cross-reference. This seems to reflect the balance between the two categories more accurately than does a straight one-for-one system that would tend to inflate the scores of authors who are frequently cited but seldom examined with any care. An author who is known but never studied intensively may be a significant minor reference point in African literature, but it is unlikely that he commands the kind of respect that would earn him a measure of distinction. Literary critics and scholars tend to gravitate toward those writers whose works interest them the most. They do not waste too much time on second-rate talents.

Table 4.1 is a list of the fifteen writers who achieved a score of at least 500 on the Famous Authors' Reputation Test and then a list of twenty-five others who achieved a score of at least 160. According to statistics gleaned from more than half a century of critical commentary,these forty names are those most consistently chosen as worthy of serious attention, constituting what could be called a High Canon and Low Canon.

But since such a list may be biased toward older writers who have been on the scene a long time, it may be interesting to look at the figures derived from the latest volume alone in order to see who among the younger writers has emerged as important in the eyes of scholars and critics in more recent years. Table 4.2 thus gives the scores for twenty writers who gained more than 150 points between 1987 and 1991 and then lists twenty-eight others who earned at least 70 points during the same period. Asterisks have been placed beside those names making the most striking short-term gains. These are evidently the most upwardly mobile celebrities at the moment, but it remains to been seen whether they will have the kind of staying power that their colleagues have already manifested.

Since some reputations have waxed or waned over time, I am presenting in Table 4.3 the breakdown of figures for the top scorers from 1977–1986 separately and then giving grand totals for each of the four categories on the scoreboard. To this, I am adding the figures for 1987–1991 separately and then cumulatively under New Grand Totals, and supplementing the original High Canon of fifteen names with those of nine up-and-coming neo-canonical or near-canonical figures of impressive statistical weight. As can be seen from the new numbers ranged in the final column, Head, Emecheta, and Rotimi have already overtaken Awoonor as all-time greats,

**Table 4.1**
**New Grand Weighted Totals, 1936–1991**

| | |
|---|---|
| 1. Soyinka | 5330 |
| 2. Achebe | 4294 |
| 3. Ngugi | 2706 |
| 4. Armah | 1081 |
| 5. Clark | 844 |
| 6. Ekwensi | 784 |
| 7. Tutuola | 778 |
| 8. Head | 619 |
| 9. Mphahlele | 607 |
| 10. Okigbo | 586 |
| 11. LaGuma | 578 |
| 12. Okot | 575 |
| 13. Brutus | 571 |
| 14. Abrahams | 563 |
| 15. Okara | 530 |
| 16. Emecheta | 467 |
| 17. Rotimi | 444 |
| 18. Awoonor | 415 |
| 19. Saro-Wiwa | 371 |
| 20. Aidoo | 366 |
| 21. Osofisan | 366 |
| 22. Farah | 341 |
| 23. Amadi | 286 |
| 24. Omotoso | 277 |
| 25. Nwapa | 275 |
| 26. Liyong | 237 |
| 27. Equiano | 235 |
| 28. Marechera | 235 |
| 29. Osundare | 235 |
| 30. Rive | 223 |
| 31. Aluko | 211 |
| 32. Chinweizu | 208 |
| 33. Iyayi | 208 |
| 34. Serote | 208 |
| 35. Plaatje | 199 |
| 36. Mazrui | 187 |
| 37. Nkosi | 182 |
| 38. Ike | 173 |
| 39. Mitshali | 167 |
| 40. Okpewho | 167 |

**Table 4.2**
**New Grand Weighted Totals, 1987–1991**

1. Soyinka          2359
2. Achebe           1831
3. Ngugi            1049
4. Armah             438
5. Saro-Wiwa         343
6. Head              327
7. Ekwensi           256
8. Clark             236
9. Emecheta          233
10. Osofisan*        226
11. La Guma          223
12. Osundare*        204
13. Iyayi*           190
14. Tutuola          188
15. Farah*           185
16. Mphahlele        179
17. Rotimi           178
18. Brutus           175
19. Okara            173
20. Marechera*       161
21. Chinweizu        149
22. Abrahams         144
23. Omotoso          144
24. Aidoo            137
25. Nwapa            124
26. Rive             124
27. Okigbo           123
28. Okot             122
29. Serote           115
30. Okpewho          110
31. Amadi            105
32. Mapanje          103
33. Ike              102
34. Okri             100
35. Fonlon            98
36. Equiano           88
37. Tlali             87
38. Mazrui            82
39. Nkosi             81
40. Ndebele           81
41. Nwoga             81
42. Ngema             80
43. Sepamla           79
44. Sofola            79
45. Sowande           79
46. Plaatje           72
47. Awoonor           71

**Table 4.3**
**Breakdown of Figures for the Top Scorers**

| AUTHOR | E | CR | RT | WT | E | CR | RT | WT | E | CR | RT | WT |
|---|---|---|---|---|---|---|---|---|---|---|---|---|
| Achebe | 190 | 151 | 341 | 721 | 216 | 230 | 446 | 878 | 591 | 690 | 1281 | 2463 |
| Armah | 27 | 68 | 95 | 149 | 80 | 102 | 182 | 342 | 132 | 247 | 379 | 643 |
| Awoonor | 21 | 31 | 52 | 94 | 28 | 55 | 83 | 139 | 65 | 150 | 215 | 345 |
| Brutus | 16 | 25 | 41 | 73 | 52 | 54 | 106 | 210 | 94 | 114 | 208 | 396 |
| Clark | 17 | 52 | 69 | 103 | 49 | 114 | 163 | 261 | 96 | 320 | 416 | 608 |
| Ekwensi | 23 | 40 | 63 | 109 | 42 | 69 | 111 | 195 | 101 | 225 | 326 | 528 |
| La Guma | 12 | 30 | 42 | 66 | 50 | 48 | 98 | 198 | 76 | 127 | 203 | 355 |
| Mphahlele | 22 | 48 | 70 | 114 | 34 | 61 | 95 | 163 | 82 | 182 | 264 | 428 |
| Ngugi | 129 | 108 | 237 | 495 | 242 | 209 | 451 | 935 | 414 | 415 | 829 | 1657 |
| Okara | 7 | 43 | 50 | 64 | 21 | 71 | 92 | 134 | 44 | 255 | 269 | 357 |
| Okigbo | 16 | 41 | 57 | 89 | 39 | 49 | 88 | 166 | 94 | 181 | 275 | 463 |
| Okot | 20 | 45 | 65 | 105 | 55 | 51 | 106 | 216 | 105 | 138 | 243 | 453 |
| Soyinka | 144 | 168 | 312 | 600 | 418 | 312 | 730 | 1566 | 737 | 760 | 1497 | 2971 |
| Tutuola | 28 | 47 | 75 | 131 | 42 | 45 | 87 | 171 | 125 | 215 | 340 | 590 |

| AUTHOR | (1987–1991) | | | | NEW GRAND TOTALS | | | |
|---|---|---|---|---|---|---|---|---|
| | E | CR | RT | WT | E | CR | RT | WT |
| Abrahams | 30 | 54 | 84 | 144 | 122 | 197 | 319 | 563 |
| Achebe | 500 | 331 | 831 | 1831 | 1091 | 1021 | 2112 | 4294 |
| Armah | 109 | 111 | 220 | 438 | 241 | 358 | 599 | 1081 |
| Awoonor | 8 | 47 | 55 | 71 | 73 | 197 | 270 | 416 |
| Brutus | 47 | 34 | 81 | 175 | 141 | 148 | 289 | 571 |
| Clark | 55 | 71 | 126 | 236 | 151 | 391 | 542 | 844 |
| Ekwensi | 64 | 64 | 128 | 256 | 165 | 289 | 454 | 784 |
| La Guma | 59 | 46 | 105 | 223 | 135 | 173 | 308 | 578 |
| Mphahlele | 40 | 59 | 99 | 179 | 122 | 241 | 363 | 607 |
| Ngugi | 266 | 251 | 517 | 1049 | 680 | 666 | 1346 | 2706 |
| Okara | 34 | 71 | 105 | 173 | 78 | 296 | 374 | 530 |
| Okigbo | 24 | 51 | 75 | 123 | 118 | 232 | 350 | 586 |
| Okot | 28 | 38 | 66 | 122 | 133 | 176 | 309 | 575 |
| Soyinka | 676 | 331 | 1007 | 2359 | 1414 | 1091 | 2504 | 5330 |
| Tutuola | 40 | 68 | 108 | 188 | 165 | 283 | 488 | 778 |

| AUTHOR | (1987–1991) | | | | NEW GRAND TOTALS | | | |
|---|---|---|---|---|---|---|---|---|
| | E | CR | RT | WT | E | CR | RT | WT |
| Emecheta | 50 | 83 | 133 | 233 | 109 | 140 | 249 | 467 |
| Farah | 53 | 26 | 79 | 185 | 92 | 65 | 157 | 431 |
| Head | 88 | 63 | 151 | 327 | 166 | 121 | 287 | 619 |
| Iyayi | 56 | 22 | 78 | 190 | 59 | 31 | 90 | 208 |
| Marechera | 48 | 17 | 65 | 161 | 66 | 37 | 103 | 235 |
| Osofisan | 57 | 55 | 112 | 226 | 87 | 103 | 90 | 364 |
| Rotimi | 44 | 46 | 90 | 178 | 100 | 144 | 244 | 444 |
| Saro-Wiwa | 106 | 25 | 131 | 343 | 114 | 29 | 143 | 371 |

but only Head has managed to break into the ranks of the High Canonicals (i.e., those with over 500 points).

The scoring method employed in the Famous Authors' Reputation Test works as follows: Entries (E) and Cross-References (CR) have been added together to produce a Raw Total (RT). Entries have been multiplied three times and then added to Cross-References to produce a Weighted Total (WT), which I regard as a more reliable indicator of reputation than a simple Raw Total. The last column—the Grand Weighted Total (GWT)—reveals where each author stood in relation to others in the pantheon of anglophone African literature by the end of 1991.

It is clear, for example, that Achebe and Soyinka have always been at the very top; that Ngugi and Armah have made impressive gains in the past decade to solidify their hold on places 3 and 4; that Clark and Ekwensi have wobbled a bit but have made game comebacks in BALEs III and IV, respectively, partly on the strength of substantial cross-reference numbers; that La Guma and Mphahlele have made modest gains; that Tutuola, Okigbo, Abrahams, and Okara, on the other hand, have experienced moderate declines; that women writers—notably Head, Emecheta and Aidoo—have made striking advances of late; that Saro-Wiwa, the most meteoric "new kid on the block," has suddenly made his way up from being an almost complete nonentity in the first three time-frames to occupying position number five in the last; that Okot and Brutus have experienced substantial instability, leaving them in a potentially precarious equilibrium; and that Awoonor, though suffering a precipitous recent drop, has retained sufficient residual numerical strength to remain, at least for now, in the top twenty on the new Grand Weighted Totals (GWT).

However, if we look more closely at the charts, taking into account the organization of entries in the data base, it is not difficult to explain some of the seismic ups and downs we see represented there. Entries under "Individual Authors" in Part Two of each volume of *Black African Literature in English* are divided into four categories: (1) Bibliography, (2) Biography and Autobiography, (3) Interviews, and (4) Criticism. If an author is newsworthy: that is, if he or she attracts a great deal of attention in the press or in periodicals as a result of notorious deeds (e.g., the winning of a prize, the losing of a freedom, the taking of a stand, the giving of a tribute, the initiation of a controversy, the ending of a life), there are likely to be numerous entries in the Biography and Autobiography subsection, each of which will garner the author three points in the Weighted Total as well as in the Grand Weighted Total, the same number of points that are awarded for a critical book or essay on the author's work. Thus, Wole Soyinka's Nobel Prize, coming at the end of 1986, was sufficient to catapult him well ahead of Chinua Achebe, with whom he had been running almost neck and neck since 1977. Indeed, had it been possible to list every newspaper article published on Soyinka's winning of this prize, the gap between Soyinka and Achebe, not to mention all the rest of the anglophone African writing community, would have been much wider. Similarly, Ngugi's detention in 1978 and subsequent political activities both in Kenya and abroad; the deaths of Okot p'Bitek, Alex La Guma, and Bessie Head; the return of Es'kia Mphahlele to

South Africa in 1978; and the deportation trial of Dennis Brutus in 1982–1983 added considerably to their individual WT scores.

In the final category, the high scores for some of the newcomers can be traced to both literary and extra-literary factors. Festus Iyayi won a Commonwealth Writers' Prize in 1988, but he also made headlines when his political activities got him sacked from the University of Benin in 1987 and arrested and detained in 1988. Niyi Osundare was the recipient of four major literary honors: an Association of Nigerian Authors Prize in 1990, the Noma Award in 1991, and the Commonwealth Poetry Prize twice—in 1986 and 1991; these successes led to many newspaper interviews and journalistic profiles of the author as well as to increased critical attention. And Ken Saro-Wiwa, who rose faster from obscurity than any other writer in anglophone Africa, was given extensive media coverage when his serialized comedy, *Basi and Company*, became one of the most popular television shows in Nigeria; in fact, Saro-Wiwa earned the great majority of his points from reportage and interviews in the Nigerian press. There were hardly any articles published on him outside Nigeria. He won his reputation almost entirely at home, not abroad. Such biographically inflated figures do not necessarily detract from the statistical reliability of the Famous Authors' Reputation Test. Notoriety, after all, is part of what makes an author famous. But remarkable variations in an author's trajectory need to be studied carefully if we are to understand whether they are the consequence of increased public attention being given to the author's deeds or to his works. Some authors may be more notorious than they are respected. A relatively high GWT score in 1991 is not necessarily an irrevocable passport guaranteeing permanent entry into an anglophone African writers' Hall of Fame. Time marches on, and if a writer's works do not sufficiently interest or engage future generations of readers after that writer is gone, he or she will eventually lose relative standing, a fate that will be reflected in a downward trajectory on later charts.

A word also needs to be said about gross numbers. More significant than a writer's relative rank in the Famous Authors' Reputation Test is the total number of points he or she has accrued. Perhaps it would help to put this in visual terms, using the GWT figures for all four volumes as the basis Table 4.4.

The dramatic disparities between the front-running troika (Soyinka, Achebe, Ngugi) and the rest of the pack are now quite apparent. Indeed, it is unlikely that anyone will catch up to them in the near future, for at each five-year interval so far they have put greater distance between themselves and their followers. In any construction of a canon of anglophone African writing, works by these three writers would have to rank high. Their reputations are very great and growing.

This is not to say that there is no hope for younger writers whose names do not yet appear on any of the charts. On the contrary, several of them have made striking gains in the past ten years, and one may expect a handful of them to keep rising in the ranks. But the only way that they and others can continue to ascend or to hold their own in future tabulations is by regularly being the subject of critical scrutiny——that is, by frequently being written about. The Famous Authors' Reputation Test shows no mercy on writers whose works or lives do not attract commentary. The

**Table 4.4**
**New Grand Totals, 1936–1991**

| 1. Soyinka | 5329 | 6. Ekwensi | 784 | 11. La Guma | 577 |
|---|---|---|---|---|---|
| 2. Achebe | 4290 | 7. Tutuola | 778 | 12. Okot | 575 |
| 3. Ngugi | 2710 | 8. Head | 617 | 13. Brutus | 571 |
| 4. Armah | 1080 | 9. Mphahlele | 607 | 14. Abrahams | 563 |
| 5. Clark | 844 | 10. Okigbo | 586 | 15. Okara | 530 |

unexamined literary career is not worth much in a noisy marketplace of ideas. To be famous, to be reputable, to be deemed worthy of serious and sustained consideration, an author needs as much criticism as possible, year after year after year. Only those who pass this test of time—the test of persistent published interest in their art—will stand a chance of earning literary immortality.

And the progress of such pilgrims toward final canonization can be assessed as easily and accurately with statistics gleaned from a citation index as with any other divining instrument. Simple numbers may not tell us the whole truth and nothing but the truth, but they can reveal something of the truth in an objective and unbiased fashion. Indeed, quantification may be the best possible method for dispassionately measuring and comparing literary reputations. To arrive at an honest, trustworthy, scientifically constructed canon, all we need to do is count and decipher the relevant numbers.

Chapter Five

---

# Five Nigerian Novels and
# Public Morality

## *Romanus N. Egudu*

It was Sir Philip Sidney (1554–1586) who once argued that the poet (the artist in general) combines the moral functions of both the moral philosopher and the historian. According to Sidney, the moral philosopher, "setting downe with thorny argument the bare rule, is so hard of utterance, so mistie to bee conceived, that one that had no other guide but him, shall wade in him till he bee olde, before he shall finde sufficient cause to bee honest; for his knowledge standeth so upon the abstract and generals, that happie is the man who may understand him, and more happie, that can applye what he dooth understand." And the historian, continued Sidney, "wanting the precept, is so tyed, not to what should bee, but to what is, to the particular truth of things, and not to the general reason of things, that hys example draweth no necessary consequence and therefore a less fruitful doctrine." To conclude, Sidney said that the poet (artist) performs both functions, "for whatsoever the Philosopher sayth should be doone, he giveth a perfect picture of it in some one, by whom hee presupposeth it was done. So hee couples the generall notion with the particular example" (qtd. in Smith 1951 200–201).

The validity (or lack of it) of Sidney's comparison and contrast is not the burden of our present discussion. However, we may quickly observe that Sidney is not fair to the philosopher, whose method of exposition is and ought to be different from that of the poet. And as David Daiches has rightly observed, "though poetry for Sidney is a more effective moral teacher than philosophy . . . the critic of poetry has to wait for the moral philosopher or the man of religion to tell him what is morally good and what is morally bad before he can proceed to judge a poem" (71–72). Nor is Sidney terribly fair to the historian, whose moral "examples" (albeit tied more to what is than to what ought to be) have been known to be of great consequence in human life and society. For history houses, among other things, "lives of great men," and the American H.W. Longfellow has appropriately immortalized in "A Psalm of Life" the fact that:

> Lives of great men all remind us
> We can make our lives sublime,
> And, departing, leave behind us
> Footprints on the sands of time.

This is true in spite of the paradoxical view of Hegel that although there are "moral teaching" and "examples of virtue" in history, yet "peoples and governments never have learned anything from history" (6). And we may hasten to remark that if people do not learn anything from history, it is not because there is nothing to learn from it; and that therefore we cannot blame the lack of that learning on history.

Nonetheless, Sidney's statement is significant to the extent that it points to the relevance and usefulness of the literary artist in society. His view is just one of the very many that have been advanced in answer to Plato's crucial skepticism about the role of the artist in his city-state. After accusing the "imitative art" of seducing other members of the state by arousing their passions instead of appealing to their reasoning faculty, and of being "thrice removed from the king and from the truth," Plato called on "those of her defenders who are lovers of poetry," saying "let them show not only that she is pleasant but also useful to States and to human life, and we will listen in a kindly spirit; for if this can be proved we shall surely be the gainers—I mean, if there is a use in poetry as well as a delight" (qtd. in Jowett 1946 367). The use that Sidney as one of such "defenders" and "lovers" of the literary art has found in it is a moral one—a use that is relevant in any human society at all times and in all places. And to look at just one dimension of this moral use (public morality) in the context of some Nigerian novels is our task in this chapter.

## THE WAR AGAINST PUBLIC IMMORALITY

The "War Against Indiscipline" (WAI) that Nigerians started waging in 1984 on the order of a military decree, is a clear testimony to the quest for public morality in Nigerian society. And most significant indeed is the fact that Nigerian novelists, through their novels, started waging the same war over two decades before the general one was decreed, and they have ever since been engaged in it. They have been fully alive to the fact that they have an ethical role to play among others, as the late Professor Kola Ogunbesan correctly noted when he observed, "African writers in general do not believe that they should abdicate their ethical role." But what is equally significant is that in each of the novels to be discussed, the war against indiscipline (immorality) is forcefully matched with the "War Against Discipline" (morality), for which we may as well coin the abbreviation, "WAD," at least in the peculiar sense of abbreviation; although the other (ordinary) sense of the word as a "roll" of currency notes may also apply.

In *Kinsman and Foreman*, T.M. Aluko creates for us one Titus Oti, who is poised with all the moral arms and ammunition available to him not only to ensure that he protects himself against immorality, but also to fight immorality in other people. Titus is an overseas-trained engineer and is appointed "District Engineer" for Ibala. The first moral problem Titus grapples with has to do with his kinsman, a cousin, Simeon Oke, who is also his foreman. Titus' mother and his uncle, Pa Joel, have persistently admonished him to respect Simeon in the office, to always act according to his advice, and above all to use his high office to protect him (Simeon). However, on one such occasion of admonition, Titus tells his mother bluntly that Simeon "is a very bad man," and "that is because he is corrupt. He steals money from his work. He collects money from the labourers whom he employs on the roads" (49). Ironically, however, his mother tells him he must pray to "God for forgiveness" for having sinned "against an innocent man" (49). Two other corrupt practices Simeon engages in are claiming a mileage allowance on his car that has been broken for months, and deploying government laborers to work on his private farm.

In the face of the opposition mounted by his mother and uncle and the pastor of the local church—an opposition meant to defend Simeon—Titus resolves:

It is my duty as District Engineer to see that no one steals any money. It is my duty as District Engineer to see that no one collects money from contractors and from workmen. It is therefore my duty to fight my kinsman Simeon and stop him from his evil practices. (50)

Titus practicalizes this resolution on two crucial occasions. The first is when Simeon is arrested for deploying government laborers to work on his private farm and for other corrupt practices. Titus boldly submits statements to the police, which confirm that Simeon is corrupt. And when Auntie Bimpe, a lady contractor who shares stolen money with Simeon, tries to persuade Titus to withdraw his statement from the police and even informs him that the "S.S.P." (Senior Superintendent of Police) is willing to have the statement withdrawn, Titus sharply retorts that "if a statement is withdrawn surely another can be made," emphasizing that he is not ready to say "that all the things that I know are true are no longer true, and that those I know are false are no longer false"(125). It is little wonder that the Chairman of the Commission of Enquiry set up to look into the affairs of the Ibala Public Works Department reports firmly that Titus, "the District Engineer of Ibala is very hardworking and, I am glad to say, his integrity is beyond reproach" (180). In spite of the overwhelming evidence against Simeon Oke, and because of the corrupt influence of Auntie Bimpe and Chris Daniels, a lawyer, the magistrate had "discharged" and acquitted Simeon Oke even before the Administrative Commission of Enquiry was set up (161).

The second occasion on which Titus demonstrates his integrity with regard to Simeon's corrupt living is when Simeon is transferred to the Cameroon's. Pastor Morakinyo, his church committee, Titus' mother and his uncle, and of course Bimpe

and Chris Daniels, all pressure Titus to avert the transfer. Titus naturally does
nothing of the sort. Rather, he tells the pastor to his face:

I tell you one thing about this man Simeon Oke whom you and your church think is next to
Jesus Christ in character. The man that is so wonderful, that must not be transferred. He is
a most incompetent person. Worse than that, he is a rogue. When he steals money from the
Government he brings half of it to your church. He pockets the remaining half. (101)

These are the firm words of one who is not prepared to give up his moral stand,
in spite of the pastor's plea in support of a corrupt and immoral man. Titus is not
ready to "steal any money to please" the pastor and his church members when they
ask him to be the "Chief Opener" at the bazaar sales" that year, which would cost
him "not less than 30 pounds." He says: "I have no money, and I'm going to be
honest." He, therefore, sends the pastor an honest "cheque for two guineas as [his]
own contribution to the Bazaar" (34–39).

Titus' integrity is also clearly demonstrated when Chris Daniel's client offers
him a bribe of twenty guineas to overlook the client's breach of the "Building Line
Ordinance" at Awana. Titus rejects the bribe to the chagrin of his friend Chris; he
is surprised that it does not matter to Chris and his client if the "proposed
development marred the orderly growth of the town for generations to come" (60).
And equally impressive is Titus' blunt refusal to award any contract to Bimpe, who
is in corrupt league with the notorious Simeon Oke. Earlier on Bimpe, thinking that
everybody is corrupt like Simeon, had betrayed the trick of her foul game to Titus:

Yes, bridge construction, why not? If you give it to me I can get someone to help me do it.
When Foreman Simeon gave me six miles of road construction in Ibana-Iwana Road last
year there were many culverts. His men constructed the road. And the men of the Yard
Superintendent constructed the culverts. . . . And I paid them all very well. . . . You, too, will
help make all the arrangements. (67–68)

On hearing this Titus is shocked out of his wits, and that seals the doom for Bimpe,
for she will never get any contract from Titus or any more from the foreman,
Simeon. Thus, right to the end of the novel, Titus stands unshakable in his fight
against public immorality, and that is, in spite of all forms of pressure from his
family, his friends, and even his local church.

Of equal moral strength, though not as fortunate in his own circumstances, is
another engineer, Sekoni, of Wole Soyinka's *The Interpreters*. The schedule of duty
mapped out by the head of department for Sekoni depicts the rotten nature of the
system in which he finds himself. His duties as a professional electrical engineer
include looking over applications for leave and putting up a leave roster; treating
some "letters for signature"; and "taking charge of bicycle advance" (25). This is
calculated not only to deny him professional relevance and job satisfaction, but also
to deprive the society of the benefit of his expertise and service.

At the next meeting of the board, of which a minister is chairman and Sekoni an ex-officio member, he boldly tells the chairman that he "cannot continue to be signing vouchers and letters and bicycle allowances." And for his punishment he is transferred to a rural station at Ijioha. In handing down the verdict, the chairman describes Sekoni as one of the "too knows" and "keen ones" and a "junk engineer" (26). This is the reward Sekoni receives for protesting the corrupt attempt to get him metamorphosed from an engineer into a clerk.

Sekoni obediently moves to the rural station, where he converts his punitive transfer into a social transfiguration. He successfully builds an experimental power station, which can supply electricity to the whole of Ijioha community. Since he achieved this by direct labor and not through an award of contract, he has saved a lot of money for the government, and has created a precedent for the much needed "direct labour" instituted by a sincere government as a sure means of conserving public funds.

But the Chairman-Minister cannot bear the shock (or truth) of this miracle of honesty, dutifulness and modesty, because his "subsidiary company registered in the name of his two-month-old niece had been sole contractor for the 'Project Ijioha' " (27). So he sets up a one-man Commission of Enquiry to probe the project. The expatriate expert who is the Commissioner is given two assignments: (a) to "probe the construction of our power station at Ijioha which was built without estimated approved expenditure," and (b) to say "in technical language" that the power station is unsafe for operation. And the expatriate expert "came to Ijioha, saw, and condemned" (26). Sekoni is dismissed; but rather than stooping to lobbying and licking the boots of the corrupt board members, he nobly leaves and engages himself in sculpturing activities.

James Booth underscores Sekoni's pathetic but ennobling experience when he says that in the novel Sekoni is "the only character to avoid 'apostasy'. He alone accepts the challenge of life and to the end refuses to acquiesce in spiritual corruption which crushes him" (135). And G.C.M. Mutiso highlights the diabolic nature of the opposing and oppressive political machinery when he observes that Sekoni "was being manipulated by the politician," and that "even worse, the villages had been led to believe that 'electricity was a government thing' and when it got ready it would provide for them" (32). Thus, in his bid to destroy the morality in Sekoni's life and actions, the politician has deprived the villages of their civic right to the electricity that Sekoni has brought to their doorsteps.

While the two civil servants, Titus and Sekoni, maintain their moral stand and stature, the third one, Obi Okonkwo of Chinua Achebe's *No Longer at Ease* (1977) builds his own moral stature only up to a point and then tragically pulls it down! Obi's temptations, like those of Titus, are created by family and social pressures; he is spared the pressure from the church. Initially, he triumphs over the carnal bribe brought to him by Miss Elsie Mark, who is in quest of a scholarship and who visits him in his office as secretary of the Scholarship Board. After Miss Mark has informed him that she did not want to suffer the fate of girls who failed to secure scholarships because "they did not see the members at home," Obi boldly and roundly tells her: "I'm sorry, terribly sorry, but I don't see that I can make any promises" (84).

By this firm moral stand, Obi raises the hopes of all the admirers of public morality; though not those of the devil's advocate, his friend, Christopher. Obi is expectedly shocked when Christopher tells him: "You are the biggest ass in Nigeria. If a girl offers to sleep with you, that is no bribery" (109). And when Obi sharply objects to his friend's immoral theory, the latter replies with nonchalant equanimity and cocksureness: "You are being sentimental. A girl who comes the way she did is not an innocent little girl. It's like the story of the girl who was given a form to fill in. She put down her name and her age. But when she came to sex she wrote: 'Twice a week'." Christopher concludes by saying, "she probably thinks you are impotent" (110). In spite of Christopher's argument, Obi is still convinced that his own action (or rather omission of action) is morally right.

However, Obi ultimately succumbs to another kind of bribe: the monetary one. His monthly net salary is "forty-seven pounds ten," and from this he has to pay twenty pounds to Umuofia Progressive Union as a monthly refund of the money they spent on his university education; he has to send ten pounds to his parents; he has to pay his brother's (John) "school fees for next term" (81); he has to pay his electricity bill which is "five pounds seven and three" (90); he has to renew his vehicle license at the cost of four pounds just for a quarter alone. Within the same month, he has to take an overdraft of fifty pounds for the renewal of his car insurance. Though his girlfriend/fiancee, Clara, gives him a check for fifty pounds later so that he can cancel the overdraft (97), he soon has to pay thirty pounds to procure an abortion for Clara (132). And to crown his financial crisis, his mother dies, and he has to foot the funeral bill. And in spite of the thirty-two pounds he sent home for that, "it was already being said to his eternal shame that a woman who had borne so many children, one of whom was in a European post, deserved a better funeral than she got" (144).

All these pressures make Obi capitulate, so that he accepts fifty pounds from a man for his son's scholarship (152). He even recants his earlier principle and accepts love from a girl seeking a scholarship (153). And because he now thinks bribery has become a matter of course and a way of life, he accepts a bribe of twenty marked pound notes! This leads to his arrest and conviction (153–154).

James Booth sees colonialism as the primary cause of Obi's predicament. He says that Europe has given Nigerians "access to irresistible material goods"; and the "people of Obi's village demand of him, their educated Europeanized son, the benefits to which his education has given him access" (96). But "Obi's civil service income is not sufficient to satisfy his fellow villagers. So, Obi must do as the Nation that he typifies does: he must live beyond his means" (97). According to Booth, one way of demonstrating one's European status is by "keeping up a life of conspicuous expenditure" (97), so that "Obi's course, if he is to continue as society demands, is corruption or massive debt" (97). And Booth concludes by saying that Obi's tragedy is therefore "inevitable."

In the same vein, G.C.M. Mutiso observes that "Obi Okonkwo succumbs to economic pressures and accepts a bribe. Although he falls, what one should recognize is the pressure put on him by the civil service system to maintain the standards of the colonial bureaucrat in terms of cars, dress and ritual, and also the pressure from his own people on one who had a white man's job" (36).

It should, however, be remarked that the fact that there is the delusive Europeanized standard of living as well as pressure from Obi's people does not inevitably mean that he must become corrupt. The major cause of Obi's moral tragedy is his lack of the moral stamina to wage a successful war against the immorality occasioned by the colonial system and social pressures. It is in this respect that he is clearly different from Titus Oti. To maintain one's integrity requires painful resistance to temptations such as Obi faces. His tragedy, therefore, results not just from the existence of temptations but from his unstable moral will.

We may now leave the civil service scene and move into the political one. Here we meet Odili Samalu of Chinua Achebe's *A Man of the People* (1966). Odili is a young university graduate whose political ambition is to bring about "a new era of cleanliness in the politics of our country" (146). This aspiration is, of course, stiffly opposed by the corrupt politicians, among whom Chief M.A. Nanga is most prominent.

The texture of the novel is woven around the two-tier oppositional relationship between Odili and Chief Nanga. The first level of this relationship is a personal or private one, wherein Chief Nanga brazenly and contemptuously appropriates Odili's girlfriend, Elsie, and takes her to bed in Odili's presence. And this takes place when Odili is in Chief Nanga's house as a guest (75–81). The second level of their relationship is a public (political) one wherein Odili is determined to capture Chief Nanga's seat in Parliament and thereby politically annihilate this epitome of corruption. Odili's response to Nanga's personal offense against him is to seek to win the love of Edna on whom Nanga has already paid a bride price as his second wife. And for this Odili has been condemned by some critics as will be demonstrated later. However, on the public (political) scene, Odili vindicates himself as a man of moral rectitude and unquestionable integrity. In the first place, Odili rejects the scholarship and the sum of £250 with which Nanga tries to bribe Odili into silence and to keep him from the Parliamentary seat. Odili's rejection comes in spite of the fact that Odili's father has pressured him to be respectful to and friendly with Nanga, and in spite of the fact that Nanga informs Odili that Max, Odili's own party leader, has accepted a bribe of £1,000 from Chief Koko and agreed to step down for him. These sweet temptations crumble before the force of Odili's moral stand and vision. For, ironically, Nanga himself confesses to Odili's face that he regards politics as "a dirty game" that should be left to "us who know how to play it" (131–133). This is ironic because, instead of intimidating Odili into submission, it invigorates his conviction that corrupt people like Nanga should be ousted from politics.

In the second place, Odili takes Max up seriously on the issue of the bribe he had accepted from Chief Koko. When Max argues that he has no genuine intention to step down for Chief Koko, that the party needs the money to fight its cause, that one cannot "fight such a dirty war without soiling [his] hands a little," and that public money is "as much your money as his" [Koko's], Odili remains unconvinced that Max should accept the bribe. He says to Max: "I think you have committed a big blunder. I thought we wanted our fight to be clean. If our people understand nothing else they know that a man who takes money from another in return for service must render that service or remain vulnerable to that man's just revenge. Neither God nor juju would save him" (142).

Here, Odili combines his quality of integrity with his consciousness of moral and social justice, a consciousness that is the motivating force behind his revenge action against Nanga at a personal level, and which, as we hinted above, has made some critics condemn him. Thus, according to Eustace Palmer, "Odili probably ranks as one of Achebe's most unpleasant characters. He is lecherous, egotistic, vulgar, shallow-minded" (79). Similarly, Gerald Moore says that Odili "is in many respects a potential Nanga" and "has a cheap desire to revenge himself on Nanga" (194–195). Also, Adrian Roscoe accuses Odili of inveighing "fickleness" in others "while showing moral weakness himself" (129–130).

These charges crystallize, of course, around Odili's revenge against Nanga's most insolent action against him. At this purely personal level, Odili can be condemned only because he has fought the vice of injustice with revenge, which is itself a vice. He cannot be condemned for the mere fact of fighting, but for the wrong method of fighting. Even though what Nanga has done to Odili is hard for a man to forgive and forget, yet in Igbo tradition, it is believed that one does not win a case by seeking revenge against his opponent. Odili, therefore, should have used an acceptable method of fighting the wrong done to him by Nanga: He could, for instance, report him to the elders of their community, who would look into the matter and settle it. But wrong as an act of revenge is, it should not blind us to that courage with which Odili has attacked the vice of bribery in the society.

With regard to Odili's public integrity and honesty, enough evidence has already been cited from the novel itself. And this has been affirmed by some other critics, among whom James Booth appears to be most unequivocal. Of Odili, he says:

His underlying integrity and high ideals never waver. It is important also to realize that despite his susceptibility, Odili remains in all essentials honest throughout the novel. . . . On the political level, he refuses to take a bribe, even when the transaction could easily have passed undetected. In this he is unique in a novel where society is built on bribery and corruption. (101–102)

We can concede to Booth the use of the word "susceptibility," for after all, no man is an angel. What is of great importance is that in spite of human frailty, Odili stands out in his pursuit of public morality. This uniqueness has also been observed by Roscoe, who notes that Odili has been endowed with "righteousness and indignation towards a hopelessly corrupt political elite and a cynical people who recognize evil yet will not revolt against it" (130). The triumph of Odili as a political moral exemplum consists in the fact that though he is finally physically incapacitated and therefore prevented even from running in the election, he undauntedly remains faithful to his moral conviction, moral principles, and moral courage. But here again those waging the War Against Discipline have immorally carried the day.

While Odili pays the price of physical incapacitation, Okolo of Gabriel Okara's *The Voice* pays the supreme price of losing his life in his own war against public immorality. Okolo is not a politician or even an aspiring one per se; he is simply a social critic and revolutionary trying to instill into both the leaders and the followers the spirit of honor, honesty, truth, and justice. This spirit he calls "it" and his ambition is to implant in the people this "it" that appears to him to be absent in them.

Okolo's major problem is that he is in quest of what most people in his society consider impossible. Chief Izongo, the overall leader argues that "no one in the past [had] asked for 'it'" and wonders why Okolo should "expect to find 'it' now that he and his Chiefs are the Elders" (24). Tebeowei, Okolo's friend, warns him that Chief Izongo and others "cannot their insides change as you change a loin cloth." And when Okolo argues that "we can still sweep the dirt out of our houses every morning," Tebeowei comes in again saying: "But the heap of dirt is more than one man's strength. . . . It may bury you" (50). A piece of mural writing in a hotel discourages him all the more: "Even the white man's Jesus failed to make the world fine. So let the spoilt world spoil" (82). Furthermore, when Okolo tells one "white man in the capital city" that he has come to find out if the "Big One" who is the ruler of the entire nation has got "it" in himself, the white man feels convinced that Okolo is mad and should go to a "psychiatrist" for treatment (88). He says to Okolo: "No one will thank you, especially one who is in authority, for telling him by implication that you are, morally, a better person" (88). And so, the dirt heap of corruption and injustice remains; but at least Okolo persists in his determination to sweep it off.

Okolo achieves some measure of success. Inspired by Okolo, Chief Izongo's messenger, Tiri, refuses to spend the money given to him by the chief as a bribe. He says "it is bad money. Bad money never brings good to anyone" (92). Earlier on, Tuere, who had been ostracized from the community for her quest for honor, pledges her unflinching support to Okolo: "I am giving you my hands and my inside and even my shadow" (56). Also, the cripple, Ukule, has been spying on Chief Izongo and his chiefs, and it is he who discovers Chief Izongo's plan to permanently exile Okolo from the town: "Izongo in this town wants him no more. If he shows his face in this town again, he and anyone like him will be sent away forever and ever" (73).

Okolo has already been banished by Chief Izongo, who vows that he "must stop his search. He must not spoil their pleasure" (24). It is this "pleasure" that is rooted in dishonesty, injustice, and oppression that Okolo insists on "spoiling" for the leadership through his quest for and insistence on honor, truth, and social justice. And so, he boldly returns from banishment and goes to meet Izongo and his chiefs frontally, that is, in spite of the threat of permanent exile. His punishment for this turns out to be not just ordinary exile but death. Chief Izongo's men tie him and

Tuere to the seats of a canoe and throw the canoe with them in it into the river where they finally drown.

That the moral quest and the death of Okolo are heroic and Christ-like is obvious. Professor Emmanuel Obiechina, for example, rightly observes that the "the moral campaign which the hero mounts right from the beginning, the morally dominated atmosphere and the inside details of the plot point irrevocably not only to an obvious analogy but to a close patterning on the passion story of the Gospels" (1972 24). Similarly, Eustace Palmer notes that Okolo is a moral "idealist" operating in a "corrupt materialistic world." Okolo is indeed a "catalyst" who challenges "the hypocrisy, spiritual sterility, and materialism of the people he meets," (1972 158) and who, therefore, endeavors to change his society for the better without allowing himself to be changed for the worse by that society. And it is to his eternal credit that though he is crushed by corrupt power, his moral philosophy, according to Arthur Ravenscroft, has positively taken root in some people, and "there is no sense of Okolo having died in vain" (114). And Tuere ensures this immortality of Okolo's influence when she says to Ukule, the cripple: "You go and leave Us. You stay in the town and in the days to come, tell our story and tend our spoken words" (127). This resembles Christ's charge to his disciples during the "Last Supper, " just before he was crucified.

## FORCES OPPOSING PUBLIC MORALITY

Thus far in this chapter, we have tried to examine the defense of public morality put up by some members of the fictional society, the heterocosm of the Nigerian novels under discussion, and we have noted their varying degrees of success or failure. We have also hinted at the struggles put up by some forces that consistently negate the quest for public morality in that society. Our next important task is to seek the answer to the crucial question: What may be the source(s) or cause(s) of public immorality and opposition to public morality in our society, as it is reflected in these novels, and in the same breath, what may be the possible solution to the problem of immorality? Generally speaking, social pressure (which includes economic pressure) and entrenched political power can be identified as two monstrous forces militating against public morality in the society of the novels. The first is present in *Kinsman and Foreman*, and *No Longer at Ease;* and the second is dominant in *The Interpreters*, *A Man of the People*, and *The Voice.*

Each of these two forces has its roots in the colonial experience, the traditional African experience, or both. The social belief that a black senior civil servant has "become" a white man and should, therefore, maintain the same standard of living as that of the white man, is a result of the establishment of the civil service by the colonialists. A story was told in the early 1960s, for example, of a coal miner in Enugu who took an undergraduate relation of his to his work place, so that he could obtain for him from the "white" boss permission to be absent from duty. The undergraduate went into the office block pointed out to him by the coal miner who, of course, was too afraid to go into the building. After a fruitless search for the "white" boss, he came out and declared his failure to find any white man there. The miner persisted in his conviction that the "white" boss was in the office, and pointed at a specific open window. The young undergraduate went back to the relevant office, where he found a black man who was the production manager of the corporation. He secured the desired permission and came out. On his telling the miner that he had not seen any white man there but that he got him permission to be absent from duty, the miner, in a matter-of-fact tone, replied: "But that black man you saw there is our 'white man.'" This belief is entirely an unfortunate colonial heritage.

Similarly, the belief that political leaders, like Nanga, should not be challenged and that their ill-gotten wealth should not be questioned is a result of the foreign partisan political system, which is fathered by Machiavellianism and sustained by capitalism. Odili understands the situation when he imagines what Nanga's mob would say about him in derision of his opposition to Nanga: "Was he not there when white men were eating? What did he do about it?" (*A Man of the People* 155). If the white men had never set up their partisan political machinery in black society, the belief that politics is a kill-and-eat affair might not have been established or nurtured in that society.

But the traditional African social system has contributed its own quota toward the social pressure that negates public morality. The expectation that one should cater to all the members of one's extended family is, of course, of traditional origin. So also is the belief that embezzlement of public funds is not a crime, as Max had argued. According to this belief, whatever does not belong to a known particular owner can be appropriated by any person. This argument was used by a certain mad man called "Jadum" in successful defense of himself against the charge of killing a vulture, and cooking and eating the meat. When he was arraigned by his people before a white Divisional Officer (D.O.), he earned his discharge and acquittal by asking the D.O. whether the vulture belonged to him or to his accusers (Egudu 1979 110). Of course, the vulture belongs to nobody.

In the same vein, the general belief that one should not engage with devotion in a job that does not belong to a known particular person, which may account for the general poor attitude to work observed among many public servants, is of traditional African origin. Indeed, the people bluntly say that "a goat owned in common often dies of hunger," for no one is going to supply leaves and grass to it in a way he would if it were exclusively his. Among the Nigerians generally, it is believed that the civil service is nobody's job, or that it is, at best, the white man's job ("white job"). It is, therefore, like a commonly owned goat, and it is nobody's business if it dies from lack of devoted tending. Thus, it is no wonder that Simeon Oke should consider it more important for the government laborers to work on his personal farm than on government projects.

## SOLUTION TO THE PROBLEM OF PUBLIC IMMORALITY

It can, therefore, be said that the causes and sources of general public immorality (or indiscipline in public life) are both within our traditional system and outside it.

And to find the possible solution to the problem, we have to look within and outside ourselves and our society. Just as Sir Philip Sidney in one of his sonnets was advised by the Muse to "look in thy heart and write," we may have to look in our hearts for the solution to the problem of public immorality in our society.

What is needed in the first instance, perhaps, is ethical resuscitation, revitalization, and reorientation. It is a common feature of the African traditional thought-system that one kind of belief is counterbalanced by another, which by opposing it moderates it in the interest of social harmony and moral good. For instance, the idea of inequality is not considered innately evil, that is, if it is a result of somebody working honestly harder than the others or a result of special or natural endowment. For example, the Igbo say that "it is the firewood gathered in youth that one uses in old age to make the fire for warming himself" (Obienyem 1975 22). Thus, in old age this person will remain superior to those who in the their youth failed to gather any firewood. And as a result of natural ordering the people also say that "the five fingers of a man are not equal" (Egudu 1972 69; Onwuejeogwu 1986 41). But though the senior civil servant is such a hardworking young man and the tallest of the five fingers and should, therefore, enjoy a high standard of living, society also believes that he should do so without stealing, and that is, irrespective of whatever pressures are brought on him. For it is said in our tradition that "one who thirsts for what his/her money cannot buy is getting ready to become a thief." Obi Okonkwo is clearly a case in point here.

With regard to the extended family system, it can be said that much as it is a source of pressure that may lead to immorality, it is also a source of moral strength. According to Professor Onwuejeogwu, "the extended family involves the development of communal interest, self-sacrifice for the common good, selfless and honest service to the community" (1986 25). And it had much earlier been observed elsewhere but in a different context (Egudu 1972 64) that the social and ethical symbiosis that is generally characteristic of the African world view, and that is engendered and nurtured in the extended family cradle, ensures mutual moral responsibility among the members of the larger community. For Example, the Igbo say, that "if the eyes weep, the nose weeps with them," and that "if one finger is soiled by palm oil, the other fingers will be affected." The extended family consciousness should, therefore, reinforce the individual's moral sense by making him constantly aware that his immoral actions will bring disgrace not only to himself but also to the entire family, and through it to the entire community. It is this sense of total involvement, for example, which compels Pa Joel, Titus' mother, and Simeon Oke to contribute the £30 with which Pa Joel opens the Bazaar sales on behalf of Titus (Kinsman and Foreman 43). This is to forestall the shame that Titus' refusal to open the sales would bring to the entire extended family. And although, as had been indicated earlier, Titus' refusal has moral merit, the family members have offset the vice of their economic harassment of Titus with this demonstration of the virtue of vicariousness: suffering on behalf of one another.

Furthermore, this consciousness of the family's honor and respectable image makes the members not expect that one should steal money in order to help the other members. It is often said that "though we expect you to help us, we do not mean that you should steal money." Besides, in Igbo tradition, generosity that results from one overstretching his means to a point where he is compelled to steal is itself considered an act of stupidity and vice. The people express this by jeering at a proverbial "woman who gave away her only kitchen knife and broke down weeping for thus losing it," and by saying that "a woman who has no restraint in carnal generosity ends up producing bastard children." Thus, the need to cater to one's extended family members should not lead one into committing acts that are immoral and undesirable.

The other problem of people regarding government funds as the white man's money or nobody's money can be combated with the traditional African belief that what belongs to an identifiable person or community equally belongs to all. That is why the narrator in Achebe's *A Man of the People* says: "The owner was the village and the village had a mind; it could say no to sacrilege. But in the affairs of the nation there was no owner; the laws of the village became powerless" (167). Since the "nation" is their own and no longer the white man's, if the nation can be made to possess enough moral mind to "say No to sacrilege," and if justice and equity can be applied to the sharing of the common wealth as is the case in the village, people's attitude to public funds is likely to change for the better. For the basic culinary ethics, which stipulates that "one does not eat while others sit by watching him," also governs the sharing of all amenities in the village.

The same principle of equity applies, indeed, to community labor. It is said that "he who accepts a share of food must also accept a share of work." The problem of apathy to public service has, of course, resulted from the fact that people do not see it as their own "work." It was in an attempt to change this mental attitude that the erstwhile sole administrator of the then East Central State of Nigeria, Chief Anthony Ukpabi Asika, rechristened public service *Olu Obodo*, that is "community work." The attempt was not entirely successful because the change in name did not bring any material benefit to the people, a benefit such as is ensured by the traditional community labor involved in the construction of a village hall, square, or road; or by the communal labor involving working in rotation on the farms of the individual members of the community. It is, however, possible that a community development project may perform the desired miracle of conversion from apathy to enthusiasm, if the project results in meaningful palpable benefits for the members of the community.

And finally, with regard to political leadership, it is not so much the ordinary people as the leaders themselves—the Izongos and Nangas—that require complete ethical resuscitation, revitalization and reorientation. For as Mutiso says in relation to Okara's *The Voice*, "the writer makes it clear . . . that the elders and the Chief, by acting in a corrupt way, are really going against tradition" (28). And to support his view, Mutiso quotes from the novel: "Our fathers' insides contained things straight. They did straight things. Our insides were also clean and we did the straight things until the new time came" (28). This shows that there is in our tradition a positive ethical foundation on which a corruption-free political system can be built.

The present day political leaders should, therefore, learn from the tradition how to say and do "straight things," which is to be honest and truthful, and to possess honor and integrity.

The relationship between the leaders and the followers in the modern political system in which the leader is lord and ruler and the masses are passive, oppressed followers, can be corrected on the basis of the model that existed in the traditional society. The Igbo, for instance, say and believe that "the King rules the people, but the people own the King." The implication, which was the practice in the past, is that the "owners" (the people) tell the "owned" (the ruler) how he must behave. There is also the implication of equal share in that ownership, as is applicable to other types of ownership, whereby even a poor member of the community can report a king's wrongdoing to other members of the community. And this can result in the king being summoned before the community to defend his action. The modern masses can also learn from the courage of such a poor member of the community.

We have all along looked into our ethical selves and roots in our quest for possible solutions to the problem of public immorality. We may now briefly and randomly look outside. According to Plato, the "best guardians" (leaders) of the people are "those who in their whole life show the greatest eagerness to do what is for the good of their country, and the greatest repugnance to do what is against her interests," who do not "change their minds either under the softer influence of pleasure, or the sterner influence of fear," and who make the "interest of the State the rule of their lives" (qtd. in Hamilton 1963 124–125). There is a fair degree of correspondence between the emphasis on the country's interests and our people's belief that the leader is owned by the people, for it is those interests that should determine the mode of operation and behavior of the leader.

And in respect to morality in general, Aristotle has said that "moral virtue has to do with pain and pleasure" and that love of "pleasure has a way of making us do what is disgraceful," while "fear of pain deters us from doing what is right and fine" (qtd. in Thomson 1970 59). In the context of this study, it can be observed that Titus, Sekoni, Odili, and Okolo have all opted for the path of pain, which has led them into doing "what is right and fine," while Obi Okonkwo, Simeon Oke, the minister in *The Interpreters*, Chief Nanga, and Chief Izongo have opted for the path of pleasure, which has led them into doing "what is disgraceful." And Aristotle imagistically captures the heroic nature of the feat that is involved in the cultivation of moral virtue in the following analogy: "Going wrong is easy, and going right is difficult: it is easy to miss the bull's eye and difficult to hit it" (66). This dictum should make it easy for us to appreciate the degree of success achieved by those characters that champion the cause of public morality in the novels under study, and by those counterparts of theirs in real life who emulate them.

Furthermore, Immanuel Kant's words regarding human actions are of great significance to the issue in point. According to him, man is forever under the influence of either the "hypothetical imperative" or the "categorical imperative." A hypothetical imperative commands actions for some "future personal results" or material gains, while a categorical imperative commands actions for the purpose of "doing the right as such," that is, for the purpose of respecting the "moral law" (qtd. in Ewing 1973 51–53). By implication, it can be said that Obi and those in his group have behaved under the influence of the hypothetical imperative, while Titus and those in his group have been influenced by the categorical one. The latter should be a model for modern society.

## CONCLUSION

In conclusion, we may say that the cultivation or pursuit of public morality is most desirable, but equally most difficult: what with the opposition from the champions of immorality, what with the natural desire for pleasure and aversion for pain eternally dramatizing innate human frailty. But equipped with the arms of ethical ideals and models from both within and outside our cultural heritage and from the fictive and real worlds of some of our novels and our society, we can still adequately face all opposing forces with dauntlessness, like Socrates did during his historic trial. When he was being prosecuted for the charge of intruding into the life of other people in his society and influencing their minds, he stood his ground and boldly admonished his persecutors thus:

If you put me to death, you will not easily find anyone to take my place. It is literally true, even if it sounds rather comical, that God has specifically appointed me to this city, as though it were a large thorough-bred horse which because of its great size is inclined to be lazy and needs the stimulation of some stinging fly. It seems to me that God has attached me to this city to perform the office of such a fly, and all day long I never cease to settle here, there, and everywhere, rousing, persuading, reproving every one of you. You will not easily find another like me . . . and if you take my advice you will spare my life. I suspect, however, that before long you will awaken from your drowsing, and in your annoyance you will take Anytus' advice and finish me off with a single slap, and then you will go on sleeping till the end of your days, unless God in his care for you sends some one to take my place. (Plato 1963 16–17)

Each of the successful moral heroes of the novels we have discussed and each of the writers that created them can be likened to Socrates as a moral "stinging fly." We may therefore pray to God to send us, in his care for us, more and more of such "stinging flies, such gad-flies" that will continuously keep waking our society from its moral slumber and torpor.

## WORKS CITED

Achebe, Chinua. *A Man of the People*. London: Heinemann, 1966.
———. *No Longer at Ease*. London: Heinemann, 1977.
Aluko, T.M. *Kinsman and Foreman*. London: Heinemann, 1966.
Aristotle. *The Ethics of Aristotle*. Trans. J. Thomson. Harmondsworth: Penguin Books, 1970.
Booth, James. *Writers and Politics in Nigeria*. New York: African Publishing Company, 1981.

Daiches, David. *Critical Approaches to Literature*. London: Longmans, 1969.

Egudu, R.N. "Anglophone African Poetry and Vernacular Rhetoric: The Example of Christopher Okigbo," *Lagos Review of English Studies* I.1 (1979): 104–113.

———. "Social Values and Thought in Traditional Literature: The Case of Igbo Proverbs and Poetry," *Nigerian Libraries* VIII.2 (1972): 63–84.

Ewing, A.C. *Ethics*. London: The English Universities Press Ltd., 1973.

Hamilton, Edith and Huntington Cairns Eds. *The Collected Dialogues of Plato*. Princeton: Princeton University Press, 1963.

Hegel, George Wilhelm Friedrich. *The Philosophy of History*. New York: Dover Publications, Inc., 1956.

Jowett, Benjamin. Trans. *The Republic*. Cleveland: The World Publishing Company, 1946.

Longfellow, H.W. *Poems*. London: Dent, 1970.

Moore, Gerald. *The Chosen Tongue: English Writing in the Tropical World*. London: Longmans, 1969.

Mutiso, G.C.M. *Socio-Political Thought in African Literature*. London: Macmillan, 1974.

Obiechina, Emmanuel. "Art and Artifice in Okara's *The Voice*," *Okike: An African Journal of New Writing* 3 (1972).

Obienyem, J.C. "*Oge*" (poem), in R.M. Ekechukwu, ed. *"Akpa Uche": An Anthology of Modern Igbo Verse*. Ibadan: Oxford University Press, 1975.

Ogungbesan, Kola. "Wole Soyinka and the Novelist's Responsibility in Africa." In Kola Ogungbesan, ed. *New West African Literature*. London: Heinemann, 1979.

Okara, Gabriel. *The Voice*. London: Heinemann, 1970.

Onwuejeogwu, M.A. "An African Indigenous Ideology: Communal Individualism" (Inaugural Lecture). University of Benin, Nigeria, 1986.

Palmer, Eustace. *An Introduction to the African Novel*. London: Heinemann, 1972.

Plato. *The Collected Dialogues of Plato*. Eds. Edith Hamilton and Huntington Cairns. Princeton: Princeton University Press, 1963.

———. *The Republic*. Trans. Benjamin Jowett. Cleveland: The World Publishing Company, 1946.

Roscoe, Adrian. *Mother Is Gold: A Study in West African Literature*. Cambridge: Cambridge University Press, 1971.

Sidney, Philip. "An Apologie for Poetrie." Eds. James Harry Smith and Ed Winfield Parks, *The Great Critics*. W.W.Norton & Company, Inc., 1951.

———. "Astrophel and Stella." Eds. E. Talbot Donaldson et al., *The Norton Anthology of English Literature*, Vol. I. New York: W.W. Norton, 1968.

Smith, James Harry and Ed Winfield Parks, eds. *The Great Critics*. New York: W.W. Norton & Company, Inc., 1951.

Soyinka, Wole. *The Interpreters*. London: Fontana/Collins, 1973.

Thomson, J. *The Ethics of Aristotle*. Harmondsworth: Penguin Books, 1970.

# Chapter Six

# *Things Fall Apart*: Problems in Constructing an Alternative Ethnography

## *Charlie Sugnet*

In a 1962 interview with Lewis Nkosi, Achebe places the genesis of *Things Fall Apart* in his dissatisfaction with Joyce Cary's "superficial picture" of Nigeria in *Mister Johnson*. He goes on to say: "and so I thought if this [*Mister Johnson*] was famous, then perhaps someone ought to try and *look at this from the inside*" (qtd. in Innes and Lindfors 1978 4; my emphasis). By and large, the critics have agreed that Achebe fulfilled his intention and that *Things Fall Apart* is a successful "inside" account of Igbo life. Both Robert M. Wren and C.L. Innes and Bernth Lindfors quote Achebe's remark to Nkosi in contexts that suggest they find it crucially explanatory. David Carroll describes the move to the British District Commissioner's point of view on the last page of the novel as "a shift of perspective from the inside to the outside," implying that everything up to the last page has been told from the "inside."

I can still recall that as a North American reader reading *Things Fall Apart* for the first time, I felt powerfully that I had seen the truth of Igbo society from the inside. I had seen, without being asked to judge, how the world made sense to Okonkwo and his people, and how the destruction of any element of their world view threatened the whole fabric of coherence in which they lived. An examination of the text provides a great deal of support for that feeling: The narrator's voice often expresses the values of Okonkwo's village; Okonkwo is the central consciousness for much of the novel; numerous Igbo words occur in the text without translation; and the narrative is densely embedded in descriptions of Igbo custom and culture.

Yet one cannot read very far in *Things Fall Apart* without encountering the voice of a narrator who has enough distance from the Igbo to generalize about them and to represent them to outsiders. In the first chapter, the narrator uses the phrases

"Among the Ibo . . . " and "Among these people. . . . " In Chapter 2, the narrator remarks that "Darkness held a vague terror for these people, even the bravest among them" (8). This ethnographic voice comes and goes in *Things Fall Apart,* disappearing into the "inside" view and then surfacing again as the narrator explains things Okonkwo's countrymen would already know, like how to plant yam (35); the role of *Ani,* the earth goddess (37); why people at home don't answer a call from outside in their own name (41–42); or what the "evil forest" is used for (38). Some episodes, such as the marriage of Uchendu's son (121–22) do not seem to advance the story, and may be there only so that Achebe can describe the *isa-ifi* ceremony, in that the bride is formally questioned about other men she may have slept with. On the other hand, Achebe does not empty out all the meanings of Igbo culture to his readers. For instance, as far as I can tell, the nature and significance of the chalk lines accompanying the kola-breaking ceremony are never explained.

A quote from Frederick Douglass about slave songs, used as an epigraph to Henry Louis Gates, Jr.'s anthology *Black Literature and Literary Theory*, helps to explain the position of Achebe's narrator: "I did not, when a slave, understand the deep meaning of those rude and incoherent songs. I was myself within the circle, so that I neither saw nor heard as those without might hear." In light of this quote, it seems obvious that a narrative like Achebe's, that is designed to "reeducate" colonized Igbo in their own culture and at the same time be intelligible to readers from other cultures, could only have been produced by crossing cultural boundaries. In the sense in that I've been using the word "view," there is no such thing as a purely inside view. From within the circle, one lives and knows a culture, but does not "view" it (or represent it enthnographically). As Stanislas Adotevi argues in his anti-negritude polemic, "Negritude et Negrologues," "You can't stand at the window and watch yourself go by in the street" (qtd. in Miller 1986 131).

Thus, I agree with Gareth Griffiths when he says that "the insideness of Achebe's vision can be over stressed," and points to the uncomfortable analogies between Achebe's project and that of the District Commissioner (qtd. in Innes and Lindfors 1978 68). On the first page of the novel's final chapter, the racist D.C. uses the same phrase Achebe used in Chapter 2 "these people," to generalize about the Igbo. And as Griffiths points out, "By the very act of writing, Achebe's stance is contiguous to that of the commissioner. Both seek to reduce the living, oral world of Umuofia to a series of words on the page, and they are English words, for Achebe as well as for the commissioner" (68). The sentence I quoted earlier, "Darkness held a vague terror for these people, even the bravest among them," could in fact be plausibly written by the likes of the commissioner. Although their sympathies and perspectives are opposed, Achebe and the district commissioner both narrate the defeat of the Igbo people by the British.

The uncomfortable parallels between their projects partly explain why Achebe fends off the commissioner with such sharp irony, and they also shape the answers he gives when pressed by interviewer Phanuel Akubueze Egejuru. When Egejuru asks why a Nigerian writer should explain the breaking of the *kola nut* to a Nigerian audience, and whether Achebe's books presuppose a foreign audience, Achebe ducks the question, saying that the glossary was the publisher's idea and was done by someone else. Egejuru continues to press the question of audience:

Q: The formula you use to introduce a proverb, for example, "Among the Igbo we say . . . " Would this imply that you are talking to an external audience?
A: No. That's not true as you must know. Because the formula of introducing a proverb in Igbo is precisely that—"Ka ndi be anyi si ekwu . . . " (as our people say . . . ). It is a matter of form and expression that varies from place to place. If you find me explaining something for the benefit of foreigners, that's a sign of underdevelopment as a writer. But I don't think you find too many examples. (1980 19)

According to Egejuru, most of the many African writers she interviewed claimed to be writing exclusively for an African audience, and denied that their work is shaped by their awareness of "a double audience made up mostly of the European bourgeois and the Western educated African elite" (19). Yet despite his typical handling of the issue, there's a world of difference between "our people" and "these people," and I believe Achebe does address an external audience.

Egejuru says that "the writer is the spokesman of his people," and should always write to and for them. Achebe, with his remark about "underdevelopment as a writer," seems to agree. I want to argue here for Achebe's artistic intuitions at the moment of composition, and against the position he and Egejuru express in the interview. It seems to me that *Things Fall Apart* has at least two narrative voices, that those two voices are evoked by the doubleness of Achebe's intended audience, and that Achebe was right to address both audiences. Or, to put it another way: given the nature of Achebe's decolonizing project and the actual historical circumstance prevailing in the late 1950s, Achebe had no choice but to speak to both audiences.

Christopher L. Miller, who argues for "traditional Africa" as a source of critical values, acknowledges that "European imperialism has changed the terms of any African discourse forever and must be dealt with" (138). From my reading of Achebe's essays and interviews, I don't think he ever attempted to deny this: He recognizes frequently that no primordial cultural purity is possible and that the future will unfold through the interaction of cultures. One of Achebe's favorite proverbs, quoted in his interview with Bill Moyers (and frequently elsewhere), is: "Wherever one thing stands, something else will stand beside it" (9). He never intended to make Igbo culture in *Things Fall Apart* an anthropologist's dream, a pure "precontact" culture locked out of time. He spoke very strongly in his 1964 "The Role of the Writer in a New Nation" against the temptation to idealize the Igbo past (Killam 1973 9), and he constructed the novel so as to make clear that Igbo culture was subject to change over time before any Europeans arrived.

What's interesting is how many of his readers do seem to want that purity. One of the things that worries me about Achebe in America is how easily Americans "assimilate" his work. Here is a man who, if I read him right, is saying true decolonization will require that Americans have less power and wealth relative to the rest of the world, and yet they're wild about him. Students love his books, department chairs are glad you're teaching him, and grants committees are pleased to fund studies of him. An African novelist recently seated next to me at dinner in the American Midwest remarked: "If you're from the third world, everybody in America wants you to write like Achebe—village life. I grew up in Dar Es Salaam. I don't know anything about village life."

Setting aside the portion of the affection that is due to his sheer personal charm, some of Achebe's popularity is due to the fact that his books construct a secure, intelligible position for a Western reader to occupy. We have only to compare the American reader's confused response to Tutuola, whose work does not construct such a space, to see the difference. If such a reader, occupying such a space, chooses to ignore the means of representation, to pretend that they are transparent, he or she can have the illusion of looking into the unbroken circle of a "primitive" society, of having a "view" of undisturbed Igbo village life, and of seeing pure, precontact Africanness. This is the attraction of the "inside" view, a false reading or a half-reading of the novel that turns it into pastoral nostalgia.

From the tenor of her questions, I suspect that Egejuru is at the opposite end of the same equation, also wanting Achebe and other writers to stick to a nationalist notion of pure "Africanness." In the section of *The Wretched of the Earth* devoted to national culture, however, Frantz Fanon describes the trajectory of the "native intellectual" and is quite pessimistic about searching for national culture in the past. "At the very moment when the native intellectual is anxiously trying to create a cultural work," Fanon argues, "he fails to realize that he is utilizing techniques and language that are borrowed from the stranger in his country" (223). Yet the native intellectual Fanon describes, with his constant changes of position and his noisy renunciations, does not sound at all like Achebe, whose choice to write in English and in a Western form has been very conscious; he didn't "fail to realize" what he was doing. As Lloyd Brown puts it, Achebe "consciously expropriates the European's literary techniques, and related perceptual values, in order to postulate an African, or even anti-European, point of view. Hence he constantly borrows European historiography in order to explode the notorious myth that Africans have no history (qtd. in Innes and Lindfors 1978 25).

Achebe consciously writes in English—and modifies the language to suit the Igbo context. He consciously chooses the novel—and alters the form in using it. Barbara Harlow opens her Preface to *Resistance Literature* (1987) with a wonderful reading of the tale of the tortoise and the birds as an allegory of mental liberation leading through language to armed struggle, and makes the point that such interpolated folktales challenge the received conventions of the European realistic novel. Nor is Igbo culture a static given; rather, it is something Achebe's writing constructs and gives his people so that they can see themselves in a better mirror than the one provided by the colonists. He's not just crossing a line between two fixed entities, inside and outside, or African and Western; he's continually negotiating a fluid boundary between cultures that are being constructed by the writing itself.

One of Fanon's more discouraging pronouncements is that "[t]he efforts of the native to rehabilitate himself and to escape from the claws of colonialism are logically inscribed from the same point of view as that of colonialism" (212). What I've just said about Achebe altering his European tools as he works may mitigate this, but in order to explain why Achebe addresses *Things Fall Apart* to Europeans as well as to Africans, I want to invoke Mikhail Bakhtin's idea of "hidden polemic" (that Henry Louis Gates, Jr. adapts to African-American literary history in "The Blackness of Blackness: A Critique of the Sign and the Signifying Monkey"). According to Bakhtin, the hidden polemic involves a prior speech act that:

remains outside the bounds of the author's speech, but is implied or alluded to in that speech. The other speech act is not reproduced with a new intention [as in parodic narration], but shapes the author's speech while remaining outside its boundaries. . . . In hidden polemic the author's discourse is oriented toward its referential object, as is any other discourse, but at the same time each assertion about that object is constructed in such a way that, besides its referential meaning, the author's discourse brings a polemical attack to bear against another speech act, another assertion, on the same topic. Here one utterance focused on its referential object clashes with another utterance on the grounds of the referent itself. That other utterance is not reproduced . . . but the whole structure of the author's speech would be completely different, if it were not for this reaction to another's unexpressed speech act. (Bakhtin 1971 187)

What are the prior speech acts that silently structure *Things Fall Apart?* We can find one of them in a type of anecdote—told variously by Gates, Cuban writer Roberto Retamar, and Achebe himself—so common it has become a sort of topos of postcolonial writing: the Westerner who expresses doubt about whether Africa (or Latin America) has a history or a literature. Retamar sees rightly that "to question our culture is to question our very existence, our human reality itself," and that the question could be rephrased as "Do you exist?" (3). Gates recites a list of black writers to his dubious questioner, but soon finds the question was really a disguised statement at the foundation of colonialist discourse: "You have no history, no literature, and no culture. Therefore you do not have human existence." (It seems characteristic of Achebe that when affronted with this position on the Amherst campus, he simply walks faster to escape his unwelcome interlocutor, but that he later builds the encounter into the opening paragraphs of his wonderful essay on Conrad.)

In the most general sense, then, Achebe's novel conducts a hidden polemic against such colonialist discourse. In a more proximate sense, *Things Fall Apart* conducts a polemic against Conrad's *Heart of Darkness* and Cary's *Mister Johnson,* two texts that are never mentioned in the novel, but hover near every page. If Conrad shows Africans as bereft of language and given only to unintelligible cries, Achebe shows them as brilliant orators and poets of the proverb, whose utterances, like all human utterances, are sometimes selfserving or mistaken. If Cary shows Africans as shallow buffoons, Achebe will show their depth and dignity. If both novelists assume that history begins with the arrival of the white man, Achebe will show historical and cultural change happening in the traditional culture before his arrival. Here is indeed Bakhtin's clash "on the grounds of the referent itself." An extended comparison of texts would show more specifically how Achebe's novel is structured by its argument against these two invisible but powerful predecessors, and how he manages to counter them without overidealizing the Igbo.

Perhaps even more proximate to Achebe's writing than Conrad and Cary is the sort of ethnography produced by the missionary G.T. Basden, or the political officer P. Amaury Talbot. Here, Achebe's polemic is less hidden, more like parody or irony, branches of Bakhtin's double voiced discourse in that the other speech act is "reproduced with a new intention." Basden and Talbot lean heavily on words like "primitive" and "native"; Basden gives forth with colonialist gems like "the ideas of the native are indefinite. He has no fixed thoughts." In the language of the district commissioner who enters the last chapter of *Things Fall Apart*, Achebe certainly reproduces the speech act of Basden/Talbot with a new intention.

The reader who is trying to occupy an invisible, privileged viewing space will encounter some challenges to his bad faith in this chapter. By introducing the language of colonialist ethnography and by ending with a book title, *The Pacification of the Primitive Tribes of the Lower Niger*, Achebe invites the reader to consider the book he holds in his own hand, to consider the process of representation and the discursive procedures that have brought him a certain construction of Igbo culture. In a way, *The Pacification* is shorthand for all the prior discourse that has shaped *Things Fall Apart,* and *Things Fall Apart* is the anti-book to *The Pacification*. Note that although the hidden polemic is structured in relation to European texts, it is not necessarily addressed only to the European portion of Achebe's readership. To the extent that Igbo people have accepted or internalized colonialist discourse (and Achebe seems to believe that this is so to a large extent), the polemic against it is addressed to them too. Achebe's working assumption seems to be that ethnographic discourse has so much power that he must produce an alternative ethnography to combat it. It is clear that, in the final chapter, he is reproducing the language of colonial ethnography with a new intention. However, at some earlier points in the novel, such as the narrator's explanation of "these people" fearing the dark, the existence of an operative "new intention" is less clear. It may be that the conventions of ethnographic writing are so strong that they occasionally overwhelm the attempt to contest them.

In "The Role of the Writer in a New Nation," Achebe expressed clearly the ultimate purpose of his fictional polemic: "The worst thing that can happen to any people is the loss of their dignity and self respect. The writer's duty is to help them regain it by showing them in human terms what happened to them, what they lost" (qtd. in Innes and Lindfors 1978 37–38). And he later told Egejuru that "[e]very colonial situation does some serious damage to the mind of the colonized. Anybody who thinks he came out of the system intact is idiotic" (Egejuru 1980 132). Achebe believed the way to repair that "damage to the mind" was to contest by hidden polemic and by parodic narrative the very territory where the damage had been inflicted—colonial discourse itself.

# WORKS CITED

Achebe, Chinua. *Things Fall Apart*. London: H.E.B. 1958.

Bakhtin, Mikhail. "Discourse Typology in Prose." In *Readings in Russian Poetics: Formalist and Structuralist Views*. Eds. Ladislav Matejka and Krystyna Pomoroska. Cambridge, MA: MIT Press, 1971.

Basden, G.T. *Among the Ibos of Nigeria*. London: Seeley, 1921.

Carrol, David. "Achebe's *Things Fall Apart*." In *Critical Perspectives on Chinua Achebe*. Eds. C.L. Innes and Bernth. Washington, DC: Three Continents Press, 1978.

Egejuru, Phanuel. *Towards African Literary Independence*. Westport, CT: Greenwood Press, 1980.

———. *Black Writers: White Audience*. Hicksville, NY, 1978.

Fanon, Frantz. "On National Culture." *The Wretched of the Earth*. New York: Grove, 1968.

Gates, Henry Louis, Jr. ed. *Black Literature and Literary Theory*. New York: Methuen, 1984.

Griffiths, Gareth. "Achebe's Vision." In *Critical Perspectives on Chinua Achebe*. Eds. C.L. Innes and Bernth. Washington, DC: Three Continents Press, 1978.

Harlow, Barbara. *Resistance Literature*. New York: Methuen, 1987.

Innes, C.L. and Bernth Lindfors, eds. *Critical Perspectives on Chinua Achebe*. Washington, DC: Three Continents Press, 1978.

Killam, G.D., ed. *African Writers on African Writing*. Evanston, IL: Northwestern University Press, 1973.

Miller, Christopher L. "Theories of Africans: The Question of Literary Anthropology." *Critical Inquiry* 13:1 (Autumn 1986): 120–139.

Moyers, Bill. "The Fabric of Memory" (interview with Chinua Achebe). *Clinton Street Quarterly* (Minneapolis) XI.1 (Spring 1989): 8–12.

Nkosi, Lewis. "Interview with Chinua Achebe." In *African Writers Talking*. Eds. Dennis Duerden and Cosmo Pieterse. London: Heinemann, 1972.

Retamar, Roberto. *Caliban and Other Essays*. Minneapolis: University of Minnesota Press, 1989.

Sartre, Jean-Paul. *What Is Literature?* New York: Philosophical Society, 1949.

Talbot, P. Amaury. *In the Shadow of the Bush*. London: Heinemann, 1912.

Chapter Seven

# Historicity and the Un-Eve-ing of the African Woman: Achebe's Novels

*Chimalum Nwankwo*

> Beatrice Nwanyibuife did not know these traditions and legends of her people because they played but little part in her upbringing. She was born as we have seen into a world apart; was baptized and sent to schools that made much about the English and the Jews and the Hindu and practically everybody else but hardly put in a word for her forebears and the divinities with whom they had evolved. So she came to barely knowing who she was.
>
> —Achebe, *Anthillls of the Savannah 96*

The historical dimension in Achebe criticism with regard to the position of women in Igbo society has not really received the careful and serious attention it deserves. If it had, an enquiry that sought to discover the faces of Eve in African literature at the 1991 African Literature Association Conference would have been absolutely unnecessary. And if it had, the call for a feminist reading of Achebe's works would find justifications nowhere except in efforts to further marginalize an African viewpoint.

*Nwanyibuife*, an Igbo female name, is not a joke. It is not a distortion or misnomer to suggest a womanhood bearing a load or burden as the black American feminists and a few uncritical African feminists are trying so hard to suggest. It is not a tautological expression of a patriarchal whim but a serious and carefully phrased affirmation of the status of woman in Igbo society. That status may be in doubt today, but precolonial indigenous Igbo society was fully aware of the total human and spiritual implications of that name. Why should any critic search for Eve in works deeply rooted in the "legends and traditions" of the Igbo? The Igbo woman does not trace her ancestry to Eve. The Igbo Supreme Being, Chukwu, is neither man nor woman. The religious roles of women as well as their spiritual stature in Igbo society are different. The attitude to sexuality is different. The history of political participation and development are different; so is the nature of social and economic deprivation. If the history of Western philosophical thought is anything to go by, with its ideational hiccups and sudden reversals, the destiny of women will remain different despite certain curiously motivated pretensions to the so-called "globalness of sisterhoods."

Let us hasten to add that it may be relevant and useful to discuss the faces of Eve in African works with direct or indirect loyalty to the Western tradition. However, in works such as Achebe's, searching for Eve will most definitely lead to the masking of certain things that remain crucial to a good reading of his works. Achebe's novels have been written with no interest in Eve when it comes to the Igbo woman's character. The best a critic of his works can really do in that regard is to listen carefully to what the author himself has insisted on repeatedly: "This is what I have set out to do: to reconstruct our [Igbo] history through literatures. This reconstruction of history has been meticulously executed by the un-Eve-ing of the woman. This means remaining as faithful as the mimetic aspect of his art can possibly permit by presenting the Igbo woman as accurately as oral and written history records it" (qtd. in Nwachukwu-Agbada 1990 122).

An archetypal eye may choose to locate a female principle in Achebe's works. This almost amounts to a parallax vision because the Igbo world that the author fictionalizes already depends on a female hypostasis in the nature of Idemili—the goddess who is ubiquitous in Achebe's works. Achebe's critics, also afflicted by the same kind of lack of awareness as Beatrice Nwanyibuife, have regarded Idemili as a god; not so reliable Igbo Anthropology and not so Achebe himself, who has a definitive chapter on Idemili in *Anthills of the Savannah*.

In *Anthills of the Savannah*, the goddess is represented as "the resplendent Pillar of Water" that "the Almighty sent to bear witness to the moral nature of authority by wrapping around Power's rude waist a loin cloth of peace and modesty" (93). Because man cannot share and hold the grandeur of divinity, Idemili is ritually recognized as "a mere stream, a tree, a stone, a mound of earth, a little clay bowl containing fingers of chalk" (95). Those symbols may look laughable, suggests the author, but not so the power of the goddess that controls all else. Even access to the all-male "powerful hierarchy of *Ozo* society begins with sacrifices to Idemili." As for the celebrant, "He is accompanied by his daughter or, if he has only sons, by the daughter of a kinsman, but a daughter it must be" (94). The significance of all this will become more obvious when we realize that in Igbo religious belief, *Chukwu*, the Great God is *Agbala*, which is manifested in the fertility of the earth and the beings that inhabit it. The same word is synonymous with *Woman* and *Spirit*.

Meanwhile, let us recognize a balancing mechanism in place within the culture of Igbo society. The material for such combination of myth and history has recently found refurbishment in the painstaking and commendable study of gender and sex in the same general area of Igbo country that Achebe constantly fictionalizes. In *Male Daughters, Female Husbands*, an Igbo woman-scholar, Ifi Amadiume, offers overwhelming evidence that these parts had "strong matrifocality and female orientations; consequently: (1) The culture prescribing industriousness is derived from the goddess Idemili—the central religious deity. (2) There was a dual-sex organizational principle behind the structure of the economy. (3) A flexible gender system mediated the dual-sex organizational principle" (27).

Commenting on another of these parts, Amadiume buttresses her own findings and conclusions with Henderson's Nri myth of origin. One of the first Igbo men, Nri, had come to settle among the Igbo people who were hunting- and-gathering communities, lacking kingship systems and the knowledge of farming. Nri became very hungry, and appealed to the Great God, who ordered him to cut off and plant the heads of his son and daughter. From the daughter's head sprang cocoyam, "a subsidiary crop managed by women" (27). Even though "yam, that sprang from the head of the son was the Igbo staple, and is still the most valuable crop in rituals and ceremonies; the ritual prerogatives . . . the secret of *Ogwuji*, yam medicine" (27) that Igbo country enjoys from Nri and his descendants remains a dual-sex principle because of the combined products of the *Ichi* scarifications from the son and daughter of Nri before they were killed. It should be noted that Chukwu demanded here a son and daughter, not a son or daughter. You may see a relationship here between this demand and the demands of the people of Umuofia in *Things Fall Apart*, when their daughter was killed by the people of Mbaino. For placation, the people of Umuofia received Ikemefuna, a boy, and a virgin who was returned to Ogbuefi Udo, whose wife had been killed. This excerpt from Nri religious myth attests to a similar attitude to males and females. Significantly, once more Chukwu is in the heart of the story:

And the earth was soft when Eri came.
Chukwu sent a smith.
Who dried it with charcoal and bellows,
The descendants of the Smith
Made hoes, knives and carving tools.
The *Ichi* marks were made on
The face of Eze Nri's son and daughter
These artists are called *Dioka*. (Onwuejeogwu 1981 69)

Amadiume cites other myths, one of which is related to Idemili, that enable her to conclude that as a matter of fact "the female gender had the more prominent place in myth and indigenous and cultural concepts—the supernatural, a goddess, is female" (Amadiume 1987 29). Behind the various forms of flexibility that charac-terize sex and gender in Igbo society are some concepts in Igbo political culture that also deserve attention in this chapter. A number of these concepts are carefully explained in Njaka's *Igbo Political Culture*. The principal among them is the well-known concept of *Oha*, which Njaka equates to Sekou Toure's notion of a communocracy (Njaka 1974 13), a system that guarantees individual protection irrespective of sex. There is, of course, the generally recognized paradox in this communality, the Igbo spiritual notion of a *Chi* or guiding spirit or destiny keeper in every individual, that mitigates any tendency toward any form of autocracy. The two other concepts closely related to this are the principles of negotiation and pragmatism. "The Igbo believes he can negotiate anything," writes Njaka. For instance, "how to negotiate with Chukwu puzzled him and he created intermediaries . . . go-betweens" (Njaka 1974 14). This idea is important with regard to the general principle behind the relationship and the nature of male and female characters in Achebe's works. It is evident that most of the major characters in Achebe's works have in one sense or the other worked out their fates in relation to this principle. So what other writers may call the "female principle," I consider something already deeply ingrained in Igbo political culture. It is more of a survival principle, which is at the root of the fundamental mathematical principle beneath universal order. Tied to the principle of negotiation is that of pragmatism."Expediency provokes reactions appropriate to the challenge of the circumstance," writes Njaka "because the nature and tradition of Igbo culture are not simply receptive to change—change is of their essence. Evidence of Igbo receptivity to change [is] frequent in stories, plays, proverbs and dances all of which stress the benefits of adaptability and competition which generate change" (51). So, central to the fortune of the characters in Achebe's works is the role of pragmatism and change in Igbo political culture. These concepts are neither alien nor borrowed but integral, and every member of Igbo society, male or female, participates in the dynamics of that system.

It is very easy to look at novels like *Things Fall Apart* and *Arrow of God* and ask: Where are the women in Igbo land when grave crises are being discussed? So also is it easy for one to look at infantrymen in all-military formations in the modern world and ask: Where are the women? The fact, as is evident in certain works, is that the nature of crisis in society determines the character of representation. In the case of the traditional Igbo society, the concept of power and the modes of power are different. Unless we recognize that essential characteristic the invisibility of conventional modes of power will create a faulty perception of the society. We will miss vital organs of the Igbo such as the *Umuada*.

Women's organizations such as the *Umuada* are very powerful arms of the Igbo polity, with responsibilities that are often as grave as the issues of war or peace. The character of the *Umuada* and the source of its power actually lie in its composition. "Because women marry outside their own *Umunna* (immediate families), the organization of the *Umuada* cuts across the units of any one level of the political structure of the state and extends upward through the hierarchy" (Njaka 1974 124). This spread guarantees the existence of an unstoppable power base when women decide to act, such as we find with the well-known Aba Women's Riot of 1929. When the traditional Igbo woman decides to act, she acts, and that cannot be said about women in many societies, especially in the Western world. "Although in general, women do not take part openly in most public affairs . . . they must not sit quietly when the Constitution is violated and the land goes ablaze. . . . Certainly, the elders will go to great lengths to avoid a confrontation with the *Umuada*, and in this way the women do, indirectly, exert a strong influence on affairs of state" (Njaka 1974 124). What we see in the Igbo society in this regard is a reflection of that principle of negotiation. It is what makes women out of certain cultural considerations inclined toward certain modes of power. What appears to be absence does not mean the occlusion that it means in many societies elsewhere.

Because of the peculiar nature of social control in traditional Igbo society, some of the problems that plague the modern world, especially the Western world, were absent in Igbo country. Chief among these is that of sexual permissiveness. At the second African writer's conference in Stockholm in 1986, Buchi Emecheta lightly touched this dormant issue waiting for exploration in the studies of women in African literature when she declared that "sex is part of life. It is not life. Listen to the Western feminists' claim about enjoying sex. . . . African feminism is free of the shackles of Western romantic illusions and tends to be much more pragmatic" (qtd. in Peterson 1988 177). One is still waiting for that African feminists' pragmatism that returns to the cultural base of the behavior of African women and men with regards to sex. It is either that current feminist studies fear the truth about sexual behavior in traditional Igbo society or they are too squeamish to broach the subject. Certainly, an understanding of the relationship between culture and literature has much to do with sexuality. It is a historical fact that premarital sex remained a *taboo* in many parts of Igbo land up to the Nigerian civil war when the Igbo world suffered its second falling apart. In his *An Igbo Civilization*, M.A. Onwuejeogwu's list of sexual taboos reflects a very stern moral code in the sexual behavior of the traditional Nri Igbo, whether they are male, female, young, old, married, or widowed.

In marriage itself, the much misrepresented traditional concept of marriage as a contract between families ensures the power of married women beyond their own family boundaries. Because the woman is no less important than the man, the system guarantees a perpetuity of protection in forms such as the unconventional retaliation enforced by Obika in *Arrow of God*, when his sister is beaten by her husband, or the form in *Things Fall Apart*, when the more conventional justice of the Egwugwu is unmistakable in the manner in which censures are evenly handed out to the families of Odukwe and Uzowulu after serious communal deliberation.

Now what do all these have to do with Achebe's works? No kind of account of literature based on Igbo country can pretend to serve its cause effectively without recording the existence of these myths and their relationship to Igbo world view. And what does this have to do with history? If a feminist program for the rectification of gender problems in the West begins with Eve and the pejorative echo of treachery and inferiority, an African feminist program could possibly justify its existence by initiating its own quest in the general character of traditional Igbo society. One ought to find good reason in this preference: The Western female mythical and historical base is negative and the African is positive. The West, through its Judeo-Christian heritage has found it necessary to evolve a female image from Eve through the notion of an intercessionary mother of God to sundry pedestalized women to the fighting New Woman. The African tradition, especially the Igbo tradition as expressed in Igbo myths, legends and history, has retained a permanent face needing only bolsters and rehabilitation from the ravage of a conquistadorial culture. The program must be cognizant of the fact that for the Igbo, *Nwanyi-bu-ife:* Woman is something because she has always been something in Igbo society. If she has ceased to be something, the task of a feminist program is to discover why such is now the case.

Bearing all these in mind, let us now reread some of Achebe's works and see how the writer conducts that un-Eve-ing of the African woman.

## DEITIES AND RELIGIOUS RESPONSIBILITIES

For reasons better expressed by Christian theology, there is no gender flexibility in Christian myths, concepts, and religious practice. In the reconstructed Igbo world we find in *Things Fall Apart*, it is clear that discrimination is virtually absent. Even a patriarchy in relation to the Great God, Chukwu, and man is absent. The Oracle of the Hills and Caves that features so prominently in the novel is male but the ministers, Chika, and then Chielo, are females. The Earth Goddess we know as the preeminent deity in Igbo society, who is frequently mentioned in *Things Fall Apart*, *Arrow of God*, and *Anthills of the Savannah*, is female but the servant is usually a male priest. *Idemili*, the "Pillar of Water," the Goddess of fertility and increase associated with the sacred python and the Igbo traditional religion as expressed in *Things Fall Apart* and *Arrow of God* is female but the serving priest in *Arrow of God* is male. In *Arrow of God*, one of the most important festivals of the people, the *Festival of the Pumpkin Leaves* has a male *Eze-Ulu* as officiating chief-priest but the chief celebrants and acolytes are women.

## SPIRITUAL, PSYCHIC, AND OCCULT POWER

In the realms of spiritual, psychic, or occult power, women are as visible as men in the Igbo world depicted in Achebe's works. If one finds the medicine man who treats Ezinma's *Ogbanje* in *Things Fall Apart* a compelling presence, the numerous references to the capabilities of women in similar roles are equally fascinating. There is *agadi-nwanyi*, "the active principle" (Achebe 1958 89) in the medicine of the people of Umuofia. There is the powerful spirit in the market at Okperi in *Arrow of God.* The market was "at first a very small market . . . then one day the men of Okperi made a powerful deity and placed their market in its care. From that day, Eke grew and grew until it became the biggest market in these parts. This deity that is called Nwanyieke is an old woman" (Achebe 1969 19). For one who is familiar with the Western world and its attitude to old people, the difference in Igbo culture should be clear. Capabilities of this nature are not restricted to mythical old women. This is clear in women such as Chielo in *Things Fall Apart*, who responds to spiritual possession without any conflicts with her secular responsibilities. Beatrice, the updated version of the Igbo woman in *Anthills of the Savannah*, despite personal ignorance and lack of awareness of her roots, exhibits a level of prophetic vision attained by no other character in Achebe's works, male or female. Nothing is ever successfully concealed from her, from the impending collapse of the dictatorship in Kangan to the understanding that it is "no matter" whether "the father named the child" (Achebe 1988 206) or whether the child who is a girl takes a boy's name. In *No Longer at Ease*, we are told of Clara's accurate sense of prophecy and persistent sense of foreboding when Clara and Obi go to the movies. Every conclusion that she anticipates in a movie is what transpires. This strong sensitivity is openly expressed by Clara when during shopping, surprised at Obi's lack of observation of details in the nature of housewares, she exclaims: "Men are blind!" (1960 74). In *Arrow of God*, Obika's wife Okuata, senses, long before her husband's tragic end, that there is some kind of danger ahead.

## EVOLUTION OF MALE AND FEMALE CHARACTERS

The male characters in Achebe's novels from Okonkwo to Odili Samalu represent a general change from intransigence to compromise, the kind of compromise that characterized the relationship between women and men according to Igbo history, legend, and tradition. In *Things Fall Apart*,and *Arrow of God*, where an older generation is depicted, the major characters, Okonkwo and Ezeulu and his son, are destroyed largely for the violations of what the Igbo regard as *odina-ani*, part of a complex of principles associated with that survival *pragmatique* that ensures that everyone in the society, man or woman, is protected at all times. It is not a surprise that Ezeulu, the priest of a male deity, is defeated by forces beyond his control. It is also not surprising that Ezidemili is victorious in a struggle that is no less difficult than that of Ezeulu. Ezidemili is the priest of a female deity and as we observe in *Arrow of God*, he successfully negotiates Okperi out of the same kind of circumstances that destroy the priest of the deity of Umuaro. In *Achebe's World* (1980) Robert Wren's suggestion is that "the quarrel between Ulu and Idemili was the quarrel of the no-longer-needed protector against the autochthonic deity;" (123) that "the autochthon Idemili [was] a god wholly incapable of dealing with the conditions of life under a European colonial government;" (123) and that "Ulu may in a complex irony sacrifice himself and his priest to secure an orderly transfer of sacred authority away from Idemili and tradition to the new order and the religion of the colonial power" (123). Should one accept this reading, what then would be the rational explanation for the ascendance of Okperi over Umuaro in the estimation of the colonial government, and why would Achebe reinvoke the power of Idemili in *Anthills of the Savannah?* Let us continue by adding that what Eze-ulu does in *Arrow of God* is really what Okonkwo ought to have tried to do in *Things Fall Apart:* to negotiate a successful exit out of an impasse. If Okonkwo was ordinarily proud, Ezeulu is, according to Nwaka, one of his rivals, "as proud as a lunatic" (Achebe 1969 217). Whatever improvement we find in him that makes him different from Okonkwo is negated by his selfdestructive tendency.

In *No Longer at Ease*, we meet another kind of man. Obi Okonkwo's historical circumstances are different, but there is a decided break with tradition, as we know in the conduct of Ezeulu and Okonkwo. Obi Okonkwo is the new Igbo man with the great potential for reinstating the power of the woman beside the man. "He was used to speaking to his mother like an equal, even from his childhood, but his father had always been different ... something that made one think of the patriarchs, those giants hewn from granite" (1960 127). The inflexible nature of his forebears is rejected in favor of a liberalism that nearly destroys him. But if Obi Okonkwo loses against the modern pressures of survival, he wins in the bold initiative he makes for a marriage that would have broken the Igbo Osu caste. In that regard, we may consider him some steps ahead of Okonkwo and Ezeulu. The forces against Obi Okonkwo are the forces represented by the inflexible president of the Umuofia union in Lagos. Rather than show sympathy for Obi Okonkwo, this spiritual descendant of Okonkwo declares: "A man may go to England, become a lawyer or a doctor, but it does not change his blood. It is like a bird that flies off the earth and lands on an anthill. It is still on the ground" (1960 150). By the time we meet Odili Samalu, the leading character in *A Man of the People*, one is no longer in doubt about the nature of the maturation of Achebe's male characters. Odili, who begins his role in the story as a philanderer of sorts, evolves through tribulations principally related to his involvement with Edna and concludes with a sense of responsibility that enables him to recognize that "woman is something." At the end of *A Man of the People* when Odili reflects on how selflessly Eunice avenges the death of her friend Max, Odili concludes that "you died a good death if your life had inspired someone to come forward and shoot your murderer in the chest—without asking to be paid" (1966 150).

In an essay entitled "Power and the New African Woman in *Anthills of Savannah*" (*MATATU:* special issue on Achebe), I have suggested that the woman in *Anthills of the Savannah* is a historical update of the woman in Igbo society. The same could also be said of the men. Ikem Osodi and Chris Oriko, two of the principal players in that novel, are distant descendants of Okonkwo and Ezeulu who were inflexible patriarchs. Ikem is completely at home with Elewa. It does not matter that he is educated and intellectual and the woman, Elewa, is not. Chris finds himself constantly responding to the power of the priestess that Beatrice Nwanyibuife exhibits. He returns to her every now and again for spiritual renewal.

I think it is the Zulu who fondly refer to *Mother* as the *Big House.* The reasons for that appellation is probably not different from the mysticism behind the Igbo declaration that "Mother is Supreme." Uchendu's explanation to Okonkwo in *Things Fall Apart* is that a man belongs to his fatherland when things are good and life is sweet. But when there is sorrow and bitterness, he finds refuge in his motherland. "Your mother is there to protect you. She is buried there" (1958 94). This whole thing, of course, goes beyond that: "To the Igbo, *Ala (Ani)* is the vault in which are interred the dead who are also the (*living*) ancestors. It is from *Ala* that the food which keeps all living things alive comes. It is assumed that any person who does not behave in accordance with the dictates of *Ala* will not find comfort within the vault. The logic resulted in *Ala* being made the constitutional deity of the Igbo" (Njaka 1974 39–40). It is this same logic that operates in the destruction of characters like Okonkwo. It is the same logic that dictates the level of moral constancy and strength in Achebe's major female characters. It is a logic that shifts from the old Egyptianism of "Man know thyself" to "Woman know thyself."

What remains clear to every reader of Achebe is that it is the men who need to change or grow, not the women, whose positions are clear within the cultural and the political system. It is ironic that the so-called feminist readers of Achebe quickly recognize that Okonkwo beat his wives, but they fail to hear the universal outcry echoed by even the inflexible Ezeulu: "It is not bravery for a man to beat his wife" (Achebe 1969 65). So we encounter declarations such as: "While Achebe's works are obvious classics within the African literary tradition, a reexamination of his work from a feminist position reveals woman as peripheral to the larger exploration of man's experience" (Davies 1986 247).

I think that what is needed is to leave Achebe's works where they are: obvious classics within the African literary tradition. It is a literary tradition that affirms that Nwanyibuife, woman is something. It is a tradition that recognizes modes of power other than that characterized by naked or brutal aggression. We see that expressed clearly in the activities of the women in *Things Fall Apart*, where the various forms of women's council are firmly in charge of all kinds of power in the community from policing the crops and farming to other religious and family responsibilities. The position of women in Igbo society has never been in question, according to Achebe's reconstruction of history through literature. The combination of priestess and intellectual in Beatrice Nwanyibuife testifies that the Igbo man is not exploring the world with women at the periphery. Rather the Igbo man and woman are exploring their world together. They are involved in the same venture in different roles. This is why Beatrice Nwanyibuife tells her story like all the other male witnesses in *Anthills of the Savannah*, and the story like all human experiences is one of struggles and triumphs. It is a story that accepts, in keeping with Igbo culture, no boundaries for the self because autochthonous Igbo society in myth and reality imposed no boundaries on her. Above the powerful voice of her story is the quizzical authorial censure for some of her kind: Does the Igbo woman know herself and her limitless potentials? Will she continue to tell her story or will her story be told by other people for her? Will she cut her own image and a distinct tradition or will she, in ignorance of who she is, posit herself before the world as a descendant of Eve? Does she know that in Igbo society *Woman is Something?* These are questions that Nwanyibuife has answered and her answers so far ought to enable the Igbo woman, nay the African woman, to find and know herself. Whether she does or not is now up to her.

Commenting on women and other minor characters in *Girls at War*, C.L. Innes concludes that "Achebe brings those marginalized characters to the foreground . . . and also focuses a much harsher light on those who exploit or ignore them" (1990 133). This is not accidental in Achebe's craft; just as it is not an accident that the world of all the female characters in his works has no room for those familiar, but alien, dreadful personages who haunt the female consciousness in some fiction and reality: the sexually depraved, the licentious wifebeaters, the evil seductresses and other variations of the traitorous descendants of Eve. They are mostly absent because they were likewise absent in traditional Igbo society. This is all the expression of a consciousness in tune with Igbo cosmology, history, and culture; it is the hallmark of a storyteller whose craft is part of the story.

## WORKS CITED

Achebe, Chinua. *Anthills of the Savannah.* New York: Anchor Press, 1988.

———. *Arrow of God.* London: H.E.B., 1969

———. *A Man of the People.* London: Heinemann, 1966.

———. *No Longer at Ease.* London: Heinemann, 1977.

———. *Things Fall Apart.* London: Heinemann, 1958.

Amadiume, Ifi. *Male Daughters, Female Husbands.* London: Zed Books Ltd., 1987.

Davies, Carol Boyce, ed. *Ngambika: Studies of Women in African Literature.* Trenton, NJ: Africa World Press, 1986.

Innes, C.L. *Chinua Achebe.* Cambridge: Cambridge University Press, 1990.

Njaka, E.N. *Igbo Political Culture.* Evanston: Northwestern University Press, 1974.

Nwachukwu-Agbada, J.O.J. "Interview." *Commonwealth* 13:1 (1990).

Onwuejeogwu, M.A. *An Igbo Civilization.* London: Ethnographica, 1981.

Peterson, Kirsten Holst. *Criticism and Ideology.* Stockholm: Uppsala, 1988.

Wren, Robert. *Achebe's World: The Historical and Cultural Context of the Novels.* Washington, DC: Three Continents Press, 1980.

Chapter Eight

# "Over-Determined Contradictions": History and Ideology in Achebe's *A Man of the People*

## *Dubem Okafor*

*A Man of the People* should be acknowledged for exactly what it is: an entertainment, written for Africans. . . . The characters are ineffectual, and Achebe's satire itself will be short-lived. The story and the characters have none of the magnitude or the nobility of those in *Things Fall Apart* or *Arrow of God*.

—Larson (1972 87)

This typical disvaluation of *A Man of the People* perpetuates the belief held by some "anthropologizing" critics that Achebe has been condemned to, and should remain within, the confines of aesthetic anthropologism that the earlier novels were said to have ably enacted. But it is a major argument of this chapter that those "flaws" for which *A Man of the People* has continued to be denounced constitute its strength and relevance. To start with, no determinism attaches to an author's choice of style or subject matter. And *A Man of the People* is the one novel where the author's ideological unarity with the people is indubitable; where antiquarian sociohistorical explanations and rationalizations are replaced by contemporary sociopolitical and ethical anatomy; where the target of his excoriation shifts from foreign conquistadors to indigenous exploiters and oppressors; and where the much flaunted artistic/technical flaws and contradictions are an expression and transmutation of the shortcomings and contradictions in society and its people. And the prophetic closure of the novel, whose publication coincided with the first military *coup d'etat* in Nigeria, while it is a textual expression of a societal demand for order and stability, constitutes, rather than cheap journalistic topicality, an incisive and attentive reading, by the writer, of the sociopolitical barometer of his society.

Literature transacts a peculiar relationship with society and ideology. This relationship can be either consolidatory or contestatory. It is also a definite reflection of the conditions of its production, with which it is so closely imbricated that it cannot be separated from them. So, while literature maintains a certain relative autonomy, it is still curiously tied up with its history and milieu. A major validation of my choice of this topic comes, therefore, from Marx's "insistence on the links between cultural creations and history," that, while "presenting the specificity" of the work of art enables us to appreciate its intertextual richness, as well as relate it to the sociocultural/historical forces of its production (Ahearn 1989 xii–xiii; Roscoe 1971 130).

Yet, this novel is not "straight history." Because the iconoclastic workers are as busily gnawing away at the foundations of boundaries as are the institutional and disciplinary masons and guardians at mending the rifts I do not intend to insist on the total collapse of the boundary between "history" and "fiction." Still, it maybe fruitful to examine some of the methodological congruencies between *historiography* and *the writing of fiction*. In doing this, I will be guided by Hayden White and Michel de Certeau, especially the latter, whose heterological project does not seek to smooth over the fragmentation of disciplines nor to espouse disciplinary co-optation. He seeks, rather, to uncover the grounds of such deep seated fragmentation and reveal the extent of disciplinary interdependence and complicated intertextualities.

In *The Writing of History,* Certeau emphasizes the concern of historiography with the "unknown other." This "other" usually takes the form of absence, silence, or void, and historiography begins with the location of this absence or past, and with separating it from the present. At the same time, however, writing continually transacts a suture of this past and the present, of the dead and the living.

But the operation of separation and suture is a discursive enterprise which demonstrates the force which discourse exercises on the shaping of the past: the past can never be known to us except as discursively constructed/reconstructed. In the shaping of this past, which always is conditioned by ideology, the historiographer, like the novelist, decides what objects, or what documents, or what events are worthy of discourse. In other words, historiography and fiction operate on the basis of the principle of *selection.* Moreover, because historiography has begun to interrogate its own scientificity, and literature finds some of its own aesthetics in the formal modes of historical inquiry, while both historian and novelist are becoming more and more skeptical towards traditional rhetoric, history and fiction are seen to be decidedly "quasi-identical" (1988 xi).

Furthermore, Certeau identifies as paradoxical, almost oxymoronic, that element in historiography that attempts to force a relationship between apparent antinomies: the *real as history,* and *writing as discourse. This* forced relationship marks the practice of historiography as fabrication that aligns, even more closely, the craft of making history and the art of making fiction. Certeau goes further to denegate historiography's pretensions to scientificity and representationality that he sees as a residue of the primitive and the mythic. For, in the first place, the *real,* "what is or what has been," which historiography presumes to represent, does not correspond to the real which determines its production. Instead, the real is occulted by the institution of history that, in return for the preservation of the hegemonic ideological status quo and the semblance of unity, stability, continuity, and progress, dispenses the largess of *legitimacy* and *authority* on its members. In this "actual case of *quid pro quo*," (1986 199ff), historiography throws over the face of the ideological present the mask of the real, that is the past. In that sense, historiography, like narrativity, is *organized, fabricated, covers its conditions of production, and selects its materials from an interested position* (1986 199ff).

The concept of narrativity is both broad and crucial. Hayden White sees the impulse to narrate, to tell a story, as a natural, human imperative in the human attempt to make meaning of apparent chaos in the social formation (1987 1ff.). He distinguishes the "social mathematizers" from the narrativizers of reality who would let the world speak itself as a story, with the narrator either absent or dissolved polyphonously among other voices. The narrativizing discourse organizes its material chronologically (even when the time scheme does not seem obvious) and produces meaning through emplotment. This success of narrative in revealing meaning, coherence, and significance legitimizes its use in historiography. Conversely, the success of historiography in narrativizing events attests to the "realism" of narrative itself.

Thus, a correlation is established between narrative as a symbolic discursive structuration and the representation of historical events. Human events are products of human actions whose effects have the structure of narrative texts. To understand these "texts," these products of actions, they need to be narrativized, that is, *re-presented* through narrative. Thus the only way the past, history, can be represented to present consciousness is through mythic/fictional/ imaginative (imaginary) discourse. Narrativized historiography, therefore, like "fiction" (a novel), fulfills our "normal narratological expectations" (White 1987 17).

This is nothing less than the normalizing and naturalizing function of ideology, in which literature plays the role of handmaiden. For our present purpose, a working definition of ideology will suffice that conflates Raymond Williams' articulation (of ideology) as "referring to the dominant ideas of an epoch or class, with regard to politics and law, morality, religion, art and science" (Ngara 1985 20) with that of Althusser, which conceives of ideology as representing "the imaginary relationship of individuals to their real conditions of existence" (1971 162). The representation of these relationships can be religious, ethical, legal, and political. Whether the necessity for this imaginary representation is thought in terms of obedience to God (through priests and despots), or in terms of the material alienation of man, what is reflected in the imaginary representation of the world found in ideology is the conditions of existence of men, that is, their real world (Althusser 1971 163–164). This existence is circumscribed by ideology from which there is no escape, human beings having *always already* been interpellated (Althusser 1971 171).

Because it is socially mediated and conditioned, literature enables us to see the nature of the ideology of an epoch from which it is born (Ngara 1985 21). It achieves this through the internal distancing of its aesthetic arm, by revealing the inherent ruptures, gaps, and contradictions. As a result, literature is able to maintain an ambiguous relationship, harmonious or conflictual, with dominant ideologies. *A Man of the People* reflects the dominant ideology, but, at the same time, contradicts it. This contradiction, which is always already over-determined even in its instances (cf. Althusser 1977 106), defines the status of the novel as well as its relationship with history and the social context. This status and this relationship are defined by irony and satire—itself a contradictory mode—saying one thing and meaning another, praising and damning in one breath (see Alexander Pope, "Essay on Criticism"). The satiric polysemy of the novel as a whole is immediately prognosticated in the ironic title that simultaneously eulogizes and undermines. For Chief Nanga, a typification of the political/moral ineptitude and degeneracy is at once populist—his roots are, indeed, rustic and among the people, and anti-populist—transplanted to the metropolis of power and transcending his humble origins, he is ensconced in palatial and patronizing aloofness. This irony defines the very structure of the novel whose textual resolution will demonstrate the ideological contradiction besetting history itself.

*A Man of the People* is concerned with contemporary society, and exploiting the long and rich Igbo satiric tradition, pokes the sharp stick into the warts on the face of decadent society. This explains the tone of humorous anguish and sardonic leer. Hence, I find indefensibly wrong and shallow the overgeneralization, by Adrian Roscoe, to the effect that "satire, one suspects, has not enjoyed a long history in Africa; and for Achebe the absence of this kind of strength at his back has been disastrous" (1971 131; but see Egudu and Nwoga, *Igbo Poetic Heritage*). *A Man of the People* is "insistently historical"; this historicity functions, not as "ideological justification" but as a satiric deconstruction of the oppressive societal (dis)order for, given Achebe's populist convictions, "irony and ironic literary forms" are deployed "as resistances to the oppression of material and historical forces, as safeguards of inner freedom" (Ahearn 1989 27, 201).

Yet, *A Man of the People* is not "straight history." The dynamics of realism, it is true, "compels a writer to represent a progressive reflection of reality" (Ngara 1985 14), but in Engels' definition of realism as consisting of truth to detail, typical characters, and typical circumstances, we are not going to insist on the first term (truth to detail). With regard to the third term (typical circumstance), however:

it relates to the writer's awareness of history and the class nature of society. Characters do not act in a vacuum. Their actions derive from social and historical conditions and are reflective of the interests and activities of a class. It is therefore the writer's duty to see what makes a particular historical moment tick, to see class struggles in their true perspective and depict them accurately, showing how the actions of individual characters are representative of classes making their impact on history. (Ngara 1985 14)

The emphasis here is on the typical, which is a conjunction of "all the most important social, moral, and spiritual contradictions of a time" and does not necessarily mean the "average" or even "archetypal" (Ngara 1985 16). The result is that the characters in *A Man of the People* are typical even as they lack individualities, the aim of the novel being, not minute characterological individuations, but indications of social development. Still, there is a double contradiction here: "a clear contradiction between reality as presented by those who hold political and economic power, and reality as seen by the creative artist" (Ngara 1985 24), on one hand, and between reality as perceived by the artist and the masses, on the other. But because in this novel, Achebe is giving a hard look at his anomalous society, and addressing Nigerians as his primary audience, in his representation of reality, he transcends the linguistic barrier by employing an idiom that is accessible to the generality of the people. Like the man of the people himself, he speaks the language of the tribe(s). In that sense, *A Man of the People* is truly both popular and realistic in Brecht's sense of the word: "Realist means: laying bare society's causal network/showing up the dominant viewpoint as the viewpoint of the dominator, writing from the standpoint of the class" that has been at the receiving end of oppression and holds the solutions to the problems of society (qtd. in Craig 1975 424).

Yet, even within this realist mode, and in his attempt to transcend the linguistic obstacle, Achebe foregrounds the pervasive insidiousness of ideological contradiction through the use of an interplay of two codes—Pidgin and Standard English—as a stylistic device not only for delineating his characters, but also for effectively evaluating their relationship to one another. On the pragmatic level, the Pidgin is a social leveler that facilitates communication, being the code that both the master and servant, minister and narrator use. But on the ideological level, the code is used to coopt the subordinated, to make them believe that the distance between them and their oppressors is only rumored, does not exist: after all, they speak the same language, a common idiom! (cf. Emenyeonu et al. 1987 240).

But we know that the gap, if anything, gets wider and wider. Thus, Chief Nanga, *the man of the people,* does speak the language of the people—Igbo *and* Pidgin, and has not undergone a "university education which [in his own view] only alienates an African from his rich and ancient culture and puts him above his people" (Achebe 1966 4); yet, he delights in the academicist connotation of his initials— M.A., and has shown "such excitement over the LL.D. arranged for him from some small, backward college" (29); and, above all, he is truly and ironically "above his people" whom he, together with others of the dominating group/class, continues to oppress and exploit. The ideological battle line is thus clearly drawn between the exploiting "haves" and the exploited "have-nots." But these two broad classes do not really have any ideological roots or linkages. On the political, superstructural level, what we have is not continuity but ideological rupture: the erstwhile dominant ideologies of the cohesive village communities do not get translated, with the coming into being of the nation-state, into a national superstructural idiom, with the result that from the beginning to the end, we have, not only ideological contradictions, but, more importantly, over-determinations in the superstructure (cf. Althusser 1977 94 ff.). As Carroll puts it:

Achebe began with the premise that the politician's role is inevitably divided. He must serve both the constituency that has elected him and the Government of the country as a whole. This is a difficult task at any time but in the novel's anonymous African state that is a conglomeration of local loyalties it is virtually impossible. These loyalties are too strong ever to be transcended by the needs of the country as a whole. (*Critical Perspectives on Chinua Achebe* 277)

So, in spite of nationalistic platitudes, the pull of primordialism remains ever strong: "Primitive loyalty, I call it" (Achebe 1966 8). This reveals a further contradiction in the appellation—man of the people—that Chief Nanga fails to assume because "the people do not [even] exist" (Innes and Lindfors 1978 34). The Western concept of nationhood had not yet congealed (in Nigeria) into coherent practical intelligibility, as the experiences and sense of tradition of the new political elite continued to be defined by the village. And the transference and application of primordial concepts and morality operate in a doubly ironic way. In the first place, they are inapplicable and, if applied at all, ineffectual; in the second, the corrupt indigenous politicians get praised, because they are "sons of the soil," for offenses and atrocities for which they would have been ostracized in the villages: "after all when the white man used to do all the eating did we commit suicide?" (Achebe 1966 161–162).

This concept of alterity whereby "ours is ours and theirs is theirs" brings up the issue of *gastrocentrism*. The historical, over-determined contradictions and conflicts are dramatized in the ideological formulaism, which receives aesthetic articulation in the diadic gastrocentric images of "cake" and "eating" that proliferate in the novel and assume a structural centrality (Achebe 1966 71, 141, passim; Innes and Lindfors 1978 63–64). The cake as a metaphoric analog of the state culls the Lacanian concept of *lack* and *desire*. As an absent center around which major conflictual actions are enacted, the cake, like the state, is not respected, worshipped, served, or maintained; being fragile, delicious, edible, and appetizing, it is scrambled and consumed, and finally egested. The coprophilic implication of this last biological activity, whose obverse is eating, and whose object is the tempting cake, is graphically aestheticized in the very heart of the metropolis where:

The attention of the Public is hereby drawn to Section 12 of the Bori (conservancy) Bye-laws of 1951:

(i) Occupiers of all premises shall provide pails for excrement; the size of such pails and the materials of which they are constructed shall be approved by the City Engineer. . . .

So disgusting did I find the bucket that I sometimes went for days on end without any bowel movement. And then there was that week when all the night-soil men in the town decided to go on strike. . . . You could "hear" the smell of the town ten miles away. (Achebe 1966 45–46)

The contradictions and the satire capsulized in this passage need no elaboration. And we are still talking about Cake! The scramble for this cake was rationalized in altruistically regional terms as one of the obligations of political representation, even though it was a clear dog-eat-dog exercise in self-aggrandizement and mindless spoliation. The control of the apparatuses of state power ensured the players a leverage in the scramble, for which they needed the "consent" and "willing support" of the people. As Althusser puts it:

In order to make its power lasting, it is necessary for the dominant class to transform its power from a power based on violence to a power based on consent. It is necessary for such a dominant class to obtain, by means of the free and habitual consent of its subjects, an obedience that could not be maintained by force alone. It is this purpose that the always contradictory system of ideologies serves. ("The Transformation of Philosophy" 23)

Hungry for independence and national self-determination—*in the last instance!*—the people gave their consent and their votes. But no sooner had they done that than they were struck by the similarity in the aims and practices that aligned the departing with the ascending/succeeding political elite, the imperial "master" and the comprador political elite, the latter even serving as *agents* of the former. A wide and deep chasm thus separated popular dreams of independence and the brutal reality of life in *independent* society. The natural result was cynicism and apathy among the masses, the working classes, and the nationalistic intelligentsia, who waited, helplessly, for the intervention of the gods. These gods were soon to come—if true gods they were—in the sartorial habits of soldiers.

Convinced of the vanguard and, ultimately salvific, role of the writer in society, Achebe, himself one of the nationalistic intelligentsia, found himself at one with the "quadrangle" of the oppressed, and *A Man of the People* became an articulation of the frustrations and aspirations of the masses. This articulation itself is defined and over-determined by contradictions. In addition to the contradictions inherent in the binaries—dreams/reality of independence, nationalism/primordialism, affluence/pauperization, and probity/degeneracy—the linguistic, characterological, and narratological contradictions are also over-determined. On the linguistic level, we had earlier noted the leveling and interpellatory functions of the Pidgin code. The level of linguistic competence generally expected of readers of the novel is such that the appeal is to a broader and wider spectrum of readers; it also marks the ideological base and, therefore, oppositional stance, of the writer. Yet, the style indicates a certain ambivalence toward the "metropolitan tongue" that both shaped the colonial status of the writer and his people, and distorted their tradition. At the same time, the same language facilitates the writer's attempt to transform the "cultural burden of England" and define his people's identity, even satirically. In effect, the language is bent, twisted, refashioned, and even *cannibalized (Calibanized)* for contestation, reinterpretation, and domestic house cleaning (Innes and Lindfors 1978 23). It is in that same contradictory manner that Chief Nanga's "colorful English" is a fraudulent facade, "unrelated to the socio-economic complexities of African culture and nationhood" (Innes and Lindfors 1978 33–34). The mixture of this colorful English with traditional aphorisms, mostly vacuous, indicates personal as well as political confusion, exposing "not only Nanga's own insincerity and irresponsibility, but the moral chaos in the world in which he lives" (Innes and Lindfors 1978 62).

This discrepancy is obvious in two ways: in the village, the use of proverbs indicates the user's integration in, and at-onement with his society; in the transitional society (Tucker 1967 91), where values are not yet coherent, which society in this instance is actually a trivial, trivialized, and trivializing one, proverbs are clearly inappropriate, not part of the cultural-linguistic *doxa* and, when they are used, become degraded and trivialized. Still, Achebe manages to use them to expose the emptiness of the characters, to "pinpoint the dangers and difficulties accompanying moral choice" and to "comment ironically on the discrepancies between the solutions of tribal past and the problems of the urban present" (Innes and Lindfors 1978 77). It is in order to say here that, because we have resisted the temptation of conflating "history" and "fiction," it is important to note that even though "referentiality . . . always reappears" (Culler 1982 250), proverbs are used as a rhetorical device to deconstruct history through anonymity and de-individualization (cf. Greenblatt, qtd. by Lentricchia in *The New Historicism* 239).

This notion of de-individualization/de-individuation brings us to the slippery threshold of characterological contradictions. In the first place, proverbs are used to delineate characters either through individuation or typification. We are able to distinguish one character from another by the proverbs they use; in the same way, because they draw their aphorisms from the same proverbic *doxa,* these sayings simply mark their users with anonymous sameness and facelessness. Thus Odili, even in his moral ambivalence, represents the dominated, counterhegemonic position, that would counter graft and self centered cavernousness with altruism and probity. But his ideas, ideals, and ideology are half baked, and his moral position proves no less contradictory and self serving than Nanga's: He is as promiscuous as Nanga is concupiscent; his motives are far from pure and altruistic; and his political vision is not clarified by his muddle-headed sloganeering. In other words, Odili, who is used to deconstruct Nanga ends up deconstructing himself through his degeneration to his antagonist's amorality (see Achebe 1966 63, 113, and passim).

This characterological contest dramatized in the pairs: Odili/Nanga, Nanga/Jalio, and, above all, that interior dramatic conflict, Odili/Odili, when translated to the "national"political level becomes clearly ideologically over-determined, in the mediate and immediate instances by the economic tussle between the dominant and dominating capitalists, fledgling bourgeoisie, and ideological hybrids, on one hand, and the dominated intelligentsia and deprived masses, on the other. Yet, the dichotomy is not as total as it would seem, for the intellectual elite are aligned with the capitalists in their material aspirations (e.g., Odili), while primordialism links villager and politician alike.

This conflict and confusion of values in the characters is reflected in the technique of narration whereby there is a constant oscillation of focalization, as well as antagonism and harmony between the narrator and flawed title-hero. Moreover, this unreliable narrator functions as satiric butt as well as authorial mouthpiece. With regard to this latter characterological functional discrepancy (Innes and Lindfors 1978 256–267), it would appear that Achebe uses it to distance himself from his persona, thus demonstrating that he is not writing *straight* history, and asserting a discontinuity between the world of the novel, the heterocosm, and the Nigerian "reality."

Commented on earlier, the oscillation of focalization is interesting because, while it asserts that the "first person narration" "is not fiction," that "first person fictional narratives are 'feigned reality statements' " it undermines that assertion by the use of the third person, indirect discourse (also used by first person narrators). At the same time, because first person narrators cannot, unlike their third person, omniscient counterparts, flit in and out of consciousnesses, they are even more unreliable (Martin 1986 140 ff). With regard to *A Man of the People*, neither the first nor the third person narrator can be privileged in respect of truth speaking. The important thing is that the constant alternation of points of view in the novel underlines the contradiction and unreliability of voices, which, as they struggle for narrative articulacy and perspectival dominance, create a textual dissonance, that some may read as "innocent" polyphony.

It is this polyphony, or, better, cacophony, since it is already over-determined, that makes it impossible to read the end of the novel in jubilantly prophetic terms. Rather than go on isolating instances of over-determined contradictions, the rapid concatenation of which led to the sudden closure of the novel—and of the sudden collapse of the First Republic—I intend to end this chapter with a critique of a wrong-headed criticism of *A Man of the People* which succeeds in underlining our theme of contradiction. It has been pointed out that the novelist's silence on the 1964 General Strike and the portrayal of "workers and peasants as clowns steeped in the bourgeois culture of corruption, although in real Nigerian life, they have no structural opportunities to receive bribes" constitutes a real structural weakness and ideological ambivalence (Onoge in Gugelberger 1985 62). We had earlier observed that the principle of selection was a prerogative that linked historiography and fiction. Achebe should be allowed that freedom. He did not set out to write a "fictionalized historical compendium" of Nigeria, that, even then would and could not include everything. Achebe's silences are as loud as his inclusions. And it appears to me that the direct discussion of the general strike, by exposing the atrocities and iniquities committed by the workers in the course of the workers' strike, and in the name of the workers, would have negated the very negations that the novel seeks to highlight and undermine. So Achebe's silence, like Derrida's silence on Marxism, aligns him ever more strongly with the cause of the working class. It is the same reasoning that dictated his silence on the Commonwealth Premiers' Conference on Rhodesia that nearly coincided with the downfall of the republic. Condemning the prime minister for hosting the conference when his own country was on the verge of conflagration would have left Achebe vulnerable to the charges of insensitivity, "imperialism," and apartheid. For who would not have wanted an end to the inhuman political set-up? Yet, the inhumanity that operated locally under *the men of the people* was no less cruel, execrable, and detestable. Again, workers are said to be depicted as steeped in bourgeois filth and corruption, whereas in real life they are innocent, unsullied, almost angelic. If Achebe's realism is to count against him, so be it; but the workers and peasants in "real Nigerian life" lack the innocence that Onoge attributes to them. To start with, corruption is not a uniquely bourgeois failing or monopoly; and one may observe that the salaried cleaner (janitor?) who would not sweep and dust the offices unless he was tipped; the messenger who would "disappear" vital documents and files and miraculously produce them on his palm being greased; the clerk/typist who would sit on urgent letters if the solicitous citizens did not promise him a-plenty; the hospital orderly who would not let a dying patient see a doctor unless he was bribed; the policeman who would turn away from a crime, or prosecute, depending on whether he was appeased or not; the bank teller who would deal sourly with, or short-change his customers because they never "gave" him; the trader who would sell detergent lather for beer; and the night-soil man who would deposit his burden in the neighborhood to cut short his trip to the sewage dump: these are real workers in "real Nigerian life!" Achebe does not deserve Onoge's strictures for not glamorizing the despicable; but he may well have been "guilty" of excess sympathy with the long oppressed.

As for painting the masses as clowns, there is surely something not funny, and definitely clownish, about villagers who would ostracize "Josiah, the abominated trader," for stealing a blind man's stick the one day, and almost apotheosize him the next for having enlisted in Chief Nanga's Vanguard. And it is surely more than ironic that the people would be recruited into the personal army of their *man of the people* whose sole purpose is the liquidation of opposition and the intimidation of the electorate, the people themselves. And if it is true that "only when the *'lower classes' do not want* the old way, and when the *'upper classes' cannot carry on in the old way*—only then can revolution triumph" (Althusser 1977 99, n.19), then, surely, the people, as apathetic and cynical as they had become, were not ready for revolutionary change, and the *coup d'etat* that brings the novel to a classic-realist close, and textualizes the downfall of the First Republic, was not a revolution but a reformation in which the *spoons* merely changed hands, while the *eating* continued. Thus while the production of *A Man of the People* took place within a particular historical conjuncture of over-determined super-structural contradictions—the economic remaining determinant, always, and not merely in the last instance—the prophetic coincidence of "text" and "history" is only an astute and correct reading of the signs of the times by the novelist. The textualized prophecy is consistent with the plot of the novel as a necessary and plausible closure for this over-determined, realist, political *bildungsroman*.

# WORKS CITED

Achebe, Chinua. *A Man of the People*. London: Heinemann, 1966.

––––––. *Morning Yet on Creation Day: Essays*. Garden City, NY: Anchor/Doubleday, 1975.

Ahearn, Edward. *Marx and Modern Fiction*. New Haven: Yale University Press, 1989.

Althusser, Louis. "Contradiction and Overdetermination." *For Marx*. Trans. Ben Brewster. London: New Left Books, 1977.

––––––. *Essays in Self-Criticism*. Trans. Grahamme Lock. London: New Left Books, 1976.

––––––. "Ideology and Ideological State Apparatuses." *Lenin and Philosophy and Other Essays*. Trans. Ben Brewster. London: New Left Books, 1971.

––––––. *Reading Capital*. Trans. Ben Brewster. London: New Left Books, 1979.

––––––. "The Transformation of Philosophy." Trans. Tom Lewis. (n.p.).

Amuta, Chidi. *Towards a Sociology of African Literature*. Oguta: Zim, 1986.

Bishop, Rand. *African Literature, African Critics*. Westport, CT: Greenwood, 1988.

Carroll, David. "Achebe's *A Man of the People*." In *Critical Perspectives on Chinua Achebe*. Washington, DC: Three Continents Press, 1978: 260–278.

Certeau, Michel de. *Heterologies*. Trans. Brian Massumi. Minneapolis: University of Minnesota Press, 1986.

––––––. *The Writing of History*. Trans. Tom Conley. "Translator's Introduction." New York: Columbia University Press, 1988.

Clifford, James, and George Marcus. *Writing Culture: The Poetics and Politics of Ethnography*. Berkeley: University of California Press, 1986.

Craig, David, ed. *Marxists on Literature*. Harmondsworth: Penguin, 1975.

Culler, Jonathan. *On Deconstruction: Theory & Criticism After Structuralism*. Ithaca: Cornell University Press, 1982.

Emenyeonu, Ernest, et al., eds. *Critical Theory & African Literature*. Ibadan: Heinemann, 1987.

Frow, John. *Marxism and Literary History*. Oxford: Blackwell, 1986.

Gakwandi, S.A. *The Novel and Contemporary Experience in Africa*. New York: Africana, 1977.

Gugelberger, George, ed. *Marxism and African Literature*. Trenton, NJ: Africa World Press, 1985.

Innes, C.L. and Bernth Lindfors, eds. *Critical Perspectives on Chinua Achebe*. Washington, DC: Three Continents Press, 1978.

Irele, Abiola. *The African Experience in Literature & Ideology*. London: Heinemann, 1981.

Larson, Charles. *The Emergence of African Fiction*. Bloomington: Indiana University Press, 1972.

Martin, Wallace. *Recent Theories of Narrative*. Ithaca: Cornell University Press, 1986.

Mutiso, G-C. M. *Socio-Political Thought in African Literature*. New York: Barnes & Noble, 1974.

Ngara, Emmanuel. *Art and Ideology in the African Novel*. London: Heinemann, 1985.

Obiechina, E.N. *Culture, Tradition & Society in the West African Novel*. Cambridge: The University Press, 1975.

Palmer, Eustace. *An Introduction to the African Novel*. New York: Africana, 1972.

Roscoe, Adrian. *Mother Is Gold: A Study in West African Literature*. Cambridge: The University Press, 1971.

Tucker, Martin. *Africa in Modern Fiction*. New York: Frederick Ungar, 1967.

Veeser, H. A. ed. *The New Historicism*. London: Routledge, 1989.

White, Hayden. "The Value of Narrativity in the Representation of Reality." In *The Content of the Form: Narrative Discourse and Historical Representation*. Baltimore: Johns Hopkins University Press, 1987: 1–25.

――― . "The Question of Narrative in Contemporary Historical Theory." In *The Content of the Form*: 26–57.

――― . "The Politics of Historical Interpretation: Discipline and De-Sublimation." In *The Content of the Form*: 58–82.

# Chapter Nine

# The True Fantasies of Grace Ogot, Storyteller

*Peter Nazareth*

Grace Ogot is one of the pioneering writers of East Africa. Having published her first story in 1963 in *Black Orpheus*, she has to date published a novel, a novella, three collections of short stories, and a popular Luo myth. Her place in Kenyan and East African literature is assured and acknowledged. "As a writer she will be remembered for her meticulous documentation of Luo customs, legends and history," says Brenda Berrian at the conclusion of her biobibliographical essay (187). But such a summation may only be the result of the fact that there has not been much analysis of Ogot's work as literary art.

The earliest influence on her writing was her grandmother's storytelling, Grace Ogot has said. She loved traditional stories when she was young and began writing some of them down. She showed her stories to the manager of the East African Literature Bureau but he "could not understand how a Christian woman could write such stories, involved with sacrifices, traditional medicines and all, instead of writing about Salvation and Christianity" (qtd. in Lindfors 1980 124). What was damned in colonial times is to be praised now. Gabriel Garcia Marquez has said many times that he writes stories the way his grandmother told them. This does not mean that Garcia Marquez does not shape his art: so we must ask how Ogot shapes the traditional story into literary art.

The very first thing she does is make the myths and legends come alive by providing details from "real life." For example, "The Fisherman" is about Nyamgondho of legend. The story begins, "The sun had emerged from the Odiado Hills, and Nyamgondho thought, 'Today it has risen earlier than usual.' He filled his mouth with water and spat at it" (59). The story is immediately believable because of the description of the landscape and the protagonist's angry toilet. The problem is that Nyamgondho has not been catching any fish:

Not so far away on the sandy beach, a group of fishermen had spread out their catch and were haggling with one another, swapping this for the other. Close to the papyrus, the kingfisher dived into the shallow water and flew off with a catch. It was a real slap in the face to realize that even the birds of the air caught their fill while he Nyamgondho had nothing to show why God had made him a man. The other day when he had made advances to his wife, Achunga had snapped at him, "At night you are all alive, but when daytime comes, you are a weakling who cannot catch a single fish to keep your wife alive." (60–61)

We *see* the scene clearly, something from the daily life of ordinary human beings: the fishermen at work, the bird flying off with a fish. We feel the anguish in Nyamgondho's mind, the attack on his manhood by his wife for his failure.

This day, Nyamgondho catches one fish. "He picked up the live fish, but the little devil wriggled dangerously, pricking his hand in the process. Nyamgondho threw it back in the boat with a thud as the blood trickled from his fingers." He was going to punish the fish for the injury. "At this, the fish tilted its head towards Nyamgondho, its blue eyes rolled round and round and it seemed drops of tears were spilling from them" (62). The eyes and the tears of the fish make the situation concrete, at the same time linking up with the tears on the face of Nyamgondho at the end.

The boat then speaks, telling him where to cast his baskets: throwing the fish back, his third basket catches an old woman, Wagai, who makes him rich with cattle. And Nyamgondho "took kindly to flattery and all forms of praise. He married many young, beautiful wives, brought to him by their fathers in exchange for a fat dowry, and the women bore him many sons and daughters. So it was that wherever he passed, people saluted him and showered him with gifts. And Nyamgondho completely forgot his past" (72). He takes to coming home late after partying, despite the pleading of his wives. "Rich people are hated everywhere, Nyamgondho," Wagai says. But Nyamgondho answers arrogantly, "I am the spring that quenches their thirst and waters their fields" (73).

One night, Nyamgondho comes home so drunk and late that no wife opens the door. He goes to the hut of Wagai and kicks it. She crawls out of her bamboo bed and opens the door. Nyamgondho insults and humiliates her. When she says so, he says she forgets he saved her from crocodiles, and she can quit if she wants to. So Wagai leaves the next morning. The cattle follow her. He chases after them, but "The last tail of Nyamgondho's last cow entered the lake and disappeared" (77). The whole clan returns to the lake shore the following morning to persuade him to come back home and start a new life. They find "His body had turned into a huge statue, his head still resting on his staff, and large blobs of tears stood where they had rolled on his face: And the people shook their heads and sacrificed for the appeasement of their ancestors" (78). The story ends:

The statue of Nyamgondho son of Ombare still stands at the shores of the Great Lake up to this day. At sunset, the chosen few among the fishermen can still hear him calling pleadingly, 'Wagai, Wagai, come back home. You are my beautiful woman." (78)

Bernth Lindfors asked Ogot whether this story was taken directly from an old myth. "I would not say it is a myth because the statue of Nyamgondho can still be seen across the lake," she replied. "We believe that when our great grandfathers lived, Nyamgondho lived with them and fished in the great lake where we are still fishing today. We believe that those events actually did happen. . . . We just say *they are true stories of events* that occurred in other generations in the distant past, at the beginning of our society" (qtd. in Lindfors 1980 126; my emphasis). Ogot misunderstood Lindfors' use of "myth," but her answer is more revealing than if she had understood it. For her, the story was true, and in her retelling, the realistic account makes the story *true*. We note, too, that the story has a lesson, for "moral impact" in literature is very important to her (see Lindfors 1980 130). Nyamgondho loses everything because he forgets his past: where he came from, how much he is indebted for what he is to others.

Another traditional story retold by Ogot is "The Rain Came." It begins:

The chief was still far from the gate when his daughter Oganda saw him. She ran to meet him. Breathlessly she asked her father, "What is the news, great Chief? Everyone in the village is anxiously waiting to hear when it will rain." Labong'o held out his hands for his daughter but he did not say a word. Puzzled by her father's cold attitude, Oganda ran back to the village to warn the others that the chief was back. The ancestors had decreed that a sacrifice of Oganda must be offered to make rains. "Labong'o burst into tears before finishing the sentence. The chief must not weep. Society had declared him the bravest of men. But Labong'o did not care any more. He assumed the position of a simple father and wept bitterly. He loved his people, the Luo, but what were the Luo for him without Oganda? (160)

We see the scene through the human touches: "breathlessly," "cold attitude," "a simple father,"and "wept bitterly." Even near the end, as Oganda is walking toward the lake to meet her fate, there is a realistic detail. "As Oganda opened the gate, a child, a young child, broke loose from the crowd, and ran towards her. The child took a small earring from her sweaty hands and gave it to Oganda, saying, 'When you reach the world of the dead, give this earring to my sister. She died last week. She forgot this ring' " (168). Henry Kimbugwe says that such small sentences "strike a sharp chord in an African mind" (23).

The story ends with rains. "There was a bright lightning. They looked up frightened. Above them black furious clouds started to gather. They began to run. Then the thunder roared, and the rain came down in torrents" (171). But the girl is not finally sacrificed, though the community believes so. Before the end, she is saved by one she loves, Osinda, who forces her to escape with him.

It is fruitful to compare this story with a previous version, the first story Ogot published, under the title "The Year of Sacrifice." The beginning and the end of the two versions are completely different. In the second version, three-and a-half pages from the beginning of the first version are deleted; the paragraph opening the newer version is actually paragraph thirty-one in the original. What is deleted is a long description of the way the people lived and the problems they faced, the last of which is the drought. The pages are very explanatory, beginning with the first paragraph: "It was a bad year for the people living around *Nan Lolwe* (the Lake of sleeping sickness, now known as Lake Victoria). It was a year full of calamities and famine brought about by a long drought" (41). By the time we get to the chief, he is only an element in solving the problem, and this applies even more to his daughter. In the new version, the focus is on the human individuals within the context of the needs of the tribes. The consultation with Ndithi, the medicine man who tells the chief that Oganda must be sacrificed, is now placed as a flashback, or, more accurately, a thorn in Labong'o's heart, so that we have been wondering for a while with Oganda why he is so upset; dramatic tension is thus increased.

There are some minor changes in the story, but the biggest one is at the end. In the original, Oganda actually sees the monster that is supposed to devour her:

The winding road ended at the lake shore so abruptly that Oganda screamed with horror as she came face to face with an enormous monster lying on a large rock waiting for its victim. It had a large body and a long tail that was lazily waggling in water. Its mouth was very wide, that [sic] it could easily swallow two people at a go. It had numerous teeth resembling those of a crocodile, with enormous eyes situated above the upper mandible. It was a frightening spectacle. (49)

The last line makes us aware of the storyteller, thus taking away some of our fear. In the newer version, the monster is not described and is more terrible because it is in the imagination. Furthermore, since we do not know whether the monster exists, the story is also more naturalistic. In the original, Osinda comes to Oganda after killing the monster and the story ends, "Unable to speak, but consumed by a man's tender love, Oganda rose to her feet. They hurried away from the sacred land, leaving the immense body of the dead monster floating at the lake shore" (50). This reads like one of the tales of King Arthur and the Knights of the Round Table; no wonder the editors of *Black Orpheus* called the story "An East African Fairy Tale." The newer ending has two differences. The first is that it rains: thus the new title. The second is that the sacrifice is not necessary, as long as the will to make it was there; neither is it necessary for the lover, Osinda, to kill a physical monster. Humanity wins out. There is the possibility of individual choice, there is no inevitability about humanity being dwarfed by events or enslaved by traditions. In terms of the use of language, many details are deleted, leaving only significant details that make the story more dramatic as well as changing the focus to individual human beings.

We now turn to a story Grace Ogot calls "a true fantasy," *The Promised Land*. "The hero Ochola and his family are people living in our generation," she told Lindfors. "Ochola's home is in Seme in Maseno Divisions. It is a family that still lives, a family that we know. They migrated in this century to Tanzania and they came back. They are people we can see and talk to. That's why we say it is a true fantasy" (qtd. in Lindfors 1980 126).

*The Promised Land* is a novel about "internal" migration, that is, migration within Africa. After his marriage, Ochola, restless, troubled by the exhausted land, decides to make his fortune across the lake like some other Luo people. He persuades his wife, much against her will, to cross the lake, settling down in Tanganyika with the help of the Luo community and becoming rich. However, he inadvertently angers a local medicine man, who puts a hex on him, so that "His body did not seem like his own and his hair had changed into long white thorns, which made him look like a porcupine!" (128). Ogot says that when she was a nurse, although she did not see Ochola's specific ailment, "there have been some other very curious illnesses and diseases of the skin answering to the description of Ochola's warts which are not mentally induced and which scientific treatment cannot cure" (qtd. in Lindfors 1980 126). The only cure comes at the end: Magungu, a Luo medicine man, removes the warts but makes Ochola and his family leave immediately, before sunset, without taking more than they can carry. So Ochola must return home almost empty handed, after tasting fabulous wealth. This is the second nightmare of immigrants, the first being the fear of getting lost far from home. Discussing his plans to leave, his family says, "You know the fate of strangers who live amongst us here? They have no voice in the running of our land. They're lonely because they're not accepted by our people. Is this what you want? . . . Why go away and be destitute, leaving your inheritance here?" (31).

And so there is a tragic sense of loss running through the novel. A harpist sings on the ship of those who left for the World War II and "remained in the land where there was no sunshine nor the warmth of a woman nor the cry of a child" (60). And in Tanganyika:

When everything had been cleared away and the tables rearranged, the traditional harpist and his followers came into the shelter. They were going to sing and entertain the visitors for the rest of the evening. The harpist was well known and had won the hearts of his people by singing famous songs, relating to the deaths of important men and women in their society. He sang of Dulo Omolo, the son of Owiti, who had died on his wedding night, leaving his bride alone in her hut. The women cried and the men bowed their heads in memory of the man whose name they knew so well. He sang of the marriage of Semo, the daughter of Okelo. When he spoke of Semo's beauty and the wealth of her people, the women stared at him with glittering eyes. His voice reminded them of their own young days when they were brides, listening to the praises showered on them by their in laws. (105–106)

We see here the sadness of a community remembering its forlorn pasts; we also understand how a community far from home remains connected. And the tone of sadness is offset the next moment by the present, showing us the Luo concept of beauty and its effect on the men and women:

As soon as these two songs were finished, a very beautiful slender woman got up. The women looked at her with some degree of jealousy, while the men beamed with happiness as if her standing before them had disturbed some hidden emotions. She could not have been more than eighteen years old. Her skin was the colour of coffee beans and her curly hair was tied with a silk headcloth, leaving some parts showing near her ears. Her cotton dress fitted into perfection and reached only to the top of her knees. Her legs and arms were well formed but dainty. Her teeth were even. The neat small traditional partition in the upper teeth completed her beauty. Her smile was bewitching and when she opened her mouth to speak, the audience held its breath. (109)

As the chief characters are people of the lake, so are the metaphors: "Ochola's compound resumed the quietness of the months before Magungu came into their lives. Not a peaceful quietness, a kind of terror: a panic that grips a drowning man whose salvation is snatched away by a powerful wave" (163). But although Ogot's primary characters are her people, the Luo, she has objectivity, a sense of cultural relativeness. This is what the unfriendly Tanganyikan medicine man thinks:

Luo people were no friends to nurse at one's doorstep. They seemed all right outwardly, yet they were so uncompromising and stubborn in their behaviour. You are a friend to a Luo so long as you accept his ideas, but the minute you want to think independently there the friendship ends. The people had given in to them long enough, and he, an old man, would not budge an inch, not like the Zangazi tribesmen who had been almost absorbed by the Luo. (95)

Our sympathies are swayed toward this outwardly strange old man for he looks on the immigration of the Luo as colonialism. "But who put it into your head that this is no man's land, for all Luo people to come and settle as they please," he says to Ochola. "You come like masters to rob us of our land. You want us to work for you, but you don't want your children to work for us. You appoint yourselves chiefs and oppress those who have no quarrel with you" (93). This is the reverse side of tribal continuity, the inability to understand the perspectives of other tribes, says the novelist. And so one of the very important functions of the storyteller is, in the words of Ogot, "If a story emerges from, say, Kikuyuland or Luoland or Kambaland, people want to read it because it helps us to learn about one another" (qtd. in Lindfors 1980 129).

Grace Ogot's strengths, then, are more than just those of retelling traditional stories. Like Ngugi wa Thiong'o, she uses her people as a base for dealing with the world. In breadth and technique, she can compete with sophisticated moderns. This is best seen in her "I" stories.

In "The Honourable Minister," the "I" is a woman from Kisumu who has moved to Nairobi with her husband on transfer. She hankers for the good life, that is, a great house and material things, but cannot get them because her husband is content being a conscientious teacher. She is desperate enough to prostitute herself and joins a "Coffee Club" advertised in the newspaper:

"It must be pretty difficult to arrange loans in Nairobi," I said, "particularly when one is new in the city. In Kisumu it would be so easy because one knew the Managers." My body felt quite warm from the long, well-prepared speech.

"It makes no difference," Mrs. Waswa told me. "You only need good contacts, that's all.

And if you or your husband know any of the Ministers, well they can fix it in no time. Ministers are very influential with the Bank Managers, and their word is as good as a guarantee."

I was dazed. It could not be as easy as that surely. Alice and her husband must have known many Ministers, and the Bank Managers.

"Do you know any Ministers well?" Her voice woke me.

I hesitated and then added shyly, "Not really, except for the Assistant Minister of Commerce and Industry, who was a classmate of my husband."

At this Mrs. Waswa pressed my hands. "No June, such matters need a full Minister. They are the only people who can help you get money over the telephone just like that. Nothing is out of the reach of a full Minister."

I looked at Mrs. Waswa wide eyed. We both giggled to hide our embarrassment. It was a look of knowing the price which one would have to pay before one could win a Minister's confidence.

Some unknown forces had drawn us quite close within a very short time of meeting. Mrs. Waswa whispered again. "You have good looks which could do with cultivation," and her smile warmed my heart. "Well, child, you have to be a little smarter than this in Nairobi." She squeezed my hand. In my normal mood I would have felt quite hurt but then learning was a painful process with many bitter tears. And if a full Minister is the only person who could secure me money from a Bank Manager without any additional guarantee, then I had to learn to be thick-skinned and daring enough to hook one. I would have to be tough and dispense with tears. (92–94)

We see in a few lines the corruption of the new society, through the experience and consciousness of a woman from the country with a conscience but too weak to resist the lure of materialism held out by the new society of the international city. She takes us through the pains and agonies of selling one's body and soul. But there is an outside world looking on and judging. When she flees the hotel where she has been with the Minister, just escaping being hacked to death by the Minister's irate wife, "The watchman who had followed me inside recognized me. He spat at me as he held the door open with his stick to avoid his hands being contaminated" (118).

The "I" in "The Middle Door" seems to be the author herself, a famous writer traveling by train to Kisumu. It is only later that we know she is Mrs. Muga. Through this deliberate "misunderstanding," Ogot implies that nobody of the aspiring new class is innocent, including the reader. She wants to be left alone in the first class compartment and cannot stand it when a woman of the people enters with a cock, a *kikapu*, and a bunch of bananas. Going to the restaurant car, she complains to the ticket examiner, who says, "In any country there are small people, middle people and big people" (26). The woman is removed, leaving the narrator free to be attacked at night by two policemen who believe she is a prostitute. She protects herself from rape by pulling out a gun. When she arrives, she is arrested for unauthorized possession of a gun; it is revealed at the police station as a toy gun she bought for her nephew. The story shows Mrs. Muga bringing near disaster on herself by distancing herself from the common people, who have paid the real price to achieve independence. In fact, she is what the policemen thought: a prostitute, though not in the usual way. She represents her class, the rising new elite willing to sell out, to distance itself from the masses. As in the previous story, the attitude of the common people is expressed by spitting in disgust: an action that becomes the climactic act of penitence in Sembene Ousmane's novel and film, *Xala* (1975).

The story could have been symbolic if Ogot had emphasized a potential symbol, the train as class system. She could have done so by cutting down the realistic details and trying to get at the reality under the surface of life by stressing the symbolism. Compare her refusal to do this here with her attempt in the earliest of her published "I" stories, "Ward Nine," which appeared in *Transition* in 1964. It begins as follows:

It was about midnight when my eyes opened. The light was so dim that the whole place was almost dark. What had Mary done to the lights? Our bedroom lights were very bright because I always worked late at night. Something must be wrong with my eyes! I opened them slowly and blinked—still there was no pain. But what I now saw frightened me. There were many beds around me; and on each bed lay a body covered up with a black Nakuru blanket. A paralyzing chill went right through me, and I cried out. It was like lying among the corpses on a battlefield. I heard footsteps, and as I turned around to look my eyes rested on a large green door. And on the door, clearly written in white block letters, were the words, "WARD NINE." (41)

The protagonist here feels an alienness in his surroundings, almost the feeling of vertigo. The details do not tie the situation down to an identifiable, familiar room: quite the contrary. The "I" does not know where he is: He could be in detention (the bright lights), he could be surrounded by death (a black blanket, corpses). What would normally be reassuring human touches become more disjointed and frightening: footsteps without people. Looking for the familiar, he finds a sinister green door and an indication that he is nearly a cipher: is he "Ward Nine"? The hospital is a metaphor; the disease is nameless. The doctors, we discover, do not believe the man is sick; the nurses are indifferent. The story was probably based on the strike by nurses at the gigantic new Mulago Hospital the year before, just after independence, as was my radio-play, "The Hospital." One may note here, in parenthesis, that many elements and even lines in "The Hospital" and "Ward Nine" are similar: the illness nobody will believe, which is really the illness of society; the callous nurses waiting to hook a rich man; the doctor who thinks only of how much money the patient is costing the system; the people who think authorities are right; the dislocation expressed by footsteps; and the reduction of people to numbers, "Nine" in Ogot's story and "Five-five-five" in my play. Ngugi told me when I played the BBC recording of the radio play to him that it was much more powerful than Ogot's story. My radio play is entirely metaphoric, nightmarish. Ogot's story begins with nightmare—consider the effect of that first paragraph read on radio. But she destroys this effect by providing naturalistic details:

At 10.30 a.m. that morning, Doctor Fish Bone arrived. He was a tall, Irish man [*sic*] with thick black hair. The thick fat hanging around his belly revealed that he liked his bottle. His scrubby moustache made him look like a First World War Sergeant Major whose photograph

I had seen at school. He wore thick rimless glasses that gave him a learned look which he did not deserve. Doctor Fish Bone lacked the gentle face of a doctor. (43)

The story ends with the patient leaving the hospital, whereas "The Hospital" is relentless: the patient dies during the nightmare operation, the suggestion being that he will be replaced by the next patient. The *effectiveness* of Ogot's story is lost because it does not remain at a consistently symbolic level, that is, the nightmare under, but created by, surface reality. Ogot's interest, and strength, is naturalism, getting at reality by selected details from externally observed life. Nightmare as reality is not her *forte* or her interest. On the contrary, she makes dreams real. It is no surprise that she has not included "Ward Nine" in any of her collections.

This is not to say that all the movement in Ogot's stories is external. Her most recent "I" story is "Love Immortalised." The narrator is herself, Grace Ogot, visiting the Taj Mahal:

Again, my eyes rested on the gigantic creation before me, its magnificent, artificial lake reflecting its size and beauty. I thought as I had done on many occasions that there was nothing material on this earth that money and power could not buy. And the part of me that always championed the cause of the masses began to get restless. I could see in my mind's eye the faces of artisans under this oppressive heat, their sweat rolling down, falling like rain drops upon the earth, the slim hungry stomachs rumbling with the smell from the rich man's kitchen, while the thin lips hunger for mouthfuls of rice that might never be got. Besides hunger, there must have been bad days when the blood streaked from the raw wounds, when the weak and the rebellious had been flogged, when the sick fainted and died and were cremated along the Holy Ganges. These things and many unnamed cruelties were done to honour the memory of lovers long dead. Could I not see that the Taj Mahal was created out of the exploitation of the masses? Their sweat, their taxes, their souls? Couldn't I see the human sacrifices that went into placating the spirit of one woman? Why couldn't I stick by my principles and denounce this as I had denounced glories and wealth conceived out of the masses' suffering? (74–75)

There is powerful description of the suffering of the masses, entirely out of the imagination of the author. It is a prose poem to all the unnamed working people who built the monuments of the world. But Ogot cannot remain at this level, for the woman within her, she says, deserted her principles. "The part of me that always hungered for affectionate love, prevailed over the plight of the masses. I was convinced that when it comes to love, there was no barrier stopping the poor from ascending the realms that flows around us free for the thinking." And so, sparked off by the love turned into "the tangible form of the fantastic Taj Mahal":

My hands resting accidentally on his broad shoulders sent emotional shivers through me, for Raj was indeed a handsome guide, polished in manners, and very well groomed. This was no place to come alone, I thought, and the face of my husband who had fallen ill on our arrival at the City of Agra the evening before, and whom I had left in the hotel prostrate with fever, flushed in my mind. I had come all this way to renew my love for him, for it was whispered that even men and women who had lived together in marriage for a life time, fell in love again head over heels, when bathed in the beauty of the Taj Mahal. (68)

A true confession? This is irrelevant. Ogot has created an "I" named "Grace Ogot" who tells her story convincingly, with an eye for external and internal beauty, aware of her own impulses and contradictions, one who moves away from the masses, while paying them full imaginative tribute. The story shows not only Ogot's ability to perceive stories in real life but also her refusal to have an ideological approach. By this term, I mean that Ogot does not approach her subject from a predetermined abstract pattern of ideas except in one story. This is *The Graduate*, a novella.

The thesis of *The Graduate* is that the white colonials who controlled Kenya are still doing so, to the detriment of the nationals. Juanina Karungaru has been made a minister, that of Public Affairs, a belated recognition of the work women have done for the independence of the country. She is determined to Kenyanize, and makes a trip to New York to convince Kenyan students to return home. Two Kenyan graduate students give up their scholarships and guaranteed jobs with American corporations. One, Ngure, married to an American girl, decides to be cautious. The other, Jakoyo Seda, quits America immediately and returns home with the promise that he can see the Hon. Karungaru as soon as he gets there. But in Kenya, it is almost impossible to see her, thanks to the bureaucratic system and the maneuverings of her English secretary. An African secretary, spotting the machinations of the white woman, talks to Mrs. Karungaru, and Jakoyo gets the job. The novel ends: "Three days later, Jakoyo Seda sat sipping a hot cup of coffee, and chatting to the Hon. Juanina Karungaru, M.P., Minister for Public Affairs, who had just handed him his letter of appointment, as Chief Engineer and City Planner designate. This was the job he would have missed if it were not for the sharp eye of Anabell Chepkwony!"

Separate sections of the novel read very well. For example, the nightmarish presentation of the blocked doors and failed hopes of upliftment:

Jakoyo's shame turned into an illness that hit his heart with a chill. The chill spread to his bones and his teeth shuddered because fever was sitting on him. He was a sick man. In his sick state of mind he saw his wife trekking from the river with a debe of water on her head, and the children sitting around the dining room table, picking at their food, thinking, hoping, longing only for when he would keep his promise and go back to collect them after signing up a new contract. He had promised them good food, good clothing, a good life, and a good education in the city. That and all his aspirations seemed to be melting out of his hands. (55)

But structurally, too many things are left hanging in the air. Having started with details of Mrs. Karungaru's life, the novella does not focus on her at the end: It is Jakoyo who seems to be the protagonist. The novella introduces Ngure in America but forgets about him. And the conclusion would let us believe that the detective work and courage of Anabell Chepkwony solve all the problems whereas the

Kafkaesque adventures of Jakoyo convince the reader that something is fundamentally alienated in Kenya, needing more than band-aid solutions. So the one time Ogot begins with a structure of ideas, she does not see the problem through, as Ngugi would have done.

Grace Ogot's most brilliant achievement is a story that in length (fifty-nine pages) and structure (four sections) is really a novella. "The Professor" touches all Ogot's bases and more. Professor Miyare returns home to Africa after qualifying. At the airport, "Miyare wanted to run, to prove to himself and to those at the waving base that he was now a free man, and that he was shedding off years of discrimination and humiliation suffered in the land of the whiteman. It requires much courage from a white professor to admit that an African student is brilliant" (192–193).

But Miyare is alienated, as seen through the eyes of the customs officer: "He had seen quite a number of these odd creatures called professors. Always absent

minded, distant and perpetually chasing their scattered thoughts" (194). Miyare feels more of a kinship with the white professors because they "had taken the same vows—a kind of academic circumcision ceremony"—than with the people of his tribe: "It was obvious that the Kolanya people were very happy to see their son back. They put much faith in education and respected a person with a string of degrees after his name" (194–195).

The story turns our feelings away from Miyare, who seems to be myopically concerned only with research and lab work to the neglect of his wife, his brother, his father and his tribe. His brother loses the election to a primary schoolteacher and falls ill; his wife is bitter because he will not visit home and because he does not care to make money, unlike his colleagues. It is in the casual details that we see the corruption of those who ought to be pursuing truth:

"The Vice Chancellor's special boy has closed up part of his house. He only uses the kitchen, study and the bedroom," reported Professor Okidi, Head of the Chemistry Department, to his colleagues in the Senior Common Room.

"What a waste!"

"Yes, the fellow is masquerading as a genius," said Professor Maru, Dean of the Faculty of Law, *and the proprietor of Uhuru Wines and Spirits Agencies.*

*"How many of us do research, write and still have time to make money?" The group which had swollen to ten laughed boisterously.*

"The Vice Chancellor should reallocate this house to somebody else with a sense of beauty," reported Doctor Kulia, Head of the Civil Engineering Department, *and a consultant to BILCO, a local engineering firm specialising on sewerage works.* (212; my emphasis)

Rosemary's friend Janet has a new list of Businesses on Quit Notice (a list of businesses taken away from noncitizens). "Money, or what we call Bank Power, is a major factor in our country today," says Janet (222). The Bata Shop in Uhuru Street, she says, nets about 400,000 Kenya shillings a month, and the commission is 30per cent. But when Rosemary talks to her husband, his eyes narrow with anger. "You nearly wrecked my work with Mwoso's politics, Rosemary," he says, "and now you want me to drop my important heart transplant project to go and run a Bata shoe shop" (223).

The absurdity makes us sympathetic to Miyare. He finally achieves what he has been striving for: he carries out the first Kenyan heart transplant operation. He now becomes a hero. When honored as Elder of the Burning Spear, first class, he is asked by the president what he wants. He asks for a smaller house, to everyone's amusement. His dedication, his refusal to be parasitic, is now seen in a different light:

That month, many academic members of staff quietly returned to their research projects which had been abandoned and locked up for months when the Odhiambo Report came out authorising all academic staff, like civil servants, to take any outside work including running businesses and large scale farming. Had the Ministry of Commerce and Internal Trade kept the statistics at their finger tips, they should have noticed that many academics from the National University did not renew their annual trading licenses. They sold out. A new awareness and re-examination of what a university stands for in the eyes of the public, generated a strong and bright light which sent bogus academics tumbling out of the University, leaving only those worthy of the honours that it bestowed on men and women dedicated in seeking the truth. (235)

Of course, things cannot end so simply. Miyare has gone against tradition in too many ways. He has caused problems by taking out a heart from one body and transferring it to a living person for, Rosemary thinks, "according to her people's religion, soul and heart were synonymous." So, she wonders, "Would the professor's father consult a medicine man to cleanse his son from such an unheard-of act that bordered on witchcraft?" (240). Much as he would like to, Miyare cannot escape the ties of family and tribe. The very tribe that places value on a string of degrees does not understand what acquiring the degrees means. His father comes to him, saying, "Education has brought luxury to every home, and filled empty bellies with food. But what about me? What has your education earned me except laughter and scorn—even from nonentities who, without their educated sons, would still be dressed in skins. . . . What kind of wisdom is this without a big car? Where is his wealth? Professorship cannot be wealth" (242). The materialist thrust from an earlier time we found in *The Promised Land* now pushes modern society into corruption. Miyare cannot resist his father's pleas, and so decides against his will that he will build a house, whereupon:

Rosemary, who had all this time pretended to be interested in a house at home, suddenly became almost violent. She sat up in bed, grabbed Miyare's hands roughly and pressed them hard on her chest. . . . Rosemary could not remember a more beautiful and wonderful night than this one, when for once the Professor was a man. (244)

We can compare Rosemary's attitude to her husband with that of Achunga in "The Fisherman." In both cases, the women link up the manhood of their husbands with their ability to bring home the bacon, or more appropriately, the fish. But here, the tone of the work is satirical compared with neutral in "The Fisherman." Miyare's downward spiral is continued by the fears of the elected member of parliament from his area who, fearing he will lose his seat to the professor, arranges for him to be promoted to dean. The vice chancellor cannot refuse the all-powerful politicians and so Miyare becomes a dean. The story ends cynically: "The clock in the Great Court gonged 2:00 P.M. Professor Miyare, E.B. and Dean of the Faculty of Medicine, dragged his weary body back to his haunted laboratory. He put his hand in the pocket and pulled out the pad on which he had boldly written 'AFRICA IS DEAD' " (249–250).

Ogot says that the story was based on her observation of the academic communities with which she and her husband have been associated since 1959. "I think that's how I got the idea for the story "The Professor"; it was through experience and contact with our friends, some of whom are devoted scientists, devoted doctors, but whom our society won't leave alone to do their work." She says. "There are often a lot of social demands made on them, and some of these men may wonder whether you can combine being a scientist and being an African, particularly if you want to be a good African" (qtd. in Lindfors 1980 127–128). True, she has observed, but she has used skill and imagination to write such a pointed story, with sharp details and frequent changes of tone and emotional point of view. The transplant operation at the heart of the story raises an important symbolic problem. Is Professor Miyare heartless to ignore the demands of his brother, who wants to win the elections so that he can get rich? Is he heartless to refuse to make money for his wife? Is he heartless to resist the demands of his father and society? Or is it the society that is heartless? What does the society profess?

"The Professor" is more ambitious than *The Graduate* and achieves more because it is better structured, because it works with Ogot's strengths as a writer, creatively combining the traditional and the modern, because it explores all the questions it raises, and because it has a central metaphor holding everything together. As Henry Kimbugwe says, Ogot "is a schooled, sophisticated intellectual, well aware of the changes taking place around her yet retaining a deep and close understanding of the traditional ways of thought and living of her people" (Kimbugwe 1969 23). This understanding cuts in different directions, undermining stereotyped and cliched responses to people and situations.

"We're all Christians, Dr. Thomson," Nurse Elizabeth says in *The Promised Land*. "But as Africans we know that there are bad spirits that cause disease, or a bad eye that causes death. European medicine has no power over these bad spirits. . . . African medicine cures them" (180). The behavior and thought processes of Ogot's characters are affected by tradition and the group, even if they live in the modern world, for if they live in the city, they retain a rural home. Whereas Gabriel Garcia Marquez makes the real world magical, Ogot makes the magical real. The village, as with Ngugi, is the geographical and psychic hinterland. But the traditional can hurt as well as help. The village girl who becomes a secretary can be exploited by the boss. A strong medicine man can bewitch a successful person. Traditional society demands materialist success, which pushes toward corruption in modern times. And not all traditional stories are reassuring about the past: violent things also happened, as in "Tekayo," who killed his grandchildren to eat their livers (47–61).

In "New York," the Kenyan Ambassador, directed to the subway by a black American, thinks, "Black people will be kind to one another whenever they meet. The Africanness within these people will never die though hundreds of years have turned them into Americans" (22). But he is followed by the black American, robbed at knifepoint and nearly killed. After drawing the worst conclusions about black Americans, he is then visited by the boy's parents who, not knowing what their son has really done, say friendly things about the ambassador; and their son ends up taking a post in Africa. So, Ogot has a complex sensibility. She combines traditional knowledge, an experience of the wide world, a feminist consciousness, and the experience of nursing. She knows how women suffer in modern society. "Elizabeth" is a girl thrown to the wolves: As a secretary, she tries to resist the advances of her boss, but he is too powerful and succeeds. When she gets pregnant, only she is blamed. Her resolution is to sneak into his home and hang herself (204). There are several stories in which Ogot creates dramatic tension out of the symptoms of illness, usually showing the anguish of the women characters. In the first story in *Land without Thunder*, Nurse Monica Adhiambo leads a strike against Matron Jack, whom she calls "the old white witch," a prejudiced white woman who refuses to understand and respect African traditions. Yet at the end, when Nurse Adhiambo is dying from advanced amebic dysentery, "showing no signs of response to the salty saline that had been put to drip through her veins to replace the water which she had lost through diarrhea" (24), it is Matron Jack who lovingly nurses her. Nurse Adhiambo was not herself free from prejudice.

Since Grace Ogot's writing is based on a selection of details from real life, climaxes are missed, and the stories weakened when she loses interest in providing details appropriately, when she changes the scene too quickly or mentions things too late. For example, look at the following paragraph from "The Empty Basket," after the terrible snake has been killed:

But Ojwang was not listening. He looked past his wife to the crowd that had gathered. Then his eyes rested on the dead serpent. The bad dream that had tormented him throughout the night started to reveal itself. He had dreamt that he attended two funerals in one day. He woke up unusually early, and when he had done the morning duties, he had asked permission to come home. (109)

To be effective dramatically, to move the story forward, the dream should have come first. Instead, it is just thrown in almost as an afterthought. Tension is lost, as in "The White Veil," when Owila is talking with John about Achola, his girlfriend:

They discussed some business for a while, and John left for safari. The examination started punctually at 9 o'clock. Achola could not eat any breakfast so she went to Standard Five and wrote all the questions on the blackboard long before the children came. (119)

The shift of scenes is too sudden, leaving the discussion undeveloped and not preparing us for change. Another example is from "Karatina": "Her heart was thudding aloud. But the take off was smooth, and she soon fell asleep—not stirring until several hours later when the air hostess was announcing that they were about to land at Cairo airport" (64). Nothing is made here of the protagonist's fears, which would have exaggerated the perils of take off. Instead, the storyteller mentions the flight as casually as a bus ride, while in *The Promised Land*, the voyage by lake steamer is presented as frightening, marvelous and exploitative of workers and peasants.

These lapses are caused by carelessness, a loss of creative energy, or a carry over of the need in reciting oral stories to give the audience an emotional break. Elsewhere, dreams do play an important part structurally, as in "The Hero"; "The Green Leaves"; " The Ivory Trinket"; and particularly *The Promised Land*, where Ochola dreams he is bewitched and wakes up to find it has really happened. And by the time of the later stories, the details are more exhaustive, that is, more relevant details are provided about particular situations than before, such that even the paragraph structure is longer and fuller. For example, in the title story of *The Island of Tears*, about the funeral of Tom Mboya, this is what the people standing close to Mboya's body see:

That day was long and awesome, and as the sun was descending to its home, its golden rays fell upon the sad island and revealed a young woman sitting with her head bowed down beside a husband who was no more. It was not a face to look at twice, for it had lost its beauty and lustre. She sat mute like a carving made out of the sad tree called *bondo* whose leaves, it is said, turned into armlike branches as a result of experiencing years of sorrow caused by the constant deaths of fishermen who drowned in the lake. She stared at the body before her without blinking. She found it painful to breathe, for she fought hard to inhale as little air as possible; thinking, why should she provide for herself generously, when the same air was denied to the father of her children? No, she needed only a little to keep her going, for what did she have to live for? (58)

The tone of loss is achieved by the maximization of relevant details about the wife, the body, the place, the people, and the relationships. The images come from the world inhabited by the people, that is, the external world as well as the recurrent pattern of their life. Once again, a son who left home is gone. There is no gap between life and fictional creation.

Does Grace Ogot, then, merely record what she sees and experiences? Unlike her fellow writer Ngugi, she does not have *a total vision* of society, that is, total in time and space into which all the details fit. To put it another way, she does not have an ideology (a set of ideas fitting into an abstract framework) of the movement of society; and therefore she is not, in this sense, an ideological writer. This explains why she cannot see *The Graduate* through to an artistically satisfying conclusion. She adopts an ideology for the purpose of this novella which is inadequate. Unlike Ngugi, although she sees corruption and the alienation brought about by Western education, she does not see the connection between the corrupt comprador bourgeoisie and the external bourgeoisie. The absence of an ideological vision as reflected in her other works explains the paucity, even lack, of criticism of her work. Critics generally find it easier to analyze works which have a clear ideology because they can then easily identify and trace patterns, growth and development.

Grace Ogot's lack of *a total vision* is actually one of her strengths. It permits her to travel around and find different aspects of, and angles to, the truth. It may sound paradoxical to say of an African writer rooted in tradition that she has an old immigrant consciousness, that is, the sensibility of a people who have long been on the move. This is only an apparent paradox. In her fiction, people move to alien places, haunted by the fear that their fate is to lose native sons. Those who do not move have the same fear for they are lake people, living by fishing. At the same time, Ogot claims the strength of the immigrant consciousness: the ability to understand different cultures, to recognize the subjectivity of different world views, to feel at home in strange lands. In this, she is very different from Ngugi, whose writing base remains the Gikuyu village; he has never published fiction set completely outside Kenya.

From the cumulative effect of her stories, we see that Grace Ogot does have a vision of society, after all, one that emerges from the work. Modern society in Kenya she sees as sick, a world in which people chase after false, materialist values instead of pursuing the truth. Not that the truth need reject materialism totally. But the admiration for materialist achievement in the past was for hard work, the pursuit of success in relation to social obligations. It did not come out of prostitution of body and soul, using one's position for undeserved material gain, consciously exploiting others. And in the past, people of the community were there to judge one's wrongdoing, as opposed to the present, where the people push one into doing wrong. But strong individuals can have an effect on society, as in "The Professor." Through such stories, Ogot is speaking for a society in which all people are respected and understood, in which people are creative and not parasitic, in which people are not prejudged by their ethnicity, and in which there is a creative dialogue with the traditions. People in the past were not unchanging, unmoving. The myths also record movements and migrations, knowledge of which reinforced Ochola's decision to leave for Tanganyika. It is a society in which women will not be exploited, at the same time having to take care of their men's natural needs. Though in many of the stories men exploit the women, in the title story of *The Other Woman*, it is the fault of Jedidah, pursuing her own career, that her husband turns for sexual gratification to the servant women.

Every good author has a special sensibility, a particular writing ability, just as the fisherman's success in catching fish depends not only on his luck but also on his skill, a knowledge of where to cast his net, and on the kind of net he has. As a writer, Grace Ogot's achievement is to write naturalistically, whether dealing with traditional life, occurrences from real life, or imagining what could happen on the basis of what is happening. Naturalism, not symbolism. She has sometimes caught the wrong fish, but has recognized this quickly and thrown it back. What Grace

Ogot is ultimately working against in all her stories can be found in three lines in the ironically titled "The Honourable Minister":

Perhaps I did not really want to change and to look like these hollow women with no souls or names. They had long ago lost their identity. Now they were merely rootless city people.

## WORKS CITED

Berrian, Brenda. "Twentieth-Century Caribbean and Black African Writers." *Dictionary of Literary Biography*. 2nd Ser. Eds. Bernth Lindfors and Rinehard Sander. Vol. 125. Detroit: Gale Research, 1992: 184–187.

Kimbugwe, Henry. "Grace Ogot: The African Lady." *East African Journal* VI.4 (April 1969): 23.

Lindfors, Bernth, ed. *Interviews with East African Writers, Publishers, Editors, and Scholars*. Athens, OH: Center for International Studies, African Program, 1980: 123–133.

Nazareth, Peter. "The Hospital." In *Two Radio Plays*. Nairobi, Kampala, Dar es Salaam: East African Literature Bureau, 1976.

——— . "The Marvelous Latin American Reality of Gabriel Garcia Marquez." In *The Third World Writer*. Nairobi: Kenya Literature Bureau, 1978.

Ogot, Grace. *The Graduate*. Nairobi: Uzima Press, 1980.

——— . *Miaha*. Nairobi: Heinemann, 1983. Translated as The Strange Bride. Nairobi: Heinemann Kenya, 1989.

——— . *The Other Woman*. Nairobi: Transafrica Publishers, 1976.

——— . *The Promised Land*. Nairobi: East African Publishing House, 1966 1974.

——— . "Ward Nine." *Transitions* III.13 (March/April 1964): 41.

——— . "The Year of Sacrafice." *Black Orpheus* XI (1963): 41–50.

Ousmane, Sembene. *Xala*. London: Heinemann, 1975.

Chapter Ten

# The Anglo-African, "the Woman Question," and Imperial Discourse

## Michael J.C. Echeruo

The instincts of women, as far as I have observed, seem to be in favour of oppressed races. Is it because they are themselves an oppressed race?
—Blyden (1971 78)

The *Anglo-African,* the first indigenous English-language newspaper in Nigeria, was established in 1863, two years after Captain Beddingfield, commanding the British Frigate, *Prometheus,* entered the Lagos Lagoon and forced the King of Lagos to subscribe to the Treaty of Cession, thereby formally making Lagos a British "colony." In fact, in the very year of its founding, the *Anglo-African* reported on an averted insurrection, following a declaration by the King of Lagos that he had not been a willing signatory to the treaty. The *Anglo-African* took a particularly ambiguous position in the case, arguing, in an editorial, that it was "too late [for the King] to complain: whether voluntarily or otherwise, he [the king of Lagos] did affix the seal used instead of signature to the articles of cession" (qtd. in Echeruo 1977 18).

The *Anglo-African* had a very short run of three years, from 1863 to 1865. In its pages during those years, we see the cross-currents at work between the African and the colonial/European contexts of the lives of some of those Africans of the mid-nineteenth century whose intellectual life was most immediately shaped by the emerging colonial experience. As its name suggests, the *Anglo-African* took its role as mediator between England and Africa quite seriously. Indeed, in its first issue on 12 September 1863, the paper's founder and editor, Robert Campbell, put on public record his attachment to the twin memories of his white father and his mother, "the offspring of a Negro." He had reason to do so because criticism was mounting against those mockingly called "half-white men": "so lost are they to all feeling of race and proper self-respect . . . proclaiming themselves cosmopolites, [and] unwilling to recognize any distinction of races and countries" (Blyden 1971 17). These criticisms were directed at those they believed were living in the afterglow of a slave culture of absentee patriarchy: of white fathers whose purported glory still ruled the minds of their children. The criticisms were directed at their unreflecting worship of colonial ideas, their inability to read themselves into the texts of the African world. Robert Campbell wanted to be different. Not only was he not inclined to reject his father, he was as anxious to acknowledge the maternal piety: "never shall we forget in the cause of the African, the love, the devotion, the sacred reverence in which we hold the memory of a mother" (12 September 1863).

Colonialism, by definition, seeks to enforce a kind of intellectual mulattoism. It requires the colonial subject to be implicated in its texts without participating in them. The colonial subject has to see himself as a crossbreed of an original native and a new foreign seed. Colonialism creates its version of the half-breed by requiring allegiance to a father who would never accept him as son. But though mulattoism properly describes Campbell and his paper, it does not quite as neatly define the ways in which this mixture of respect and reverence worked in practice. Few Western writers on the colonial and postcolonial condition appear to understand the process by which the colonized rereads the imperial text by inserting his (till then) absent self into it, by making his being an interested presence in the reconstitution of the text's meaning, by understanding the difference between what the imperial text seeks to do and how it is itself revealed by the colonized.

The process is never a simple one; nor is its course always the same, of course. It cannot, therefore, be adequately elaborated from just one instance. But basically, even allowing for the Derridean truism that all readings are renderings of omnivorous difference, it can be claimed that the presumption in imperial discourse is that the colonized subject is not, himself, part of the primary readership/audience, the constituency of the discourse. Imperial discourse does not solicit the participation of the colonized, but only acknowledges his object-status as the one/thing referred to. Indeed, this is the ultimate mode of differentiation, the only relevant meaning that one can give to the concept of the colonized "Other," namely, that the colonized subject is not expected to function in the system that creates the meaning of the text. The colonized reader/auditor is always confronted with a text that makes no prior provision for his presence but still addresses him as its object. For the colonized reader, to read the Western text at all, he has to inject his subject-status into it; and read the text not from just another point of difference, but to reread it *as if* he were, from the start, part of the putative constituency, the map of moments and signs that precipitate meaning. In other words, his presence, hitherto ignored by the text, is now openly claimed by him without his having to rewrite the text; and with this consequence, that meaning is realigned and redirected to ends both conformable to the integrity of his subject-self, and, by implication,—to the extent that such texts are demeaning of his being—actually subversive of the original political purpose of those texts. This is also to say that Derrida's questions in *Margins of Philosophy*: "What differs? Who differs?" are both framed in the context of a multivalency that an imperial/colonialist *noumos* must reject, considering that, in principle, the colonized is not part of the "who" of the interrogation itself (66).

It is not simply, then, as has often been claimed in much postcolonial criticism, that the so-called native person was the undifferentiating and helpless victim of imperial discourse. Rather, I want to suggest that the colonial reader was, in fact, a competent, circumspect and sophisticated reader, even if not an infallible one. He was certainly conscious of himself as both subject and object: subject of his own, and the object of white colonialists', discourse. He knew, as the editor of *The Eagle* (a contemporary Lagos newspaper) put it, that "like all other nations of the world, or any other part of Africa, the people will follow power and influence, and imitate the manners and customs of the conquerors and superiors." In that sense, and to that extent, the paper's correspondent recognized that the balance of "influence [was] decidedly on the side of the English" (31 March 1883).

That acknowledgment itself is an indication of a consciousness of his peculiar status in the exchange, even when, as happened often, the reader is himself overwhelmed by the pressure of that influence. One reader who wrote to the *Anglo-African* on 30 July 1864, although obviously very much on the defensive, was clearly not just echoing the voice of the imperial master. Amidst the debate on the civilizing influence Europe had a mandate to bring to Africa, he was alarmed that Africa would return to the "turgid waters of superstition, ignorance and depravity, dark and dismal as a funeral pall [should] *all* white influence" be removed from the continent. The warning was that of a patriot, not of a slave; and it was not addressed to the colonizer either. "I have done my duty, and can console myself with the reflection, '*Dixi et salvavi animus meum.*' " Hence, it did not take impossible effort for the colonized to also re-construct a system of meanings for himself out of the very texts of imperial (usually, also white) discourse. My argument is that that process also included an uncanny awareness of the many faces of European "civilization" and European racism; and, accordingly, a generous deconstruction of the deeper layers of that imperial discourse.

It was the policy of the *Anglo-African* to reprint excerpts from foreign journals on a variety of social, philosophical, political and even lighthearted matters, excerpts that give some indication of matters considered important and topical to the contemporary readership. That policy was required by the very fact of colonialism in which system the absorption of other lands and other peoples into the *regime of the metropolis* also meant the enforced harmonization of social, political, ethical, and moral conditions: language, religion, dress codes, marriage customs, and even domestic humor. That was the reality of the colonial condition, and to live under it was to accept the presence of an active imperial override of a dominated but real "native" organism. The humor, for example, of the excerpt published by *The Anglo-African* on 15 August 1863, on "How to Quarrel with Your Wife," lay, essentially, in the miracle by which the new African can join the English in the celebration of the social rites of their cherished homeland. It is the point of colonialism to make an adopted citizen of its colonial subject, to implicate that subject in its cultural and (as we shall see) intellectual enterprises without having to deal with him as an active consciousness.

One such enterprise, with which the *Anglo-African* was involved, was the "Woman Question." That the subject featured at all in the colonial press (indigenously owned and edited by people like Mr. Campbell) must speak to its more important place in the discourse of the mother country. But, as must be self-evident, the colonial reader in Nigeria was not himself raising the issue independently of that metropolitan event. Hence, then, the participation of the *Anglo-African* in the affair, and its responses, were precipitated (and even compelled) by the pressure of European intellectual history. In this chapter, we will discuss four of these excerpts: "The Power of Women" (15 August 1863), "On the Education of Women" (7 November 1863), "Women and Children" (15 August 1863), and "The Female Intellect" (10 June 1865).

"The Power of Women" (referred to subsequently as "Power") appeared on 15 August 1863:

Whatever may be the customs and laws of a country, the women of it [*sic*] decide the morals. Free or subjugated, they reign, because they hold possession of our passions. But their influence is more or less salutary, according to the degree of esteem that is granted them. Whether they are our idols or companions, courtesans or beasts of burthen, the reaction is complete, and they make us such as they are themselves. It seems as if nature connected our intelligence with their dignity, as we connect our morality to their virtue. This, therefore, is a law of natural justice; man cannot degrade woman without himself falling into degradation; he cannot raise them without himself becoming better.

The passage speaks to a subject that encompasses the character of the relationship between universal man and woman; woman and society; society and morals, as well as between morality and progress. Its rhetorical style allows woman to be goddess and patroness; blessing and subsidizing man's noble enterprise, even while in the process sacrificing herself to man as harlot and slave ("courtesan" and "beast of burthen"). On the face of it, then, all societies can subscribe to the manifesto, if *society* is defined here as any community of men (with their women and children in tow). African men could presumably be party to the argument, on the supposition that they, too, are the male "owners" of society.

And yet, as the colonial reader saw it, man (as so often in that century) did not always include the African. Not only were "educated" Africans aware of the European theories that sought to exclude them formally from the common roll—the pre-Adamites, the polygeneticists, and in a few more years, the theorists of "the missing link" (see Popkin 1973 245–262)—they could hardly have had any personal doubt that they were men. Hence, they read the imperial text as if they had been party to it in the first place; and having done so, made new/different/other meaning from it. Whence, another layer to the discourse on the woman is made patent. It can then be seen that the excerpted passage is not as concerned with the *power of woman* as it is with the miracle of *European progress*. The passage argues that European society has made its phenomenal progress *because* of its espousal of the freedom and dignity of its women. It claims that because Europe loved and honored its women, it has prospered and progressed. The proof of this assertion is not to be found in any microstudy of particular European societies but in the global differentiation of peoples. The proof, in other words, is located not in social history but in cultural anthropology. What begins as a general statement on the nature of the civilizing function of woman in society becomes a mere prelude to a celebration of difference within the "great divisions of the human race." The advanced races are those in which women are loved and honored. The barbarous civilizations are those in which women are slaves. The "imperial" text concludes as follows:

Let us cast our eyes over the globe, and observe those great divisions of the human race, East and West. One half of the ancient world remains without progress or thought, and under the load of a barbarous cultivation; women there are slaves. The other half advances towards freedom and light; the women are loved and honoured. ("Power" 15 August 1863)

Against this assertion may be placed the comment of an irate Lagosian writing in the *Lagos Weekly Record* of 1899. His reading of that social history, as Europe would have it, tells him to expect a story, not of progress but of degeneracy in Africa. But, for example, when the consequences of European monogamy are taken into full historical account, so his argument ran, polygamy would actually be seen as a healthier arrangement in honor of womanhood:

No African who has had the opportunity of visiting Europe and encountered the demorali- zation to be met in the streets of England at night, or who has visited the houses of public prostitution in France, and witnessed the depths of degradation to which woman has reached, can ever be convinced that monogamy . . . is better than polygamy. (16 September 1899)

In its maiden issue, the *Anglo-African* carried an extract from the *Atlantic Monthly, that* addresses itself to the issue of women and the territory of motherhood. The article, "Women and Children," indeed, sets out to reject the proposition that "the nursery is the mother's chrysalis," and to argue instead that God never intended woman to "wind herself up into a cocoon. If He had, He would have made her a caterpillar. She has no right to bury her womanly nature in the tomb of childhood" (15 August 1863). The paper's readers had reason to be interested in the argument. In various issues of Lagos newspapers, and clearly reflecting a trend in popular discourse, the "education" of women was proclaimed to be important to Africa because it provided for the *future* of the continent. In the schools established for girls in Lagos during this period, the subjects taught were, appropriately enough, those:

directed to make [girls] useful in their homes and generation, and no one would doubt that a greater proportion of responsibility rests on those engaged in imparting education on the daughters of our soil than there would be on the sons. On the daughters rest in after life the bringing up of, and early instilling in the infant, first impressions of the future generation. (*The Eagle* 30 June 1883)

In effect, the woman was to be educated so that Africa's children might see the light. The problem was that that high-minded role was also seen as confounding the woman's role in society. Women were to be educated, apparently, in order that they would function well in the confinement of the home. Therein, indeed, lay the double jeopardy: that her education actually "condemned" her to childbearing and child rearing. The "imperial text" reads:

You hear of them about six times in ten years, and there is a baby each time. They crawl out of the farther end of the ten years hollow, wrinkled, and lank—teeth gone, hair gone, roses gone, plumpness gone; freshness and vivacity, and sparkle— everything that is dewy, and springing, and spontaneous, gone—gone—gone for ever. ("Women")

At issue, actually, in the original European text, was the very soul of the transitional European woman: "transitional" because the passage does not address itself to woman-in-general, but specifically to the "scores and scores of women [who] leave school, leave their piano, and drawing, and fancy work, and all manner of pretty and pleasant things, and marry and bury themselves" ("Women"). Home and marriage are the death and burial of the new European woman; the loss is to the bourgeois community of pianists and artists and decorators. For such a community, the seclusion of the nursery is much more than a return to caged life of childhood; it is a virtual entombment of the soul. The "educated" woman, to the extent that she assumes the unequivocal role of mother, is as impoverished as the altogether "uneducated" woman: "She wraps herself in the robes of infantile simplicity, and burying her womanly nature in the tomb of childhood, patiently awaits the sure-coming resurrection in the form of a noble, high-minded, world-stirring son, or a virtuous, lovely daughter" ("Women").

The excerpt, thus, questions the primacy of this "ancient" sense of female/maternal duty. It was the mind and soul of the individual new woman, not the well being of the children of the nation that needed to be secured first. A "womanly nature" was given to the female: "to sun itself in the broad, bright day, to root itself fast and firm in the earth; to spread itself wide to the sky, that her children, in their infancy and youth and maturity, that her husband in his strength and his weakness—that her kinsfolk and neighbours, and the poor of the land, the halt and the blind, and all Christ's little ones, may sit under its shadow with greater delight" ("Women").

Woman shall then become what she was created to be (but has been prevented from becoming): the great tree of life under whose shadow all shall seek pleasure and refuge. The European text was setting up a condition for the proper functioning of the woman, which was actually and totally at variance with what Africa expected of its woman and its future.

Although these excerpts speak of the "woman" in universal terms, it is clear also that only a very closely defined kind of woman is invoked. This is made even more apparent in a piece from *Victoria Magazine,* "On the Education of Women," which was republished in the *Anglo-African* of 7 November 1863. The "woman" of contemporary discourse was in fact a white, educated, middle-class person who had little need to earn a living by working for it. That class of women, as the periodical press represented it, was beginning to show signs of mental breakdown, not from overwork but from frustration and idleness. Indeed, the article takes the trouble to refute the argument that "an enlarged course of study would, by overworking the female brain, eventually produce widespred [*sic*] idiocy." On the contrary, the article argues that "mental disease is produced by want of occupation as well as excess of it." One of the authorities cited in support of this argument is a physician "at the head of a large lunatic asylum near London, having under his charge a considerable number of female patients of the middle-class." To cure women of these "melancholy diseases"—the "hysteria and nervous affections" afflicting "so large a proportion of women in the well-to-do classes"—it was previously the habit of doctors to prescribe an "interesting occupation, change of scene, anything in fact, that may divert the mind from the dull monotony of a vacant life." No longer. A new remedy was proposed: the "stimulus" of "higher intellectual culture" (7 November 1863).

Woman, thus, becomes the name for the new sick European female of the well-to-do classes; and the education of women (the stimulation of "higher intellectual culture") a form of preventive therapy for various aberrations peculiar to that kind. Education could save those women "denied a healthy outlet for their energy" from indulging "in unhealthy extravagance, simply because it is a necessity of their nature to be active in some way or other." In any event, "the fast women and the masculine women are not those who sit down to their orderly course of study." On the contrary, "the hard and cold women are precisely those whom a consciousness of their unimportance to the world in general has made callous to everything but their own petty, personal interests, and in whom the sense of duty and responsibility, or, in other words, the conscience, has been deadened and seared by fashionable frivolity" ("On Education" 7 November 1863).

The tenor of "native" thought suggested a different conclusion. This evidence supported the more general view that Africa would go the way of Europe, if it continued to espouse the ways of Europe. As a contemporary correspondent put it:

In the trail of European culture there has followed a host of social disorders the existence of which is rendered impossible under purely native regime. The sanctity of domestic relations—those of parent and child, of husband and wife, of master and servant, and of proverbial chastity of the female sex—these and other social gems, so dear to the native mind and so strictly and jealously guarded under patriarchal rule, have been sacrificed as holocausts to the fascinating bubbles of European civilization which are of short durability and transient glory. ("Editorial" *Lagos Weekly Record* 27 August 1904)

Perhaps the most revealing of these articles excerpted from the foreign press and published in the *Anglo-African* is that on the "Female Intellect" (10 June 1865).

The piece, originally published by the (English) *Saturday Review,* is remarkable for the elegant and urbane manner in which it manages to phrase its insults to women. We "often meet with men who not only understand what they see and hear and read, but can go on and make inferences and discoveries for themselves. But we seldom meet with men who can thoroughly understand and appreciate anything that is set before them, but have never in their whole lives thought out any matter for themselves." The quality of the compliment to men is a measure of its denial to women. Indeed, as the article sees it, "intellectual giantesses are still rarer than intellectual giants," though the article "suspects" that "intellectual dwarfs, painfully common among both sexes, are still more common among men than among women" ("Female Intellect" 10 June 1865).

The argument seems to be that while men and women are alike in having their fair share of geniuses and idiots, there would seem to be a marked evidence of the innate incapacity of the female sex to handle intellectual property:

It seems inexplicable, that where the receptive power exists in so high a degree, the creative power seems absolutely wanting. You have not the same difficulty with men; they either do not understand at all, or they do something more than understand. To show a brilliant power of appreciation, to take in, without difficulty or hesitation, instruction of a hitherto unknown kind, but stop at this stage of reception and appreciation, seems a position exclusively feminine. ("Female Intellect" 10 June 1865)

In this instance, the argument, in so far as it relates to women, seems to discover a pattern in what men actually "observe" in life that confirms a deeper suspicion about innate female deficiencies. The article notes that the capacity to learn languages has been "observed" to differ from that required to learn mathematics; and that such a difference can be seen in the different ways men and women master both disciplines. "Every man endowed with moderate philological power will probably not work out Grimm's Law for himself in all its fullness, but he will, without any help, find out fragmentary portions of it," unless he is one of the sort who may be "set down as having no head for the subject at all." With women, the matter is different. They will "learn several languages without finding out anything of the sort:

Though the moment the theory is set before them, they will grasp it in all its fullness, and work it out in detail with a clearness and thoroughness of appreciation that, to a male teacher, is not only pleasing and surprising, but altogether perplexing." Such a male teacher, "half-charmed, half-puzzled, with his female disciples," will ask "If [women] can thus perfectly understand everything that is set before them, why on earth have they never found out anything for themselves?" The reason, the article explains, is two-fold: "the incapacity is partly the result of nature, partly of education" ("Female Intellect" 10 June 1865).

Recent criticism is beginning to document what was all too apparent to contemporary African readers of the European thought, namely that European attitudes to women and to Africans had close parallels. On 30 July 1864, the *Anglo-African* carried a report on a recent meeting of the British Anthropological Society at which Bouverie Pusey read a paper "On the Negro and His Capability for Civilization." Pusey contended that Negroes possess "the power of attaining a high degree of civilization, and that the condition of slavery . . . is the principal cause of their degradation." But the paper also published the comments of some other members of the society who thought otherwise; in particular the view of a certain Dr. Hunt that "all the evidence adduced of the capacity of the negro for civilization was derived from the association of the black man with the white, and that it depended on individual instances only. There can be no doubt that at the present time the negro is an inferior race." On 21 October 1865, the paper reprinted an article from *Macmillan's Magazine* on "Hereditary Talent and Character," that argued that man's "mental habits in mature life are the creatures of social discipline, as well as of inborn aptitudes, and it is impossible to ascertain what is due to the latter alone, except by observing several individuals of the same race, reared under various influences, and noting the peculiarities of character that invariably assert themselves." Whatever the paper's readership may have thought of the soundness of this general statement, it would have had little difficulty in responding to that part of the article that specifically mentioned the African—especially as it was in order to draw attention to that part of the article that the piece was reprinted in the first place. According to *Macmillan's Magazine:*

Take, for example, the typical West African Negro. . . . [He] has strong impulsive passions, and neither patience, reticence, nor dignity. He is warm-hearted, loving towards his master's children, and idolized by the children in return. He is eminently gregarious, for he is always jabbering, quarreling, tom-tom-ing, or dancing. ("Hereditary Talent" 21 October 1865)

The article claims that these qualities in the race are as ingrained as comparable traits in the sexes. "They are transmitted, generation after generation, as truly as their physical forms. What is true for the entire race is equally true for its varieties" (*Anglo-African* 21 October 1865). Similarly, Alfred Wallace could, on one hand, uphold a general truth of the "wonderful power, range, flexibility, and sweetness, of the musical sounds producible by the human larynx, especially in the female sex" but, on the other, argue that "[female savages] . . . seldom sing at all. Savages certainly never choose their wives for fine voices, but for rude health, and strength, and physical beauty" (45). The effect of this climate of thought on the African reading of the "Woman Question" is that woman appears in two categories of being: the white woman, although inferior to the white man, is nevertheless, by definition, superior to the both the African man and the African woman; the argument claims nothing whatsoever for the black woman who is placed below all others. The irony is telling. The language used to characterize the supposedly inferior people is then applied to characterize white woman, as a subset of the superior races. According to "The Female Intellect," the female mind is "naturally receptive but not creative." No amount of power that it manifests "in the way of merely understanding and appreciating" can imply "any proportionate power of original discovery." Such a mind requires external stimulation for it to begin to act. Such a mind "will take a keen delight in working out the application of a law, though the law would never have suggested itself without external help." This state of affairs turns out actually to be consistent with what it claims is the "doctrine that all men and most women hold as to the position of women in the world." That position is one of intrinsic subordination to men, not only in practice but also in essence:

A man of intelligence and information wishes to find, in a wife or sister or female companion of any kind, one who is in some sort his intellectual equal, and yet in some sort his intellectual inferior. He does not want a teacher, a disputant, an overthrower of his first principles; he has male friends and male enemies who will do all these services for him. But he wants one who is essentially receptive, who can understand, appreciate, and develop what he sets before her, who can act as a keen critic of details, who can even point out his flaws and inconsistencies, but who will not boisterously attack the principles from which he starts. ("Female Intellect" 10 June 1865)

We should find in this formulation, a concise statement of the purpose of differentiation and the ends of imperialism. The nature of the female intellect is made to accord with the functions determined to be appropriate to woman. Or, more exactly, in the language of the article, the female intellect satisfies man's very wishes for woman: "If, as the Apostle tells us, the woman is created for the man, this is exactly the sort of woman that a man would wish to have created for him" ("Female Intellect" 10 June 1865).

Contemporary Africans were quite familiar with this kind of rhetorical and political gesture. The European theorists of the later nineteenth century spoke and argued to make their world accord to their best wishes for themselves and their kind, which is the very definition of imperialism. It amounted to a high minded quest for a kind of order that would best accommodate difference under the auspices of a *permanent* (imperial) ruling group. In nonimperial settings, white men constituted that ruling group; white women the oppressed, or colonized, group. Women were intelligent enough to be associated with men, but should not be independent minded enough to become a threat to men. The function of woman (as of the nonwhite races in the imperial sphere) was thus "a most amiable and honourable" one. It "manifestly requires a very high development of those faculties that we have called receptive, while it would be inconsistent with the presence, in any strong degree, of those powers that we call creative—those by which *men act as teachers and rulers of the world"* ("Female Intellect," my emphasis).

In his book, *From West Africa to Palestine*, Edward W. Blyden argues that "there is, perhaps, no other people in Europe among whom the caste feeling is more deeply seated than in the English middle classes" (78). This judgment is further restricted to English *men*. As Blyden specifically phrases it, "there is no class of men whom it is less interesting and agreeable to meet in travelling than ordinary Englishmen out of England" (78). Blyden's "people" is transformed into "middle classes" and then into "ordinary Englishmen." What makes the reductions particularly interesting is the contrast that Blyden immediately suggests between ordinary English men and ordinary English women. Although adopting a phrase of much common Victorian currency to describe English women ("the gentle sex"), Blyden is not as sanguine about this Victorian rhetoric as might otherwise appear, for he goes on to raise the Woman Question in the language usually reserved for race-related discourse. "The instincts of women, as far as I have observed, seem to be in favour of oppressed races. Is it because they are themselves an oppressed race?" (78). As far as I know, this linking of women and oppressed races through a naturalizing of their "instincts," had never before then been phrased in this manner.

Still, Blyden's is only a question, not a proposition; but it clearly redefines the status of "men" and "races" so profoundly that "white men" are set radically apart in both instances as the oppressors. Blyden's piece, in a representative way, is a rewriting of the entirety of the dominant discourse of womanhood in its imperial context. His "women" in this instance, are actually white women. In a formulation based only on gender and localized to European (white) society, white men would indeed be the "oppressors" of white women just as, following that logic, African women would be the oppressed in African society. But, based on race and extended to empire, in a sphere in which it was eminently possible for the African to introduce his subject-self, white men were the oppressors of African men *and* women. On that basis, however, white women were not subject to any oppression by African men. Blyden's remark would then, if reconstructed, amount to an assertion that the women of the oppressing races identify with the peoples (men and women) of the oppressed races because, in their own domestic circumstances, they know what it can mean to be oppressed. What Blyden's formulation does is to construct two parallel categories of oppression based on gender and race. The fact of sympathy does not, however, collapse the categories into one in which the oppression of European women is made identical with that of non-European races. There is no equivalent to this construction in any European text that I am aware of. In this sense, Blyden's is a contestation of those European interpretations of human history that would otherwise have been entertained under the aegis of contemporary feminist argumentation. It is a sophisticated rereading.

I have used Edward Blyden both to have a name and a sense of authority lacking in newspaper editorials and commentaries for this rereading. But Blyden's sentiments can be gleaned in varying degrees of precision and force, from a variety of unsigned and "unauthorized" comments in the *Anglo-African.* It is inconceivable, then, that contemporary Africans, like Blyden, who lived under the rule of white governors and the patronage of white teachers, and read the outrageous things European "thinkers" had to say about their race would not have understood the parallels that the logic of the European discourse of women had with their own. The same arguments used to qualify the intellectual abilities of women were used to question the capacities of Africans. To the proposition that the success of Africans in European universities was proof that Africans were not intellectually inferior to Europeans, the answer came as it did for women: the exception cannot be the rule. The irony was that imperialism required that colonial subjects become foster children and learn the ways of the European household: to dress, think, eat and generally behave like the European, but never to presume to equal status with the European. In part, the need for this arose from the very mission of civilization in which imperialism was engaged. This was especially so because local colonial institutions, themselves modeled on the English system, offered African women only "that sort of smattering education, that is comprised solely in playing on the piano, and a fondness for dress" (*The Eagle* 30 June 1883). In that tradition, "proper" education was provided only in English schools: there "French is taught by a Parisienne. Tuition also includes a sound English Education, German, Music, Dancing and all modern accomplishment" ("Advertisement" *Observer* 4 June 1887). The double irony of the situation was that the judgment of the period on the colonial woman who acquired these skills was anything but favorable. Europe thought her presumptuous and foolish. "[T]hat foppish and mongrel class of our English speaking population that have done more to damnify English education than any other cause" ("On the Education Ordinance" 31 March 1883). Africa regarded her as a ruin and a mockery. The "Woman Question," then, was essentially redefined as an imperial and a race question. Africa's own "Woman Question" had to be dealt with at a different time and within a different framework of ideas, and under the aegis of an entirely different momentum, namely of a Negritude seeking to claim its own woman.

## WORKS CITED

"[Advertisement]." *Observer*, 4 June 1887.

Benjamin, J.B. "[Editorial]." *Anglo-African,* 12 September 1863.

Blyden, Edward W. "An Address before the Maine State Colonization Society, Portland, Maine, June 26th, 1862." In *Black Spokesman: Selected Published Writings of E.W. Blyden.* Ed. Hollis R. Lynch. Cass Library of African Studies: Africana Modern Library. London: Frank Cass & Co. Ltd., 1971.

———. *From West Africa to Palestine.* Freetown, Sierra Leone: T.J. Sawyer; Manchester: John Heywood; London: Marshall & Co., 1873.

Brantlinger, Patrick. "Victorians and Africans: The Genealogy of the Myth of the Dark Continent." In *"Race," Writing, and Difference.* Ed. Henry Louis Gates, Jr. Chicago: University of Chicago Press, 1986.

Callaway, Helen. *Gender, Culture and Empire: European Women in Colonial Nigeria.* Urbana: University of Illinois Press, 1987.

Campbell, Robert. "[Editorial]." *Anglo-African,* 12 September 1863.

Curtin, Philip D. *The Image of Africa: British Ideas and Action, 1780–1850.* Madison: University of Wisconsin Press, 1964.

Darwin, Charles. *The Descent of Man and Selection in Relation to Sex.* 1st ed. London: John Murray, 1871.

Derrida, Jacques. *Margins of Philosophy.* Trans. Alan Bass. Chicago: University of Chicago Press, 1982.

Echeruo, Michael J.C. *Victorian Lagos: Aspects of Nineteenth Century Lagos Life.* London: Macmillan Education Ltd., 1977.

"[Editorial]." *Lagos Weekly Record,* 27 August 1904.

"The Female Intellect." Reprinted from *Saturday Review. Anglo-African,* 10 June 1865.

Gates, Henry Louis, Jr. *"Race," Writing and Difference.* Chicago: University of Chicago Press, 1986.

Gilman, Sander L. "Black Bodies, White Bodies: Toward an Iconography of Female Sexuality in Late Nineteenth-Century Art, Medicine, and Literature." In *"Race," Writing and Difference.* Ed. Henry Louis Gates, Jr. Chicago: University of Chicago Press, 1986: 223–61

Kopytoff, Jean Herskovits. *A Preface to Modern Nigeria: The "Sierra Leonians" in Yoruba, 1830–1890.* Madison: University of Wisconsin Press, 1965.

Levine, Philippa. " 'The Humanising Influences of Five O'clock Tea': Victorian Feminist Periodicals." *Victorian Studies* 11.2 (Winter 1990): 293–306.

"On the Education of Women." Reprinted from *Victoria Magazine. Anglo-African,* 7 November 1863.

"On the Education Ordinance." *The Eagle.* Lagos, Nigeria. 31 March 1883.

Popkin, Richard H. "The Philosophical Basis of Eighteenth-Century Racism." In *Studies* in *Eighteenth-Century Culture: Racism in the Eighteenth Century.* Ed. Harold E. Pagliaro. Vol. 3. Cleveland: Case Western Reserve University Press, 1973: 245–62.

"The Power of Women." *Anglo-African,* 15 August 1863.

Schiebinger, Lora. "The Anatomy of Difference: Race and Sex in Eighteenth-Century Science." *Eighteenth-Century Studies* 23.4 (Summer 1990): 387–406.

Spitzer, Leo. *The Creoles of Sierra Leone: Responses to Colonialism, 1870–1945.* Madison: University of Wisconsin Press, 1974.

Wallace, Alfred Russell. *The Action of Natural Selection on Man.* University Series, 6. New Haven, CT: Charles C. Chatfield & Co., 1871.

Chapter Eleven

# Impersonation in Some African Ritual and Festival Performances

## Sam Ukala

Impersonation in the theater may be defined as the imitation of the appearance, speech and behavior of a character. It is the nucleus of realistic acting, designed to communicate artistic truth as truthfully as possible through the instrumentality of the actor's disguised body and voice. It is an aspect of "mimesis," defined by the *Chambers 20th Century Dictionary* as "imitation or representation in art"; but while mimesis includes the imitation and representation of setting and other environmental factors, such as light and nonhuman sound, impersonation excludes all those and entails the imitation and representation of only the character in a play. For, of the literary, creative arts, namely, drama, the novel, the modern short story and poetry, only in drama does impersonation occur.

In drama, the fully delineated character has three dimensions, which Lajos Egri calls "physiology, sociology and psychology" (1960 36–37). Physiology refers to the character's physique, appearance, gait, and clothing; the character's status, occupation, and interpersonal relationships constitute his sociology; his psychology comprises his mental and emotional states—intelligence quotient, complexes, motivations, temperament, and so on. In the play script, these dimensions are represented by means of written words—words describing the character's looks, status, actions, emotions, etc. in the stage direction; words in the dialogue and speeches of the characters, portraying their own feelings, motivations, intelligence, and so on. In performance, the character's physiology, sociology, and psychology are bodied forth by means of impersonation: an actor, whose physique may resemble that of the character, is costumed, made up, carries properties, assumes a gait and voice, and generally acts as appropriate to the character. Impersonation, therefore, cannot be achieved without the joint efforts of the visual artists (including the costume designer, maker and makeup artists) and the actor. In this regard, it assumes a slightly different nature from acting, essentially achievable by means of the actor's body and voice, whether or not they are disguised. In other words, while an actor in his work clothes can convincingly act as a king, the impersonation of the king would be unrealistic, incomplete, and unconvincing, without investing the actor with the royal regalia and appearance as represented in a costume and makeup.

Yet perfect impersonation goes beyond a technical imitation and representation of the three dimensions of the character to a point at which the actor is so intellectually and emotionally immersed in his role that "'I am impersonating someone's ends, and if I am such and such a character, what is the nature of my feelings and what are the correct physical movements for me now?' begins" (Stanislavsky 1967 95).

It is really at the point of finding a correct answer to this question that the true psychology of the character begins to be realized by the impersonator.

Though impersonation is more vital to realistic acting, it has remained basic to most of the nonrealistic styles also, from the classical or formalistic through the expressionistic, the romantic-cum-fantastic to the surrealistic. It is relegated by performance art and related current paratheatrical experiments, but in mainstream theater, it remains a more dependable parameter for drama than the mere imitation of action or scenery, than plot (with its surprise and suspense), than ability to edify or enlighten or entertain, than even the context of relaxation. Though important factors in drama, imitation, plot, edification, entertainment and context are not, like impersonation, exclusive to drama. They are found, in different combinations, in poetry and in the novel. Even movement and gesture are not exclusive to drama. De Graft (1976) mockingly reminds African cultural nationalists of this:

We talk patriotically about "our heritage of indigenous drama and the richness of our dramatic traditions." At such times, the term "drama" seems to cover almost every form of social expression that may be said to incorporate movement and gesture: singing, drumming, dancing, all ceremonial behaviour, enstoolment and destoolment of chiefs, child naming, circumcision rites, hunting, drinking palm wine, and eating goat's meat—literally everything. I know of no easier way of reducing to nonsense one's thinking about drama. (3)

The African cultural nationalists had been engaged in a worthwhile endeavor to prove that there was drama in Africa before the white man arrived there, that there were literature and history. If their concepts of these were apparently overembracive, they, nonetheless, attracted further research into the forms conceptualized, consequent upon which the international recognition of indigenous African ritual and festival performances, art, literature, and history has been won. It can not now be determined how strongly the apparently overembracive concepts of the African dramatic heritage influenced the movement in European and American theater since the 1960s (involving performance artists, such as Eugenio Barba, paratheater practitioners, such as Jerzy Grotowski and John Fox), which aims at converging theater and ritual, abolishing the audience-performer polarization, and blurring the art-life distinction. But Schechner notes, rightly, that what is a "movement in

Europe and America is the most widespread kind of theater and dance in many parts of Africa and Asia" (1988 122).

But the aesthetic principles of African ritual and festival performances, which spur theater experimentalists abroad, have seldom been gainfully adapted to modern African literary drama and theater. Wole Soyinka has shown the keenest interest in doing this. Several of his plays, notably *A Dance of the Forest, The Road, The Strong Breed, Kongi's Harvest,* and *The Bacchae of Euripides,* pulsate with ritual and festival presence. Soyinka's cyclical plots, sparse narrative content, large numbers of characters, characterization that hardly elicits empathy, cryptic language, symbolic music, oracular dances, sometimes by masked figures, are all borrowings from African rituals and festivals. But it can hardly be rightly guessed which particular ritual or festival any of the plays is based on. For, out of the vibrant richness of his imagination, Soyinka often truncates and grafts festivals; uproots, transplants, and crossbreeds mythic essences; and tumbles and reverses sequences of familiar rites (see Ogunba 1970 8–10; 1978 106). This results in the complexity of much of his theater and its unpopularity with the African audience (see Adedeji 1971 140–142, 147; Okpewho 1983 218). The audience can hardly recognize and identify with its aesthetics, and directors are unsure of the appropriate performance style. Perhaps, to avoid Soyinka's pitfall, a number of African theater practitioner—J.P. Clark Bekederemo, Efua Sutherland, Femi Osofisan, and Sam Ukala, among others—prefer to explore and adapt the more comprehensible aesthetics of the African folktale.

The African ritual or festival is, indeed, more composite and complex than even Soyinka's theatre. It combines visual art, myth, theater, religion, magic, and life. It cannot, therefore, be completely grasped from a single perspective (of, say, the anthropologist). Such narrow perspectives have yielded, at best, brilliant general descriptions, which leave the interested theater artist with little more than a smattering knowledge of specific aspects of the forms described.If the current search by African scholars and playwrights for an indigenous dramatic aesthetic principles is to be fruitful, if the experiments in African, European and American theaters, which are influenced by the African ritual and festival, are to have integrity and be intelligently assessed, a thorough understanding of the various aspects of the African ritual and festival may be necessary. And this may derive from studies of a more limited scope, concentrating on one or two aspects of the performances at a time, in the same way as exhaustive chapters in the criticism of conventional literary theater focus, respectively, on language or acting or scene design or costume or characterization or lighting, and so on. Hence we are, in this chapter, concentrating on impersonation, which we have shown to be the distinguishing core of, and litmus for, mainstream theater.

We shall begin with two examples of ritual performance, the *bori* of the Hausa and the *orukoro* of the Kalabari. For descriptions of the *bori,* we shall rely on Andrew Horn's "Ritual, Drama and the Theatrical: The Case of the Bori Spirit Mediumship" and Dapo Adelugba's "Trance and Theatre: The Nigerian Experience." (1981) Adelugba's essay deals, in addition, with the *orukoro.*

The two forms share the same mode of performance: They employ trance and possession. In describing the *bori* performance, Horn tells us that the *mai bori* (literally "owner of *bori*" but which may be translated as the "*bori* medium" or "*bori* actress") is costumed in clothing reminiscent of the *iska* (the "spirit" that regularly possesses her). She also carries "the *tsere*, a fetish, contrived from objects and clothing associated with the particular *iska*," which functions as more than a stage property, as it is "the vehicle through which the spirit possesses the medium" (190). If she is to function as a medium, "the *mai bori* [in her dance] will assume the demeanor of the spirit and her movements, voice, words, knowledge and power will be those of the *iska* 'riding' her. If she is not a medium but is merely possessed, she begins to dance, to move erratically, to jump in the air and land squarely on the buttocks with legs splayed apart, or to jerk wildly about. The spirit is now presumed to have occupied her body and, in the image of bori, she is said to be 'ridden', 'mounted', (*hawa*) by the *iska*; she becomes the '*mare*' (*godrya*) of the spirit . . . there will be no fully realized characterization of the occupying spirit and the performance will simply be a display of ecstatic hysteria with a musical accompaniment" (190). At the end of her dance, observes Onwuejeogwu, the medium

falls exhausted and is covered with a cloth. During this state she may foretell the future. Spectators wishing to obtain a favour from or appease the spirit that has mounted her, place their gifts and alms on the mat. Then she sneezes, the spirit quits her, and she becomes normal. During this period she is never referred to as herself but as the spirit. (qtd. in Adelugba 1981 204–205)

Adelugba's description of the *orukoro* has many correspondences with the description of the *bori* spirit mediumship. The *orukorobo* (priest or priestess) is dressed in white and red cloths, the usual ceremonial colors of African priests, priestesses, and medicine men. The other items worn by the *orukorobo* are also generally worn by the functionaries just named: coral bead necklaces, wristlets, anklets, and Indian bells. The *orukorobo* also carries objects, which cannot rightly be called props: an elephant tusk, symbol of authority and that, like the *tsere* of the *mai bori,* may be a vehicle through which the *orukorobo* is possessed; "a saucer containing a fresh egg, some alligator pepper and/or kola nuts and coins which significantly are part of the sacrificial offerings" (211). While dancing, the *orukorobo* makes ritual sacrifices and incantations. As he or she becomes deeply ecstatic, he or she is "transformed into the essence of the god. Thus a priestess who in ordinary life is known to be very effeminate, old and weak, can be transformed into a fierce, agile, bold and awe-inspiring character capable of commanding the worship" (210). The *orukorobo* becomes "capable of the prophet's sight, communicating with man as a first person representative of the deity" (210).

The common element resembling impersonation in the two ritual performances just described is the assumption, by the "performer," of the behavior of the "character." But this is done beyond the scale of creative and conscious imitation, which is vital to impersonation in drama. According to Albright et al. (1967) most systems of acting are subsumed in two schools of thought: "a psychological school of 'inner response' and a mechanical school of 'external technique'" (84). To employ the external technique, the actor needs only to present the "external manifestations" and "assumed behaviours," using more or less known and dependable bodily attitudes and gestures combined with "a rather arbitrary and mechanical mode of line delivery" (84). It is believed that, with this technique, the actor can adequately communicate the character's emotion and thought to the audience whether or not the actor himself "feels" the emotion or "thinks the thought" (84).

With the technique of "inner response," on the other hand, the actor strives to feel the emotion and think the thought of the character as a prerequisite for the achievement of "perfect vocal and bodily expression" (84). The intensity of the actor's emotional and intellectual involvement in relation to the character is quite low with the external technique and incomparable with a state of trance. With the technique of inner response, however, the intensity of the actor's emotional and intellectual involvement is so high that the actor could almost be said to be possessed by the role he is playing. Here lies the danger in adopting *in toto* the technique of inner response: the actor may be so engrossed in the character's emotion and thought that he would stray from the overall design and tempo of the play. He may actually weep, fall in love, hate, and kill or, in common parlance, generally overact. On the other hand, he may be unable to express the emotion or thought if he had never experienced it in real life. Hence Albright et al. do not recommend a strict adherence to the technique of inner response or to the mechanical one, which "sometimes leads to excess of insincerity and artificiality" (84). Rather, they observe that "the typical actor uses both the psychological and the mechanical approach, to the degree and at the time that each serves him best" (86). This means that, contrary to the impression created by Stanislavsky's statement, the real intensity of the character's "feelings" and its "correct physical movement" cannot be truly assumed by the impersonator using the psychological technique. He can only approximate to them. On the other hand, it is possible to adopt solely the mechanical technique, if the goal is "insincere" or "artificial" impersonation.

Whichever technique is adopted, the impersonator has a dual personality: at every stage of his performance, he is himself, planning, executing, and controlling; he is also the interpretation of a character. But in the *bori* and *orukoro* spirit-mediumships, the performer possesses a single personality at every stage. He or she begins as himself or herself and later transforms into the god or goddess or spirit that possesses him or her. While himself or herself, he or she is a mere individual dancer, a priest or priestess performing a ceremonial function (for example, offering a sacrifice), communicating with spectators as man with man; he or she cannot, at the same time, assume the behavior of the god or goddess or spirit. Conversely, once transformed into the god or goddess or spirit, he or she completely loses his or her own personality and communicates with spectators as god with man.

Writing about "magical drama," by which he refers to such ritual performances as the *bori* and *orukoro,* J.C. De Graft states:

what distinguishes magical drama from all the other forms of drama that derive from it is the element of possession in magical drama, the trance state *for which the impersonator in all the derivative forms of drama substitutes conscious intellectual and emotional control during the act of impersonation.* [The impersonator strikes] a fine balance between his awareness of the fictional world of the character impersonated and his awareness of the work-a-day world of his audience and his artistic self; he knows that no matter how deeply he immerses himself in the role of the fictional character there is always a psychological point of safety beyond which he dare not go, lest he be swept out of his depth and get carried away on the uncertain currents of hysteria and ecstasy. In simple theatrical terms this means that the actor loses control of himself and, with that loss of control, his grip on the role and on his audience, if it is an artistically sensitive audience. (1976 6)

Thus, there is no impersonation in the *bori* and the *orukoro* as they do not allow for the conscious imitation and representation of a character's sociology and psychology. Although, it may be argued, with regard to the *bori,* that there is physiological imitation, since the *mai bori* is costumed in clothing reminiscent of the *iska*, it is important to realize that costume is neutral until it is appropriately invested in the dual personality of an impersonator-cum-character's representation, an interpreter-interpretation. The hood, they say, does not make the monk. When an impersonator wears it and plays the role of the monk, then it is the costume of the monk, but if the impersonator plays the role of the devil, the costume assumes a fake value, becomes the costume of a sly villain. Before the *mai bori* is possessed as well as during her trance, she impersonates no one. At the first stage, she is dancing as herself and the costume on her has no dramatic value; at the second stage, she *is* the *iska* in its customary work-a-day clothing. At no stage is she a dual personality. This, perhaps, explains the appearance of the *orukorobo* in the typical ceremonial regalia of the African priest or priestess, which cannot be confused with the costume appropriate to the mermaid. For in the African folk memory, the water goddess or mermaid is a longhaired half-woman-half-fish. There is, thus, no attempt by the *orukorobo* to assume the physiology of the "character," as this may have been considered unnecessary. In our third example, the *owu* masquerade performance (also of the Kalabari), which has grown less ritualistic than the *bori* and the *orukoro,* the water people (*owu*) are represented in "many cloths" sewn together and decorated "wooden head dresses which cover the dancer" (Horton 1981a 97). This interest in appropriate physiological imitation probably arose in the nineteenth century when the *owu* ritual performance became remarkably deritualized. Horton informs us that in some of the *owu* masquerades:

recreation seems to have broken loose from religion. The motives of dancers and audience in the drum-answering competitions are no longer focused on concern for the gods; even less so were the motives of nineteenth century *Owome* chiefs who combed the Eastern Delta for new plays to devastate their rivals. True, most of the performances involved are preceded by prayer and offerings to the gods represented. But in some cases these seem to have become little more than precautionary measures to ensure that no accidents mar the play . . . there is little doubt that a secular dramatic form was beginning to emerge from the religious practice. (101)

The *owu* engage in three broad kinds of performance: character-sketching dance, reenactment of a historical episode, and the playing of "a game of risk." An example of the first kind centers on Igbo who falters "in the serious business of dancing. He rushes off for a lecherous advance upon some pretty girl in the audience." This depicts the major character trait of the *owu* being represented by Igbo, "a lascivious good time 'bluffer' who can never resist using up all the family funds in buying the favours of a woman when his father sends him up-river to buy yams" (99).

The conflict between Agiri and Sabo is an example of a historical event reenacted. The conflict arises from the attempt of Sabo to prevent the marriage of his sister, Data, to Agiri, whom he considers ruthless in nature (99).

The "game of risk" involves the masker and the young men of the village. In a performance at Bile, described by Horton, for example, "the masker alternately slashes with a machete and hurls heavy staves in long, well-directed volleys" at the young men, "the supply being kept up to him by a retinue of attendants carrying bundles of these staves." The young men "compete in creeping as close to the menacing figure as possible" while escaping harm. The game is intended to portray the water people as powerful and ruthless (100).

The artistry in the entire performance is underlined by the fact that, since the *owu* are gods, not ancestors, their reenacted lives, character traits, and encounters are fictitious. There is a clear attempt by the maskers to creatively imitate and interpret the (imagined) roles of the gods, and the maskers are always consciously engaged in a competition as they strive for virtuosity. For, not only is bad performance a disgrace to the masker's lineage, virtuosity is "one of the most admired achievements in the [Kalabari] community" (98). Clear-eyed skill is necessary to achieve virtuosity. Hence the incidence of possession is much lower in the performances just described than in the *owu* divination rites (not discussed in this chapter), which are similar in nature to the *bori* and the *orukoro*. It can even be claimed that part of what looks like possession in the few *owu* masquerade performances is nothing more than an intense emotional and intellectual engrossment of the actor in his role to the extent that he stays, for some time, at the brink of possession and exhibits what Horton calls "possession behaviour" (107) while retaining the control of himself. Yet, if at any point, actual possession occurs, impersonation ceases, the masker transforms from an actor to a medium. It should be stressed, though, that the transition, in this case, is from impersonation to possession and not from ordinary dancing to possession or from normal personality to mediumship as in the *bori* or *orukoro*.

Thus, the *owu* maskers in the performances just described are impersonators, maintaining dual personalities, imitating the "powerful and ruthless" characters' physiologies through their costumes, which are so elaborate that Horton describes them as *Wburdenw* into which the masker slowly "vanishes" (97); their sociologies through the reenactment of interpersonal relations and actions; and their psychologies through the remanifestation of their drives and temperaments.

Apparently, there is a sense in which the nature, aesthetic function, and context of a performance may be indicative of the possible occurrence of impersonation. For example, while the *bori* and the *orukoro* are essentially ritualistic—the former is "primarily concerned with the healing and prevention of illness, but also more generally with [foretelling] good and bad luck" (Horn 1981 186); the latter is "essentially a performance of worship," which also leads to prophesying "with the voice of the god or goddess" (Adelugba 1981 209, 211)—the *owu* is essentially aesthetic, its immediate context being that of "game" and "play," and its essential function being to entertain and to edify man. Thus, while communication in the *bori* and *orukoro* is between god and man, in the *owu* it is between man and man. The three forms are ritual, but *owu* is ritual and drama at once.

Let us now examine some African festival performances. Though a number of ritual performances, such as the *owu*, are events in the African festival and may also be called African festival performances, a majority of them, for example the *bori* and the *orukoro,* are often scheduled outside of the festival at the discretion of the cult or sect that "owns" them. Most traditional African festivals take place once a year, and performances, which conventionally occur in them before an indiscriminate audience, are our concern here. Those other performances, which take place under the cover of night and/or are a taboo to the public audience cannot really be regarded as theatrical in intent: they are often more deeply ritualistic and cultic than the *bori* and the *orukoro* and their methods are often gruesome and diabolical. Anyone who set eyes on the rites of an *Ekpo* mask of the Efik/Ibibio in a night outing, for example, was sure to be pursued and slaughtered (Enekwe 1987 63). The *Egungun* and the *Gelede* societies of the Yoruba also have ritualistic performances at night, which are out of bounds to the public (Beier 1967 243–244).

Examples of public festival performances, which we shall examine here, are the *Osun* of Owu/Ijebu, *Ogun* of Ondo, *Agbegijo* of Dahomey, *Mmonwu* of the Igbo and *Ikaki* of the Kalabari.

The *Osun* performance takes place during the *Osun* festival of the Owu/Ijebu of Western Nigeria. It is an imitation of the capture of Olusen by Iganmigan, a dead ethnic [Yoruba] hero. This hero is imitated by chief Asipa, as the chief advances in dance to pay homage to the king, seated at one end of the arena.

As the Asipa dances on, he makes penetrating moves at the audience, butting in and withdrawing hastily as in a military encounter. . . . It is by far the most tense of the dances, thus showing the fierceness of battle. When the music changes again, . . . there is the relaxed feeling of success. (Ogunba 1978 14)

Olusen, Iganmigan's enemy, who later becomes his captive, is not bodily represented except vaguely by the audience. And there is no indication that Chief Asipa is costumed and made up to look like Iganmigan.

The *Ogun* of Ondo is similar to the *Osun* in some respects. The action imitated is a battle between Ogun, the war god, and an unnamed enemy. However, neither Ogun nor his enemy is represented by an individual: dancers in a procession represent Ogun while the spectators represent Ogun's enemy. As the dancers move along the route, they make "dashing, mock attacks at the audience with their swords, the latter receding good-humouredly and then coming forward again as the 'attacker' withdraws" (Ogunba 1978 21).

Again, it is not indicated that the dancers imitate Ogun's physiology. They are a guild of hunters, to whom Ogun is patron-god; on ceremonial occasions, they turn out in the guild's usual ceremonial dress.

The *Osun* and the *Ogun* contain dramatic action, a conflict developed in plotting or in characterization (Albright et al. 1968 22–24). Such a conflict normally presents the characters with various stimuli to which they respond, thus utilizing their physical endowments, confirming their sociology, and revealing their psychology. It also provides the impersonator with the opportunity to fully realize his art by roundly but consciously imitating the three dimensions of the character. In the *Osun* and the *Ogun,* the conflict is, however, not developed in that the protagonist, in each case, is not confronted with a contrarily motivated antagonist. The good-humoured "receding" and "coming forward" of the audience rather than a more realistic simulation of battle between two great warriors, reduces the battle to too easy a ride and denies the plot the essential elements of surprise and suspense, which are vital to plotting in the conventional theater.

But this is, perhaps, deliberate, for the faith of the owners of the festivals may be weakened by a narrow escape for their heroes. In their imagination, the conflict developed in waves toward a climax with the increasing intensity of the dance; the peak of the battle was the crescendo of the music. Most members of the audience are familiar with the details of the reenacted action, the violent boasts and altercation of the warriors, and will be satisfied with a symbolic and formalistic demonstration of the clash and its outcome by individuals (including the audience itself) playing their normal roles in the festival in their personal, ceremonial dresses. The bodily contact of two impersonators embroiled in combat is, therefore, superfluous. Hence impersonation in each of these performances is monodimensional, aimed only at the representation of aspects of the sociology of the hero, particularly, his status and action. The ultimate aim of impersonation here is not to lead to an understanding of the character or elicit empathy with him as in realistic drama, but to rekindle the people's awe of him, their devotion to or faith in him. The surest way to demystify a character is to make him understandable.

In several respects, the nature and function of impersonation in the *Osun* and *Ogun* are akin to those of performance art. Usually not based on a script, it has no "character," no "actors" in the conventional sense. It has only a "performer" and "performers are themselves, exist in real time, and perform or 'do' the various tasks or activities that the piece requires. Actors impersonate others, exist in stage time, and respond to their characters' inner psychological promptings" (Mehta 1990 189).Though Mehta warns that the difference between the performer and the actor is not absolute, since performers can "demonstrate character types in Brechtian fashion and sometimes also act illusionistically" (189), he stresses that, unlike the impersonator, the performer is not expected to present "a coherent personality developing consistently through time." Rather, he "may sketch out a social type inside an image and then vanish midsentence into another image" or return simply to "'himself' doing a task in real time" (190). Performers are, therefore, not disguised to look like the character.

Chief Asipa, the dancers in a procession representing *Ogun,* and others like them in several other African festival performances may be called performers, but it may be wrong to dissociate them from impersonation. It may be more correct to say that their impersonation is monodimensional but suited to the style of performance that they are engaged in, in which the performer, in his/her ceremonial attire, basically dances as himself/herself, performing his/her ceremonial duty in real time while sporadically or, at some point in the dance, imitating symbolically but with all solemnity a mythic or historical personage in action. The impersonation covers only the sociology of the personage — particularly his/her action. There is no necessity to imitate his/her physiology and psychology or to represent the actual number of persons involved in the original action.

A performance of the *Agbegijo*, an outfit of the *Egungun* cult of Dahomey (West Africa), exemplifies a two-dimensional impersonation. In it:

The masks imitate leopards, monkeys, crocodiles, snakes, tortoises and other animals. Each animal has to act his part: the monkey scratches; the leopard climbs on the roof of a house and pounces down on a chicken. Often there is a whole scene between a hunter and a leopard. Others imitate people. These may be funny because of abnormal features. They make fun of ethnic groups; the Hausa man, the Fulani woman, the Dahomey warrior. One of the most amusing masks is usually the European. They wear masks with long pointed noses, their smooth black hair is made from a Colobus monkey skin. They walk around, stiffly shake hands and say "Howdoyoudo." (Beier 1967 224)

Generally, a headpiece appropriately carved, an appropriate animal skin, beak, horn or any other appropriate item of costume is used to represent animals. Each ethnic group or race or calling is represented in its traditional attire and with an item or items usually associated with it or with a mask depicting the peculiar facial features of its members. In addition to these, mannerisms of each group are also imitated in the performance just described. There is no conflict, unless one considers the hunter and the leopard as a protagonist and an antagonist. Even then, such a conflict would provide no prospects for character growth. Characters are also not individuated. If, for example, all monkeys scratch, then scratching is insufficient to delineate a particular monkey. And do not all colonialists on official business "walk around, stiffly shake hands and say 'Howdoyoudo' "? There is, therefore, no attempt to probe any individual's or group's psychology. Impersonation in the performance is, therefore, only of physiology and sociology. But it is also generic, superficial, and light-hearted, intended to generate, not awe or empathy, but laughter.

The same objective and style are patent in a performance of the *Mau* (actually *Mmonwu*) of the Igbo, described by G.I. Jones, even though, in it, there is an attempt at tridimensional impersonation:

A white-faced mask with a calvary moustache wearing white ducks and spotless sun-helmet, stalks into the arena and casts a supercilious eye over the scene. The play stops, the mask languidly signals them to proceed and strolls over to sit among the audience in the seat of honour. This character is Oyibo the White Man. (qtd. in Finnegan 1970 511)

The physiological elements—"calvary moustache," "white ducks and spotless sun-helmet"—foreshadow the foppery and supercilious behavior of a colonial master in the mood for relaxation. The action of the character substantiates this foreshadowing. His signal for the play to proceed is languid because of his low opinion of "savage" entertainment; he strolls in order not to ruffle his dignity and gorgeousness; he takes "the seat of honor" without being ushered to it because, among the natives, he claims honor as of right. His preeminence and action are his sociology; his superiority complex is his psychology.

In spite of his tridimensionality, however, the white man is flat. There is no conflict for him to grow in. Therefore, we cannot know the depth of his psychology. Only his frivolous actions are parodied, as in the *Agbegijo* performance. These contrast with the grave actions that the characters in the *Osun* and *Ogun* performances are engaged in, actions upon which the continued existence of the performing communities once hung. To the *Osun* performers, Iganmigan is an illustrious ancestor, hero, and savior; to the *Ogun* performers, *Ogun* is a god. But the white man, the monkey, and the other characters in the *Agbegijo* and the *Mmonwu* performances are of no such importance to the *Agbegijo* and *Mmonwu* dramaturgy and performers. Expectedly, they are treated without awe and solemnity.

Thus, the value of the character and the nature of its action determines the kind and function of characterization and impersonation. Superficial and caricaturish characterization and impersonation are required in the *Agbegijo* and *Mmonwu* performances because they are closely related to farce, which "aims at producing laughter by exaggerated effects of various kinds and is without psychological depth. Characterization and wit are less important than a rapid succession of amusing situations. . . . Probability is not much regarded" (Boulton 1960 153).

For our final example, we return to the Ekine society of the Kalabari. It stages the *Ikaki* masquerade, which reenacts relatively long stories, elicits empathy, and makes a moral statement. Although, like many other African masquerades, the myth behind it is not reenacted, the *Ikaki* masquerade reenacts imaginative stories based on the essence of *Ikaki* (Tortoise), the central, deadly figure in the avoided myth. Horton relates the avoided myth (1981b 481–482). He also describes the *Ikaki* masquerade performance, which lasts for two days and comprises six scenes. Four of the scenes are enacted on the first day, with a lunch break after the first two. The fifth and sixth scenes are enacted in the afternoon of the following day. For convenience, we shall identify the scenes as: 1. the conflict-on-the-sea scene; 2. the fake-loan-recovery scene; 3. the looting scene; 4. the scene of the arrival of Aboita (Ikaki's wife) and Kalagidi (Ikaki's favorite son); 5. the palm-tree-climbing scene; 6. and the elephant-hunting scene. A story is enacted in each of the scenes, except scene four, which is mainly one of dance and mime. There are four major actors and one major "actress" in the performance and they represent Ikaki (Tortoise), Nimite Poku (his "Know-All" son), Nimiaa Poku (his "Know-Nothing" son), Kalagidi (his favorite son), and Aboita (his flirtatious wife, actually played by a man). Horton's description of the performance of the scenes fills nine pages of a book and cannot be reproduced here. But its highlights shall unfold as we examine the nature of impersonation in it.

Let us begin, then, with the physiological elements. Of the five major players, only Aboita's physical appearance is not explicitly described, but it is suggested by the adjectives, "silly" and "flirtatious," by which Aboita is repeatedly qualified:

Ikaki himself, though fairly simply dressed, is readily recognizable by his hunchback and by the schematized tortoise body which is his headpiece. . . . Nimite Poku [is] dressed mainly in a soiled blue and white sheet topped with an old felt hat. . . . Nimiaa Poku [is] dressed if anything more shabbily than his brother. (1981b 483–484.)

Ikaki is also said to be suffering from "elephantiasis of the scrotum—a disease usually regarded as a mark of an evil life" and his "enormous testicles" are represented by a "wooden slit-gong" (490). Of course, each of the major players wears an appropriate headpiece constructed by specialist-members of the *ekine* society. These physiological elements disguise the players and clearly distinguish one from another.

The plot is long enough to depict the characters' sociologies and psychologies as well as whether each is round or flat. At every stage of the performance, a particular emotional attitude toward a character is evoked in the spectator. We are anxious for Ikaki and Nimite Poku in scene one, when Ikaki's boat is almost capsized through the negative action of Nimiaa Poku; we laugh Ikaki to scorn when, in scene two, he is unable to swindle money off the spectators by claiming, falsely, that their freshly deceased father owed him a large sum of money; we dislike him for tricking the animals and looting their food in scene three, and so on. At the climax of the story in scene five, the palm-tree-climbing scene, the spectators' earlier emotional whiffs are distilled into a profound feeling:

But whilst Ikaki is at the top of the tree, blissfully praising himself and extolling the virtues of palm-fruits, . . . Nimiaa Poku has got hold of an axe, and is amusing himself by trying to cut the tree down. Aboita, silly as ever, is flirting with the *ekine* people, and so doesn't see what her son is up to. Kalagidi makes one or two attempts to stop Nimiaa Poku but without effect. At last Ikaki looks down and sees what is happening. With an alarmed shriek, he throws his palm-cutting instrument at Nimiaa Poku. But it misses Nimiaa Poku and knocks out his beloved Kalagidi. Ikaki is beside himself. He says he will never come down again.

He will hang himself in the tree. [He wails in song for his favourite son.] While Ikaki wails at the top of the tree, Nimiaa Poku rejoices at his escape and dances happily about below. The feckless Aboita . . . joins him in the dance. Ikaki looks down, sees both his son and wife rejoicing in the midst of his misfortune, and redoubles his threats to hang himself. (Horton 1981b 489)

In spite of our earlier emotions of scorn and dislike for Ikaki, we can hardly fail to empathize with him here. His motivation for climbing the palm tree is to exhibit a positive character trait, which we could have sworn he did not possess. He climbs the palm tree, not only to show that he can perform the feat of climbing it, but also to work for his own food and wine in contrast to his usual habit, already dramatized, of swindling or looting other people's possessions. Our empathy derives partly from our understanding that, having earlier (in scene one) attempted to drown Ikaki, Nimiaa Poku deserves a punishment for his latest attempt at patricide and partly from the message of the play, which is apparent at this point: Repentance of one's evil ways and/or the doing of good is no guarantee for a life without pains. And Ikaki's pains, in this case, are compounded by his rash reaction to Nimiaa Poku's attempt to fell the palm tree. The palm-cutting-instrument, which he throws at Nimiaa Poku, can kill rather than correct an erring son, and the ironic twist of the instrument missing its target and knocking out Ikaki's beloved Kalagidi is designed to teach temperance even in the face of gross provocation.

All this sounds somewhat like the hermeneutics of Aristotelian drama, complete with its plot of a certain magnitude, arousal, and eventual purgation of fear and pity, clear and full delineation of character, definite structure of conflict development and resolution. Hence impersonation in the *Ikaki* is similar to that in formalistic drama—largely realistic and three-dimensional but with only essential details; deeply psychological, thereby accentuating individuation, yet allowing for the wearing of masks, necessary to create aesthetic distance and universality.

In all, our findings may be graphically represented in Tables 11.1 and 11. 2.

Using impersonation as our parameter for drama, we thus eliminate the *bori* and the *orukoro,* both spirit-mediumships. By the same token, we eliminate all other African performances that "use" art but in which the performer is entranced or possessed beyond physical, emotional, and intellectual control. But the other performances may be drama of the kind shown in Table 11.1. Though many of them may occur as part of a festival, often lasting several days and serving, primarily, a religious or ritualistic end, the microcosmic context of each within the festival is that of relaxation in the same way as the drama competitions of the fifth century B.C. took place in a special artistic context within the overall ritualistic context of the City Dionysia (Gassner 1967 5). It should be stressed that by relating the traditional performances to approximate Western theater forms, we are not trying to legitimize the latter with the former. Performance art, which emerged in the Euro-American theater in the 1960s, for example, could not be used to legitimize the *Osun* and *Ogun* performances, which have existed for centuries. We have named approximate western theater equivalents with the hope that knowledge of them may aid some

**Table 11.1**
**Kinds of Impersonation in African Ritual and Festival Performances**

| Performance | Kind of Performance | Kind of Impersonation |
|---|---|---|
| *Bori* of Hausa | Ritual | None |
| *Orukoro* of Kalabari | Ritual | None |
| *Osun* of Owu/Ijebu | Festival | Monodimensional |
| *Ogun* of Ondo | Festival | Monodimensional |
| *Agbegijo* of Dahomey | Festival-Masquerade | Two-dimensional |
| *Mmonwu* of Igbo | Festival-Masquerade | Three-dimensional |
| *Ikaki* of Kalabari | Festival-Masquerade | Three-dimensional |
| *Owu* of Kalabari | Ritual-Masquerade | Three-dimensional |

**Table 11. 2**
**Approximate Equivalent of Western Theater**

| Performance | Western Theater Equivalent |
|---|---|
| *Bori* of Hausa | None |
| *Orukoro* of Kalabari | None |
| *Osun* of Owu/Ijebu | Performance Art |
| *Ogun* of Ondo | Performance Art |
| *Agbegijo* of Dahomey | Superficial/Caricature |
| *Mmonwu* of Igbo | Superficial/Caricature |
| *Ikaki* of Kalabari | Realistic/Formalistic |
| *Owu* of Kalabari | Realistic/Formalistic |

readers to better understand African theater performances that relate to them. As we have seen in Table 11.1, the more ritualistic the ritual or festival performance, the more profound and comprehensive the impersonation in it. The performances in which two-dimensional impersonation occurs are farcical; while those in which three dimensional impersonation occurs may be either farcical or formalistic, depending on the depths of the psychological representations. Thus, while the occurrence or absence of impersonation in an African ritual or festival performance is useful in determining whether that performance is drama or not, the kind of impersonation suggests the style or kind of drama.

## WORKS CITED

Adedeji, J.A. "Oral Tradition and Contemporary Theatre in Nigeria." *Research in African Literatures* 2.2 (Fall 1971).

Adelugba, Dapo. "Trance and Theatre: The Nigerian Experience." *Drama and Theatre in Nigeria: A Critical Source Book Yemi.* Ed. Ogunbiyi ed. Lagos: Nigeria Magazine, 1981: 203–218.

Albright, H.D., W.P. Halstead, and L. Mitchell. *Principles of Theatre Art.* 2nd ed. Boston: Houghton Mifflin Company, 1968.

Beier, Ulli. "Yoruba Theatre." *Introduction to African Literature.* London: Longman, 1967.

Boulton, Marjorie. *The Anatomy of Drama.* London: Routledge and Kegan Paul, 1960.

De Graft, J.C. "Roots in African Drama and Theatre." *African Literature Today* 8 (1976).

Egri, Lajos. *The Art of Dramatic Writing.* New York: Simon and Schuster, 1960.

Enekwe, O.O. I*gbo Masks: The Oneness of Ritual and Theatre.* Lagos: Nigeria Magazine, 1987.

Finnegan, Ruth. *Oral Literature in Africa.* Nairobi: Oxford University Press, 1970.

Gassner, John, ed. *A Treasury of the Theatre.* Vol 1. New York: Simon and Schuster, 1967.

Horn, Andrew. "Ritual Drama and the Theatrical: The Case of Bori Spirit Mediumship." *Drama and Theatre in Nigeria: A Critical Source Book.* Ed. Yemi Ogunbiyi. Lagos: Nigeria Magazine, 1981: 181–202.

Horton, Robin. "The Gods as Guests: An Aspect of Kalabari Religious Life." *Drama and Theatre in Nigeria: A Critical Source Book.* Ed. Yemi Ogunbiyi. Lagos: Nigeria Magazine, 1981a: 81–112.

——— . "*Ikaki:* the Tortoise Masquerade." *Drama and Theatre in Nigeria: A Critical Source Book.* Ed. Yemi Ogunbiyi. Lagos: Nigeria Magazine, 1981b: 481–494.

Mehta, Xerxes. "Performance Art: Problems of Description and Evaluation." *Journal of Dramatic Theory and Criticism* 5.1 (Fall 1990).

Ogunba, Oyin. "Traditional African Festival Drama." *Theatre in Africa.* Eds. Oyin Ogunba and Abiola Irele. Ibadan: Ibadan University Press, 1978.

——— . "Traditional Content of the Plays of Wole Soyinka." *African Literature Today* 4 (1970).

Ogunbiyi, Yemi, ed. *Drama and Theatre in Nigeria: A Critical Source Book.* Lagos: Nigeria Magazine, 1981.

Okpewho, Isidore. *Myth in Africa.* Cambridge: Cambridge University Press, 1983.

Schechner, R. *Performance Theory.* New York: Routledge, 1988.

Stanislavsky, Konstantin. *Stanislavsky and the Art of the Stage.* Trans. David Magan. London: Faber and Faber, 1967.

Chapter Twelve

# Exile and Home: Africa in Caribbean Theater

*Osita Okagbue*

## CHILDREN OF SLAVES

West Indian society is a peculiar society because of its very peculiar historical origin. The society as we know it today came into being in the service of Western European plantation capitalism. The autochthonous American Indian population was almost wiped out because of its unwillingness to serve Western European capital, and so a labor vacuum was created in the plantation economy that had to be filled. Slavery provided the cheap labor force that the plantations needed in order to become hugely profitable, and so began the infamous slave trade across the Atlantic, which over a prolonged period forcibly transported an estimated five million Africans across the middle passage to begin the harsh and inhuman life as plantation and house slaves in the West Indies and the two Americas. One can see, therefore, that West Indian society is a transplanted one and has remained a cultural/racial melting pot all through the centuries.

Life in the plantations was from all accounts harsh and inhospitable, but for the unfortunate African slaves, it was one long nightmare. Essentially, therefore, and of more relevance to the argument of this chapter is the fact that West Indian society is one that today still bears the scars that the slave experience inflicted on the minds of both the slaves and their descendants. The psychic injury of slavery over the years manifests itself in various forms of alienation, and these have become the central concerns of much Caribbean literature and theater. A persistent quest for identity, a feeling of being perpetual exiles, plus an ever present desire to migrate: these are the facts of life in the West Indies, facts that poet-playwright, Derek Walcott, has in mind when he says:

The West Indian mind historically hung-over, exhausted, prefers to take its revenge in nostalgia, to narrow its eyelids in a schizophrenic daydream of an Eden that existed before its exile. Its fixation is for the breasts of a nourishing mother. . . . Slaves, the children of slaves, colonials, then pathetic, unpunctual nationalists . . . we have not wholly sunk into our own landscapes, as one gets the feeling at funerals that our bodies make only light, unlasting impressions on our earth. . . . The sprout casually stuck in the soil. The depth of being rooted is related to the shallowness of racial despair. The migratory West Indian feels rootless on his own earth, chafing at its beaches. (1972 19–21)

In the quoted passage, Walcott asserts the existential paradox of the African Caribbean man: the classic dilemma and tension arising from, and between, the need to search for roots, and the desire to escape alienation of exile through migration.

On the whole, one notices that wherever they are, and in whatever circumstance they find themselves, the children of Africa, dispersed throughout the Caribbean and American diaspora, have always retained a deep and very strong psychic connection with mother Africa. This is the thesis that Emmanuel Obiechina eloquently articulates in his incisive study of the slave narratives of Olauda Equiano, Ottobah Cugoano, Ayuba Suleiman Diallo, Abu Bakir al-Saddiq, Ali Eisami Gazirmabe, Omar Ibn Said, Salih Bilali, Ukawsaw Gronniosaw, and Ignatius Sancho. Of these narratives, he writes:

Africa was a vibrant reality in the soul of her expatriate children during the era of the slave trade, a source of sensations in which memory was indistinguishably mixed with anguish. From the testimony contained in the narratives . . . it is clear that the natal home remained deeply etched in the consciousness, not only as something of pure pleasure and joy, but as part of themselves, a part of their emotional and spiritual existence without which their integrity as human beings would have simply disappeared. (1986 101)

It is against this theoretical backdrop that one can begin to appreciate the psychic as well as transitional pressures that feature so prominently in Caribbean literature and theater, especially those impulses and agitations that the characters experience in their quest for an understanding of both the self and society. It is my intention in this chapter to extend Obiechina's thesis by suggesting that the undying memory and presence of Africa in the consciousness of her children in the diaspora is responsible for the persistent feeling of exile and rootlessness of the African Caribbean, and that it is a feeling that, very often, is matched by a nostalgic longing to return home to mother Africa, that "lost paradise" before the misery and emasculating experience of the "middle passage" and slavery. This is more so in the West Indies and is powerfully reflected in the literature and theater of West Indians of African descent. For the purpose of the present analysis, I will focus on the plays of Derek Walcott, and specifically on *Dream on Monkey Mountain* and *O Babylon!*, two plays that, for me, best illustrate alienation and existential anomie within the context of black life and experience in the Caribbean racial and social melting pot. However, I hope to make occasional references to other plays like

Dennis Scott's *An Echo in the Bone* and Edgar White's *Redemption Song*. These are plays that also deal with these essential dilemmas and with the anguish of being black and poor in the West Indies.

## EXILE AND ALIENATION IN CARIBBEAN THEATER

The theme of home and exile is a prevalent one in the literature and theater of the West Indies because, as I indicated, it is unavoidably part of life and living in the Caribbean. Of the corpus of West Indian plays, the three that typically reflect the feeling of alienation and a sense of being exiles and outsiders in West Indian society are Walcott's *Dream on Monkey Mountain*, *O Babylon!*, and White's *Redemption Song*. White's play deals with alienation and exile of a different nature. Legion, its central character, pushed by poverty and desperation at home, migrates to England where he encounters greater hardship, racism and, finally, the ultimate humiliation of imprisonment. He decides to return to Redemption City to take up his paltry inheritance. But sadly, he can no longer feel at home in his island community and so he becomes an outsider who, having experienced two exiles, feels at home in neither. His alienation can end only in one way, death; and appropriately he is stoned to death by his rival Fowler and his policeman son, Simon. Legion's tragedy is that, unlike Makak, he does not have any other home away from Redemption City, nor does Africa provide him with a spiritual home to which he can escape in order to recharge his psychic battery. And so he is a doomed man who only tries to escape his shadow but tragically fails in the end.

But the Walcott plays, and to some extent Scott's, fundamentally link this feeling of rootlessness and outsideness to an underlying feeling for *Africa-as-home,* and besides, the three express this feeling and desire at two very distinct levels: that of the personal in *Dream* and that of the collective in *O Babylon!* and *An Echo.* Indeed, *Dream* has been described as a play that:

identifies the fantasies about whiteness and ancestral connections with Africa as the major fantasies that preoccupy, confuse and shape the psyche of West Indian man. [Its] central character is caught between the two fantasies. His vision of himself as a descendant of African kings and as a revolutionary saviour of his tribe is ironically inspired by a white blonde goddess, symbol of that very whiteness that is the anti-thesis of his ordinary perception of himself as black, ugly and undesirable. (Dabydeen and Wilson-Tagoe 1988 35)

As I have pointed out elsewhere (1990a 37), Caribbean playwrights focus on the Caribbean blackman now; they are interested in his world, his life, his values, but above all, in his psychic alienation in the present. Like very many Caribbean plays, *Dream* is a quest that involves a journey into the self, an examination of an individual consciousness in order to discover the alienation that is believed can be found in the past, but that, by and large, affects life in the present. It is a journey to the center of self in order to resolve an individual as well as a collective psychic dissociation. Makak, the central character, has an identity crisis born of his racially induced feeling of inferiority. And because he sees himself as "this old man walking, ugly as sin," he opts for a reclusive life in his lonely mountain hut where he dare not look at himself in the mirror or at any reflection of himself. But structurally, the play is "a rite of passage as well as a pilgrimage for Makak and his traveling companions who go in search of their individual and collective identities as Black people in the West Indies" (1990b 16). It is significant that the entire action, like the dream that it is, takes place in Makak's mind. The other characters are mere figments of his tortured imagination, the "bananas of his mind" who, in the end, become externalized symbols that represent the contradictory aspects of his schizoid personality. So it is possible to see the play as an elaborate and intricate ritual designed to purge and/or harmonize those warring aspects of a complex individual so that he can overcome his alienation.

Makak is black, considers himself ugly and undesirable because of that, and so turns himself into a recluse seeking isolation and refuge behind the mists of Monkey Mountain. He finds neither a place for, nor an acceptance of, himself in his West Indian society because deep down he sees himself as an African, whose rightful home is in this idealized African arcadia where he was a king or descendant of kings before his forced exile. This is basically the subject of his dream, which he dramatizes with the help of his cellmates and the mulatto police corporal, Lestrade. The scene in the forest/Africa is used to recollect and reflect Makak's past greatness and ancestry, a greatness that he needs to relive periodically in order to overcome his alienation and feeling of inferiority. The scene is redolent with accounts of his great deeds and eloquent passages of praise poetry. Makak is "King of Limpopo, eye of Zambezi, blazing spear. . . . Who has bundled the tribes like broken sticks" (308–309).

This is almost an apotheosis of the "ugly" Makak whose humanity can only be realized in or validated by his African homeland. That is, the dream or the reality of Africa provides Makak with the humanity that he lacks in the West Indies, a humanity that alone can make life worth living. And until that happens, he must remain the reclusive exile and outsider in his West Indian home.

The second play, *O Babylon!*, deals with a group of slum dwellers on the outskirts of Jamaica, who, because of the extremely poor and dehumanizing conditions of their island home, find no love, no peace, nor any meaningful life. The unjust social structure that is a legacy of slavery and colonialism consigns them to the periphery of society where they've become social lepers who idly nurse their vain dream of a mass return to Africa with the emperor-god, Haile Selassie. The play is actually preoccupied and set within a frame of the activities and anxieties surrounding the state visit of Selassie to Jamaica and the list being compiled of those who will qualify to accompany the emperor home. The major tension of the play arises from this and eventually explodes into a violent act of arson, when Aaron discovers that his name has been omitted from the list of the chosen ones. Aaron, an exconvict and hot-tempered petty criminal, sees the journey to Africa as his only hope of salvation and a meaningful life. Like Makak, it provides him with the only means of escape from the terrible prison of his skin color and race, and it is in the context of this that one can understand and sympathize with his despair and rage at being left out. Fed constantly on a dose of the Rastafarian doctrine of "peace and love" by their exconvict leader, Sufferer:

the Rasta commune in *O Babylon!* see themselves as children of Zion suffering bondage and exile while waiting on the outskirts of oppressive Babylon for the glorious dawn of repatriation to a deserved African paradise. They'll have nothing to do with their Jamaican home that they have judged and denounced in the hope of an Ethiopian utopia reserved for the chosen children of God. (Okagbue 1990b 15)

Theirs represents a kind of mass alienation, "a psychological state in which a group of individuals have become estranged from, or made unfriendly toward their society and the culture which it carries" (Nettler 157 672). It is their overwhelming sense of despair and exile that stokes their dream of migration and mass return to an African "homeland."

What one finds, therefore, in most West Indian literature and theater are characters who, because of centuries of oppression and humiliation in a racially unjust social order, feel like outsiders and aliens in their own Caribbean homes. For some of the characters, especially those who see their predicament and suffering mainly in economic terms, the overriding desire is to migrate to anywhere, but away from the islands. But for a great many, the Africa in the soul calls very strongly since it offers the only worthwhile antithesis to the racially determined social structure and the blatantly proEuropean images of their Caribbean society. For these, therefore, the idealized African home is the only place where a black man or woman can ever hope to walk tall and free. Romanticized and overly deodorized as this notion and image of Africa might be, it significantly has its uses for traumatized individual and communal psyches searching for the origin and meaning of self after so many years of dehumanization and cultural immolation.

## A RETURN TO EDEN, OR A LONGING FOR UTOPIA?

The idea of a physical return to Africa has always remained with her children from the moment of their capture and subsequent removal to the New World. Even on the slave ships and in the tribulations of the middle passage, Africa's slave children never gave up hope of one day seeing their home countries. This hope has survived in generations of slave children in North America and the Caribbean. In the past, there have been movements like the Marcus Garvey "back-to-Africa" or recolonization movement that conceived of a mass return of most peoples of African descent to Africa; there have also been individual odysseys and a long list of West Indians who have made cultural pilgrimages to Africa. Of these, some such as Dennis Williams, Jan Carew, Neville Dawes, the two Brathwaites from Barbados and British Guyana, and Patrick Wilmot have stayed and worked in different African countries, mainly Nigeria and Ghana. Wilmot actually became naturalized and taught in Nigeria for a long time before his deportation in the late 1980s. But for many, Africa is of the mind, and this explains the psychic nature and the psychological level at which Makak's journey in *Dream* and the collective trip of the wake-keepers in Scott's *An Echo* take place. Makak's Africa is of the soul, a home within which he visits in order to discover himself, and to which he drags his companions in order for them, too, to discover their origins.

For Walcott, the longing for and the acceptance of Africa as an ancestral home is useful because it provides the Caribbean black with a hope for an inner black "Atlantis buried in a sea of sand" and filled with vibrant communal archetypes and solid memories of race. The enduring image of the archetypal black slave being ground through the inhuman mill of plantation slavery is deeply etched in the unconsciousness of every child of the slave experience. And it is the confrontation with and acceptance of the communal ancestor that every Caribbean person must periodically make in order to come to a true and meaningful understanding of race and self in the seemingly harsh conditions of an unjust social order that slavery left behind in their West Indian island societies. And herein lies Walcott's differing attitude in his handling of the notion of Africa in his two plays.

In *Dream*, as in *An Echo*, Africa is a thing of the mind, and involves a psychic journey by the Black characters to an Africa that is at the center of the self. Makak undertakes this journey in his dream while being detained overnight in a police cell for unruly behavior. Scott's play deals similarly with this psychic journey into the beginnings of Caribbean history, that again leads inevitably to the period of slavery. As Walcott sees it, it is, indeed, a journey to the communal psyche, "For us in the archipelago the tribal memory is salted with the bitter memory of migration . . . the degraded arrival [that] must be seen as the beginning, not the end of our history" (40).

The Caribbean black is a product of the slave encounter between Africa and Europe and it is not surprising that inscribed in the unconscious of every Caribbean Black person is the painful memory of the middle passage, and so any movement into the self or into the communal past invariably ends at the navel point of this racial scar. Makak talks about the "belly of the boat" and the "sound of suffering;" while slavery and its consequences for the Caribbean Black provide the central dilemma and tensions of Scott's play. In effect, these plays use these gruesome memories of the past in order to put the present in proper perspective. For Makak, discovering and reclaiming his "kingly ancestry" is necessary before he can begin to rid himself of feelings of inferiority and a debilitating anti-black neurosis. And for the assembled Black congregation at Crew's funeral wake in *An Echo*, bringing up the painful details of slavery and the not very savory images of Africa of the past seems to me to be an attempt by Blacks to use them to enable the present generation to fully understand where and when the suffering began. Slavery, the plays suggest, was the genesis of Black misery in the Caribbean, and it is hoped that the resurrected slave scenes would help relieve some of the characters of their wild longing to go back to an Africa that has become hazy, and that, incidentally, had also contributed to their present predicament. This seems to be the central message of several

Caribbean plays; for whose writers, and for Walcott especially, the idea of a physical return to Africa is an unrealistic and impracticable dream.

This, perhaps, explains Walcott's anger, that is so evident in his depiction of the Rasta commune in *O Babylon!* For him, the longing represents an escapist utopian nostalgia for an African mother who would call all her children to her comforting bosom. It is an enervating dream that seems to paralyze the characters in the second play. Sufferer and his group idly sit on the edges of their Caribbean society with their dreamy semi-drugged eyes fixed on a perfect African homeland, while they do nothing to pull themselves out of the cycle of oppression in which their racial history has placed them, nor do they use their African inheritance as an anchor and a hammer to smash the Babylonian structure that keeps a majority of the children of African descent in perpetual penury. Walcott appropriately lambastes this escapist inertia that the Rastas constantly feed with dreams of a never-never escape to an idyllic Africa, an Africa whose outlines have since become blurred in their collective racial memory. Perhaps, for Walcott as well as for other Caribbean playwrights, such a psychic journey into the center of being as Makak embarks upon in *Dream,* or the one by the group in *An Echo* in their ritual of remembrance, such longing for and claim of Africa as home may well be in order, may, in fact, be necessary; but the hope of a physical return that the Rasta commune entertains is impossible and ultimately ineffectual as a means of dealing with the experiential dilemmas and anguish of Black life in the Caribbean. Walcott criticizes Sufferer and his doctrine of "peace and love" that prevents the rastas from rising as one in order to dismantle the structure of Babylon. He uses Mrs. Powers to denounce this drugged dream of Zion that constantly provides a protective cloak behind which they hide, and which keeps them from contributing toward the creation of a new Jerusalem for all, a new Jerusalem that will function as an antithesis to the present, racially oppressive regime of Babylon: "Mrs. Powers: It's time to cut the umbilical cord that joins them to Zion. . . . If they want to build Jerusalem, let them get off their arses and lift a bloody shovel" (262).

This represents a very clear articulation of the playwrights' attitude to the African factor in Caribbean consciousness. Africa must be acknowledged, for it is, without doubt, the ancestral homeland. Walcott himself in an interview in January 1989 acknowledges this ancestorship when he says that "life in this archipelago is a mirror of the one on the other side," and that the "interior rhythms" of black Caribbean people are reflections of the undeniable presence of African blood in the genes and an African cosmology that still influences life and living among black people in the diaspora.

## CONCLUSION

But having said that and by way of conclusion, there seems to be a general agreement by Caribbean writers that home is the Caribbean, and that Africa should remain a home of the mind that is necessary for making their geophysical home really home. The slave experience had all but wiped away the memory of history and race from the minds of the descendants of the unfortunate slaves. And to fashion out a new meaningful life and a new image of self in the land to which they have been uprooted and which they now must accept as home, the black children of slaves have to understand their history, their origins, the crossing that will forever remain the dominant image in the collective unconscious of Caribbean black people. Walcott's *Dream* is an examination of this essential dilemma and the anguish of being Black in the Caribbean for it is:

in part, about West Indian man's rejection of his home, and therefore of himself. It is about the psychology of mental and cultural emigration . . . the psychology of the Black bush recluse who is, in the play, a mental and cultural emigrant to an Africa of the mind. . . . Makak, crazed by loneliness, futility and longing for psychological status and self respect, makes a dream escape from the prison of his island and condition and emigrates to a dream Africa. (Hopkins 1977 79)

Walcott, and other West Indian writers as well, seem to be saying that it is essentially the urge to escape from their present harsh reality, to find an anchor and a new meaning in their lives, that make characters in Caribbean plays in their dreams or in moments of trance reach back to slavery and to an Africa only dimly remembered. And for the writers, these gruesome realities and moments have to be revisited and sometimes relived and understood to enable black West Indians to move forward in their present home. This is the resolution in *Dream*, where Makak, "within the dimension of reality," reemigrates to his Caribbean island home where he has been freed from his prison of complexes. It is also the outcome in *An Echo*, where the journey back to slavery of the mourners at the wake helps them to understand the tensions and festering communal rage that had pushed Crew to kill Charles, the white plantation owner.

A physical return to Africa, the central theme and guiding philosophy of the Rastafarian movement, is shown in *O Babylon!* to be a hopeless dream, a mere escape from reality. Africa, therefore, while it ought to remain in black Caribbean consciousness and dreams, must be acknowledged for what it *actually* is: a psychic/psychological root that goes deep and that acts as an anchor. But the Caribbean people must accept the Archipelago as their *actual* geosocial home, because it alone is the reality that they have, even though it is a home that has been fashioned out of elements from two former homes: Africa and Europe. For, as Louis James rightly points out, "whatever they found germane in Africa, few West Indians have found there a complete answer to their quest for identity. The facts of the middle passage across the Atlantic, the centuries in the Caribbean racial and social melting pot, and the different environment of the West Indies, form a gulf that cannot be recrossed" (7).

## WORKS CITED

Dabydeen, David and Nana Wilson-Tagoe. *A Reader's Guide to West Indian and Black Literature*. London: Hassib Publishing Limited, 1988.

Hopkins, Slade. "*Dream on Monkey Mountain* and the Popular Response." *Caribbean Quarterly* 23.2 (1977).

James, Louis. *The Islands in Between.* London: Oxford University Press, 1968.

Nettler, G. "A Measure of Alienation." *American Sociological Reviews* 22 (December 1957).

Obiechina, Emmanuel. "Africa in the Soul of Dispersed Children: West African Literature from the Era of the Slave Trade." *Nsukka Studies in African Literature* 4 (January 1986): 101–160.

Okagbue, Osy. "Aspects of African and Caribbean Theatre: A Comparative Study." Unpublished Ph.D. dissertation, University of Leeds, 1990a.

Okagbue, Osy. "Identity, Exile and Migration: the Dialectics of Content and Form in West Indian Theatre." *New Literatures Review* 19 (Summer South): 1990b.

Walcott, Derek. *Dream on Monkey Mountain and Other Plays.* London: Jonathan Cape, 1972.

———. *The Joker of Seville and O Babylon!: Two Plays.* London: Jonathan Cape, 1979.

———. "The Muse of History." *Critics on Caribbean Literature.* Ed. Edward Baugh. London: George Allen and Unwin, 1978.

———. Interview. "Profile of a West Indian Writer," *The South Bank Show* (15 January 1989).

# Chapter Thirteen

# One Year in the First Instance

*Biodun Jeyifo*

Does the university as a sensitive centre feel the existence of a rich literature in the local tradition? How is the sensitivity expressed? Is there any kind of cross-fertilization between the literary developments in the two sectors of literary experience? Is there a continuing dialogue, and how is the dialogue articulated? What kind of presence does Nsukka have in the literary artifacts that are fashioned in the University of Nigeria? Has the environment itself advanced or impeded the development of literature in the university?
—Emmanuel Obiechina, "Nsukka: Literature in an African Environment"

Wherever I am, there Germany is!
—Thomas Mann (qtd. in Brink 1983)

The uneasy ruminations that will be encountered in this chapter owe their inspiration to a short, highly, provocative article published by Emmanuel Obiechina in the journal *Liberal Education* in March–April 1992. Though the article represents a mere tip of the iceberg of Obiechina's productive and, in many ways, seminal career, it is, nevertheless, a uniquely appropriate general statement on which to base this contribution to a volume celebrating African literary scholarship, of which Obiechina himself is a luminary exemplar. This article, titled "The Dilemma of the African Intellectual in the Modern World," is, as far as I know, Obiechina's first major critical statement since his relocation from the University of Nigeria, Nsukka and theAfrican University system(s) to North America. Moreover, the article sharply reenacts what may be described as the strengths and weaknesses of the peculiar brand of proto-Fanonist theorizing on the important transformative historical and social significance of literature and the arts that we find in virtually all of

Obiechina' s books and essays. Rather imprecisely, I describe this proto-Fanonism as a canny, muscular but sensitive propensity for striking a moral high ground in defense of the African continent, its most vital indigenous traditions and, especially, the fate of its most marginalized and dispossessed groups and classes. But more on this point shortly.

This reenactment in this short article of many of the themes and propensities of Obiechina's works is expressed not only in the substantive issues that the article raises but also in the sweep of mind and spirit displayed within its very short, condensed discourse, and in the resonance and suppleness with which it negotiates, strengthens, and transmutes the underlying sentimentality of its informing rhetoric. This indeed, as I see it, stands as perhaps the mark of Obiechina's personal enunciative register, the quality that makes the power of his work and thought so much greater than the unyielding directness and clarity of much of his writing. For if it is the case that no homage to Obiechina would be complete, or even adequate, without due cognizance being given to his secure, immovable habitation in the house of clarity and directness, it must also be recognized that always, between and within and around the controlled, tidy motions of his prose is secreted intimations of a romantic intuition that meaning is often greater than the additive sum of the parts within the made-to-order lucidity of his writing.

In other words, at one level, perhaps the primary level, Obiechina is always at his most compelling in the issues that he raises, issues pertaining to the quality of life in Africa, and of Africans in the face of large historical experiences of trauma and transformation, stultification and possibility, and issues dealing with the response, through the imagination and the spirit, of both Africa's greatest writers and intellectuals and its teeming masses. However, at another level, these issues are compelling in Obiechina's works not only in their own right, and not only in their pellucid organization within a personal prose idiom that generally and rigorously eschews stylistic, metaphoric, and semantic self-indulgence, but also because the breadth of sympathies and sensibilities evoked often exceeds the confines and limits of his judicious, conscionable prose to hint at matters that may be merely implied but, nevertheless, achieve a fecundity in suggestiveness. This particular quality makes much of Obiechina's work highly susceptible to symptomatic reading, that mode of Marxist hermeneutics that seeks to uncover the inescapable perturbations of the social whole on the bits, pieces, and fragments of social reality that cannot "know" themselves as effects and consequences of the whole since this "whole" likewise cannot "know" itself as an efficient, systemic totality.

What follows in much of this chapter is an attempt at such a symptomatic reading of "The Dilemma of the African Intellectual in the Modern World." As I hope to demonstrate, this kind of reading is entirely consistent, on an ideological level, with an aspect of Obiechina's work that is much-heralded and much-acknowledged—but only with a deafening silence: the solid, left-identified, Fanonist proclivities that undergird the pan-Africanist rationalist-nationalist orthodoxy of the central ideas of his works.

It ought to be stated right away that it is not the strengths and weaknesses of what I describe here as the rationalist-nationalist orthodoxy of Obiechina's central ideas, as reformulated in "The Dilemma of the African Intellectual," that I wish to examine in this chapter. Rather, I am more interested in reading that article for its hints at other anxieties, other discontents. Nevertheless, it is useful to state what features constitute this orthodoxy. This has an inherent interest in itself; it also has the additional advantage of opening up for our scrutiny the considerable tension of this orthodoxy with Obiechina's Fanonist leanings as these are applied in "The Dilemma of the African Intellectual" to an indirect, sublated confrontation with the re(dis)location of African academics in North America that began as a steady stream in the early to mid-1980s.

One crucial nexus of closely connected themes and idiologemes revolves around Obiechina's conception of an ideal type of the modern African intellectual, with its roots in the eighteenth century, its valorization of the application of reason and intellect to the cause of African self-assertion in the face of historic Western denials, its seminal figures, and its classic texts and books in such disparate disciplines and genres as historiography, imaginative literature, ethnophilosophy, social theory, theology, and linguistics. Central to this composite nexus of ideas is the notion of the continuity of the tradition that has produced the ideal type of the modern African intellectual, and Obiechina does not hesitate to supply a galaxy of representative names and figures from the eighteenth century to the present: Olaudah Equiano, Edward Wilmot Blyden, James Africanus Beale Horton, Joseph Casely-Hayford, Reverend C.C. Reindorf, Reverend Samuel Johnson, Chiekh Anta Diop, K.O. Dike, J.F. Ade Ajayi, Adu Boahen, Frantz Fanon, Amilcar Cabral, Kwame Nkrumah; and writers like Chinua Achebe, Wole Soyinka, Christopher Okigbo, Ngugi wa Thiong'o, Leopold Sedar Senghor, Mariama Ba, Aminata Sow Fall, and Mongo Beti. (We can see parenthetically but suggestively, that though there are two women in this list, this "ideal type" of the African intellectual inscribes a national-masculine genealogy.) In our own day, according to Obiechina in this article, creative writers represent the most powerful and inspirational embodiment of the decisive elements that shape the formation of men and women who accede to the status of this ideal type of the modern African intellectual while, conversely, critics have strayed the furthest from these elements.

It is no doubt highly, and perhaps deliberately, provocative to suggest, as Obiechina does in this article, that creative writers stand at the top of his bricolage of the ideal modern African intellectual while critics and theorists lie prostrate at the bottom. If this contention does not exactly yield what is orthodox about Obiechina' s central ideas, the manner of its articulation provides a means of extrapolating this orthodoxy from his contentions in this article. The issue turns, at a general level, on writing, and at a more specific level, on writing (and thinking, and imagining, and theorizing) in the European languages of colonial derivation. In Obiechina's view, the best African writers are incomparably more authentically African while writing in European languages, while the critics and theorists consistently lose their African selves in these languages and their received intellectual systems. (Historicism is given a particularly caustic treatment by Obiechina in the article; he virtually assimilates it into Eurocentrism tout court, and locates the roots of both in the Enlightenment.) To argue this point, Obiechina deliberately makes more categorical a commonplace of conventional postcolonial African literary criticism, to wit the notion that the best of our writers successfully preserve an African resonance in the derived European linguistic medium. The corollary to this, mostly implied but, all the same, mooted by Obiechina, is that most of the African critics and theorists do not achieve this consummation. This widely believed but tactfully orthodox rubric of African literary-critical discourse Obiechina makes more categorical by infusing into it an idiosyncratic deployment of the term "double consciousness": "These writers are products of a double consciousness; in their works, African realities and experiences are competently assimilated to one or another European language. They are sufficiently in control of both their African realities and their European linguistic medium to make the language serve them by carrying their African experience with aesthetic elegance" (1992 20).

It is, I believe, important to grasp the essentials of Obiechina's special slant on the notion of "double consciousness" in his profile of the "ideal" modern African intellectual, since this is not only crucial for the way in which it throws considerable light on the tensions as well as productive contradictions in his positions, but also, in fact, runs counter to most "modernist" and dialectical accounts of the formation of intellectuals. Definitely, Obiechina's deployment of "double consciousness" runs counter to W.E.B Du Bois' insistence, in *The Souls of Black Folk* (1965), on a fundamental split in the very fabric of the "doubleness" theorized in the psyche or the "soul" of African-Americans. It also runs counter to the notion of a necessary "alienation," a historically grounded self-objectivization of the African intellectual from indigenous traditions as a precondition for effective confrontation with the challenging and reifying pressures of modernity that Abiola Irele advocates in his famous polemical work, *In Praise of Alienation* (1987). The very notion of a split, or a dissociation in consciousness or psyche, is for Obiechina the sign of a crippling cultural and psychological malaise:

This dilemma is sharpened by the African intellectuals' tendency to be both "self" and "other" simultaneously, to be subject as well as object in the same process. The lack of affectivity as a result of the intellectual's inadequate integration within the traditional world and its system of knowledge creates a serious crisis of confidence and renders intellectualism itself precarious. A state of intellectual schizophrenia results from inadequate induction into either or both traditions. The obverse is the African intellectual who is adequately formed in the African tradition before becoming the best interpreter of the African experience, culture, literature, religion and ethics, and philosophy and thought. The critical factor here is the degree of exposure to the African and Western traditions. (1992 18)

If "double consciousness" for Obiechina thus implies a rejection of the axiomatic alienation or self-division that most authoritative accounts of intellectuals and "intellectual labor" in capitalist societies elaborate, it is important to recognize that Obiechina is, indeed, in the company here of a whole tradition of cultural theorists of the ex-colonial, developing societies who enjoin on all "native" intellectuals who wish to be historically and politically relevant to "return to the source." This is a crucial element of Obiechina's notion of "double consciousness" and his peculiar articulation of this orthodox staple of cultural theories of Third World emancipation is worth noting. For Obiechina advocates not just equal integration of the African intellectual into the African and Western traditions, within this stipulation he inserts an insistence that the African intellectual be "adequately" formed in the indigenous African traditions before being inducted into the Western intellectual systems. It may be noted in passing that this particular insistence, stated with deliberate forcefulness and bluntness in the article under discussion, would effectively dele-gitimize the work of many Africanist scholars without any prior "adequate" grounding in African traditions before professional specialization in Africanist scholarship; this, indeed, would include quite a good number of African Africanists! Indeed, it could be fairly and convincingly argued that the passion and angst of "The Dilemma of the African Intellectual" derives from an unstated suspicion that most African Africanists of the younger generation, especially those located in the "metropole," in North American and European institutions and academies, increas-ingly fall within this particular form of total separation from, or grossly inadequate shaping within, indigenous African tradition and its foundations.

Two closely linked notions that are crucial elements of the rationalist-nationalist orthodoxy under scrutiny here are worth emphasizing at this point since we shall presently engage them more directly. These are the notion of an indigenous African intellectual tradition and its sources and institutional locations as well as its scions and exemplars, say the Dogon sage of Marcel Griaule's classic text, *Conversations with Ogotemmeli* (1965), and the notion of a putative continent-wide centeredness and unity of this tradition. Meanwhile, it is necessary to observe that Obiechina's insistence on a necessary foundational grounding of the "ideal" modern African intellectual in this African tradition also runs counter, in an apparently overstated fashion, to those currently influential Africanists in North America like Valentine Mudimbe and Anthony Appiah who, under the sign of one school of cognitive postmodernism or another, insist that no modern Africanist discourse, in any discipline and of any ideological expression (including Obiechina's own brand of vigorously nationalist orthodoxy!) is possible outside of a Western epistemological framework. Indeed, I believe the fire of Obiechina's nationalist orthodoxy is apparently directed at this particular formation of North American-based "postmod-ernist" Africanists in hortations like the following in "The Dilemma of the African Intellectual":

Fourth (dilemma) is the African intellectual's self-alienation that results from being educated in Western schools and inducted into the Western intellectual system. In adverse cases, this process alienates the intellectual from the indigenous tradition. *The African oral tradition is the encyclopedia of African values, attitudes, history and ethical models. The intellectual cannot be ignorant of it and remain seriously African.* Such ignorance places the intellectual outside the centre of "the order of knowledge," the delicate sensitivities that sharpen the individual's responses to the totality of a human system. Ultimately such alienation creates problems of vocalization, definition, and discourse when the African intellectual assumes the role of interpreter of the African way of life or relates African realities to the non-African world. (1982 18; my emphasis)

It will be readily observed in the foregoing quotation that Obiechina, in "The Dilemma of the African Intellectual," consistently writes of the African tradition in the singular: he writes of an encyclopedia, of a "center," and of the African "way." What needs to be observed concerning this point is that this centralizing, totalizing impulse is part of what makes the major ideas being extrapolated here orthodox and that this does not arise from a willful forgetting on Obiechina's part, either in this article or in his other works, of the diversities and heterogeneities of the historical experiences of the ethno-linguistic groups that make up the African peoples, or the considerable differences in the specific sociohistorical realities of the African nation-states. Indeed, as demonstrated in at least three of his works—*Culture, Tradition and Society in the West African Novel* (1975), the monograph *Literature for the Masses: An Analytical Study of Popular Pamphleteering in Nigeria* (1971), and some essays in *Language and Theme* (1990)—Obiechina is one of the foremost historical sociologists of modern African literature and he is particularly attentive to the multiple, contradictory, and contingent forces of capitalism and class formation, the rise of literacy, and the chaotic growth of urbanism as they impact on the institution of African literature. It is thus rather a matter of an ideological and metaphysical pan-Africanism, of a particular form of rationalization of indigenous African matrices and traditions, the kind at work in Soyinka's *Myth, Literature and the African World* (1976) and Ayi Kwei Armah's *Two Thousand Seasons* (1973) and *The Healers* (1979), that Obiechina insists that, behind and beyond the diversities and pluralisms of historical experience in Africa and attempts to conceptualize and codify it, there is a putative unity, a common ground, a mainstream, indeed, a center.

This center, though obviously metaphysical, is ideological to the extent that while it may be "imagined" and is in the process of being constructed or consolidated, the necessity for it, and its eventual consummation as a respected, useful, and widely deployed tradition are beyond question. Beyond question that is, except, according to Obiechina, for the growing ranks of African intellectuals who either have never been seriously invested in the construction of this tradition and its mainstream, or who, in fact, question its existence, even its possibility, while easily yielding to the Western Other's intellectual mainstream that is no less "imagined" though, apparently, more "real," more powerful, and hegemonic. Obiechina's harshest censure, as well as his most idealized ideological musings in "The Dilemma of the African Intellectual" coalesces around this particular issue:

African intellectuals have no centre yet from which to draw strength. Their would-be centre is in the thousands of dispersed villages where African masses are, where they subsist within the age-old cultures, where they experience a sense of community and the warmth of communal values, linking destinies and feeling one another's heartbeats. The new theories that currently are being promoted, aggressively and resonantly, are an extension of age-old Western individualism. The language is electrical and the conceptualization is magical, but it has with it the makings of hard liquor. It intoxicates and ultimately will overpower the weak. And Africa is in a weakened state now. In the absence of an intellectual mainstream, or the equivalent of an Eurocentrism, what protection has the continent from wayward theories? (1992 21)

Unquestionably, Obiechina in this particular tirade aligns himself with that movement of contemporary intellectual culture that has come to be known as "theory and its discontents," to the point of enacting that "movement's" charac- teristic double gesture of a violent disparagement of the de-centering poststructu- ralist, postmodernist theories and discourses while at the same time bearing witness to their dazzling appeal, their widespread influence, and their fashionableness. But it ought to be noted that Obiechina does this on his own peculiar terms. For him these theories and discourses, for all their devastating anti-foundationalist, de-cen- tering assaults on the mainstream of Western post-Enlightenment humanist thought, are part of this mainstream and serve basically the same historic function of that mainstream with regard to the rest of the world, the non-West:

The speed with which African critics absorb the new critical tools of the West does not augur well for the creation of an intellectual tradition in Africa. Europe already has a mainstream intellectual tradition, whatever the new movers may do or say. The Graeco-Roman-Judaeo- Christian tradition, alias Euro-American mainstream, remains as solid as ever. New move- ments will play about its margins but will not replace it.. The central dilemma remains how the African intellectual can get out of the Eurocentric shadow. The writers have managed somehow to do so. One hopes others will. (1992 21)

There is obviously much to say about these Obiechinian assertions and hortations on contemporary Euro-American theories, on the nature of intellectual legacies (as essentially asserting their effectivity and hegemonic power primarily as unified mainstreams), on the chasm between, on one hand, the achievements of African imaginative writers in the construction of an intellectual "mainstream" and, on the other hand, the massive failures and the vapidities of the critics. Some of these issues have indeed been joined and thrashed out in other contexts like Miller's (1972) and Soyinka's (1994). What I wish to address here is what I see as a reenactment in "The Dilemma of the African Intellectual," on another level and in a new context, of a basic tension that runs through all of Obiechina's writings between those aspects of his thought that apparently derive from a discriminating, relativizing historical sociology of art and culture and those that obviously flow from the totalizing, visionary, and partisan of the subaltern groups and classes in Africa. I wish to construct my discussion of this antinomy around a question posed by Obiechina in the article under discussion, a question the like of which is hardly ever posed in these days of a postcolonial "Afropessimism" and a postmodern, "post-marxist" celebration of an absolute lack of any guarantees in all ideological and political affiliations, a question that may indeed be regarded as quintessentially Obiechinian as is demonstrated in this quotation from the same essay:

Finally, there is the question of commitment. *Trapped within Euromodernist contexts and theories, the African intellectual frequently is dogged by the bogey of society's expectations.* African peoples emerging from colonial domination expect their intellectuals to be in the vanguard of those providing solutions to economic, social, and political problems; restoring their arts, cultures, histories, and traditions; and helping them to regain their confidence and respect in the world. These intellectuals also are expected to play important roles in interpreting Africa to the world. . . . In such cases, we may well ask: On whose side is the African intellectual? An honest worker in the service of people, society and culture or an indentured laborer in the vineyard of Westernism, of esotericism? A modern-day Rip van Winkle toiling assiduously in other people's farms while his own is overrun by weeds? (1992 19; my emphasis)

We can very well imagine that while most intellectuals in postcolonial Africa (and indeed in most of the postcolonial societies) would readily accept the intellectual tasks enumerated by Obiechina in this quotation as part of the composite agenda of reconstitution after historic colonialism, many would vigorously refuse to recognize themselves in the new forms of "indenture" and servitude drawn by Obiechina in this grim profile. Many would indeed ask: which particular phalanx of African intellectuals "feel trapped within Euro-modernist contexts and theories" and are "dogged" by the terrible unease of "toiling in other people' s farms while their own are overrun by weeds?" This question might indeed be raised to a level of generality that would apply to all postcolonial intellectuals wherever they may be plying their trade: Are we all, from Nsukka to Delhi, from Dakar to Ithaca, from Colombo to Cambridge, Massachusetts, and from Sydney, Australia to Berkeley, "trapped in Euro-modernist contexts and theories" as the new form of Western epistemological hegemony? Is this what Obiechina has in mind? Is this his take on Fredric Jameson's theory of postmodernism as not just one cognitive school and artistic period style out of the plethora of available contending schools and styles, but indeed the very cultural logic, the "cultural dominant" as he puts it, of a fully globalized transnational, late capitalism? (see Jameson 1991).

I would find it surprising if Obiechina were to agree unequivocally to the view of postmodernism as the "cultural dominant" of late capitalism that uniformly holds sway over all of us. I think Obiechina would be more likely to assert that different regions and nations and societies of the world live unequally and asymmetrically within the sway of postmodernism and its irruptions into both "high literariness" and the popular culture promoted globally through the electronic mass media. If this is the case, we would have to look elsewhere for where the shoes would fit so that those who do feel trapped within "Euro-modernist contexts and theories" would wear them willingly and fittingly (or rather, seek ways to replace them with more "befitting" ones). This means in effect that the eloquence and vehemence of "The Dilemma of the African Intellectual" derive from, and address a particular location where the metaphoric shoes would, so to speak, fit. This particular observation takes us right into the heart of the much-debated and unresolved disputes over the consequences of the ever-increasing number of leading African postcolonial intellectuals (of all disciplines but more notably in the human sciences) who are located in the universities and institutions of North America and Europe. I reveal no hidden secret when I say that Obiechina is a prominent figure within this general phenomenon; his presence in Geneva, New York, at the Hobart and William Smith Colleges "robs" the University of Nigeria at Nsukka of his towering, inspiring presence at that institution. [Professor Obiechina duly retired from Nsukka after his term as the Director of the Nigerian Universities Office in Washington, DC; Editor's note.]

I would argue that within the highly heterogeneous group of postcolonial intellectuals of a "metropolitan location," Obiechina speaks for only a fraction, for many do not feel themselves "trapped." And not all of these are of an extraction that can be easily and superciliously sneered at as fellow travelers of Vivek Dhareshwar's celebration of something he calls "immigritude" as the fundamental situation of the truly postcolonial intellectual at the present time. Most acknowledge dislocation and displacement, but many, indeed, feel some kind of "liberation" and tremendous ideological and intellectual empowerment in some of the very same "Euro-modernist wayward theories" that Obiechina so roundly excoriates. Most of these, one imagines, would find Obiechina's tirades simply passe, if not exactly philistine. Indeed, to postcolonial intellectuals of this particular theoretical orientation, nothing could possibly be more passe and self-deconstructing than declarations from Obiechina like the following: "African intellectuals have no centre yet from which to draw strength. Their would-be centre is in the thousands of dispersed villages where African masses are, where they subsist within the age-old cultures, where they experience a sense of community and the warmth of communal values, linking destinies and feeling one another's heartbeats" (1992 21).

By a kind of (deconstructive) reading of this passage, there is an all too apparent self-dissolution of his "identitarian" certitudes when Obiechina writes of a "would-be centre" that exists through "thousands of dispersed villages"; this bespeaks fragmentation and de-totalization rather than integration and centeredness. Extending the logic of this reading further, the projection of villages as the center of intellectual renewal seems benightedly escapist at the very historic moment when villages and rural populations in Africa are at the worst receiving end of the social and spiritual ravages wrought by the economic decline throughout the continent and much of the developing nations that began in the 1970s. This reading is indeed enhanced by Obiechina's infusion into his "villagization" of intellectual renewal in late twentieth century Africa of sentiments and images of organic communities and solidarities that are historically associated with a precapitalist "moral economy" that predates the worldwide generalization of commodity production, exchange value, and capitalist market mechanisms as the fundamental mediating forces of all human social and economic relationships and, as some theorists aver, even the deepest and most subliminal human desires and fantasies. Surely, of all places in a present-day devastated postcolonial Africa, Obiechina's native Nigeria would be hard put to provide a single example of a significant survival or residue of such a village "moral economy"! In light of this particular dismantling of the textual self-misrecognitions of Obiechina's village idyll, it is not putting the matter too strongly to read into these projective solecisms a flight into crypto-transcendental-ism as a means of overcoming personal and collective experiences of severe dislocation and a terrifying sense of the inexorable slipping away of the historic initiatives that, initially, independence from colonialism seemed to promise. This may be the reason why "The Dilemma of the African Intellectual" is dominated throughout by a tone of modulated lamentation that is rather rare in Obiechina's writings.

But this particular set of disconstructive readings cannot, should not, supply the last words on these troubled and troubling matters (Deconstruction, after all, does not accept the closure implied in "last words.") Great intellectual centers have been built and have prospered in villages, in rural outposts of the expanding megalopo-lises built by the architecture and social engineering of capitalist modernity. Villages and rural-agrarian redoubts, Marx's dictum on "rural idiocy" notwithstanding, have sometimes borne the weight of creative alternatives to, and centers of intellectual challenges to, the urban nightmares and dead ends of capitalist "modernization" in all the main stages of its historical unraveling. Some of these factors formed the basis of the spectacular successes of the land-grant universities and colleges in an earlier period of the history of the university idea in the United States. Indeed, the University of Nigeria at Nsukka was at its inception based on this model; the first epigraph to this chapter comes, indeed, from an earlier article of Obiechina's that contains an optimistic but sober and realistic exploration of this Nsukka ideal in the area of literature and the arts (Obiechina 1990). At a much more general historic, probably metaphysical level, Obiechina is certainly not the first, nor will he be the last, to suggest that Africa, and different regions of the developing world, and indeed planet earth itself, would do well to preserve a considerable degree of village life and its ethos and best traditions for the moral and spiritual renewal of the species.

It is instructive to speculate why basically the same sentiments, the same enthusiasms and hopes on such broad historical and cultural issues can generate such totally divergent textual inscriptions as between the disciplined optimism of Obiechina's earlier essay, "Nsukka: Literature in an African Environment" and the fretful, if eloquent jeremiads and improbable ante-capitalist (as distinct from anti- or non- or post-capitalist) prognostications of "The Dilemma of the African Intellectual." In concluding this chapter—which, for all its critical engagement with, is a sincere tribute to the unsurpassable and indubitably seminal example of Obiechina's work—I cannot go into all the possible ramifications of this question. One ramification that I will have to skip, regrettably, in the present context is the enormously significant and complex factor of the ever-deteriorating material and institutional environment for academics in Africa to obtain even the minimal requirements for both the practice of their profession at home (that includes the reproduction of the next generation of "homegrown" academics) and to connect with developments in other regions of the world of scholarly research and intellectual innovation. It is not too difficult to see that in an indirect way, Obiechina's 1992 essay, written and published in his North American "relocation,"is profoundly inflected by this factor, even though not a single word is expressed in the article about the material and institutional crises of African universities and the re(dis)location of leading academics in all disciplines. Rather than get deeply into this issue, I wish to focus in my concluding observations on that aspect of the matter that pertains not to the travails of the academic vocation on the continent itself at the present time, but to the condition of those who have "migrated," those who, like Obiechina, now live and "profess" in North American academies and institutions as probably the advance guard of a phenomenal "season of migration to the North" among professional African academics in the 1980s and 1990s.

I suggest that among this expanding, relocated and incompletely "diasporicized" academic community, Obiechina's 1992 article represents a first tentative, frank but rather awkward application of the proto-Fanonism of his earlier works, as evidenced by the 1978 essay, to the consequences and pressures of re(dis)location. By the classic terms of this proto-Fanonism, the intellectual and the community of which s/he considers her/himself an "organic" part live in the same place, geopolitically, and in terms of actively expressed moral-ideological solidarities. This point can be stated in much stronger terms: no physical or institutional dislocation can be deemed to rupture this conception and tradition of "belongingness" that is best encapsulated by a mixture of the phrase from Mira Nair's film *Mississippi Masala*, "home is where the heart is" and A. Sivanandan's more combative identification, "the heart is where the struggle is" (1990). In a different but quite apposite analogy, this tradition of the self-idealization of the intellectual's commitment to "community" is captured in the famous riposte of the then exiled Thomas Mann to the Nazis' takeover of Germany: "Wherever I am, there Germany is!" (qtd. in Brink 1993).

This kind of self-idealization that, I suggest, silently but powerfully underwrites Obiechina's "The Dilemma of the African Intellectual," is totally negated by the connotations of a canard that is currently circulating as part of the underground folklore of the growing community of Nigerian academics "relocating" in North American universities and colleges. As the story goes, upon being asked how long a first, probing study leave in a North American institution would last, the prompt, wryly self-deprecating and glib response is—one year, in the first instance! This "one year" is, of course, the regulation duration of an earned sabbatical, or an unpaid leave that, however, by unspoken acceptation, everyone expects will stretch into two, three, maybe five years and, if things really work out well, into a tenured appointment that would then be seen as a "deserved" mid- or late career achievement.

The flood of African academics migrating to the North American universities parallels similar "floods" from other parts of the world such as South and East Asia, Latin America, Eastern Europe, and even Western Europe; all seek, singly and collectively, to avail themselves of the considerably better institutional, financial, and research facilities that seem more assured in the United States (as the very epicenter of transnational capitalism), for the practice of the profession than in most of these other regions of the world. But African universities and African countries are worse served than other parts of the world by these academic "labor migrations" precisely because both university and nation-state in Africa have the least consolidation as viable historical entities relative to other parts of the world. Consequently African academics, I believe, are particularly prone to the negative and dispiriting feelings of rats abandoning sinking ships that this "flood" generates in most re(dis)located academics in North America. Thus, it seems that the canard of "one year—in the first instance!" connects with Freud's insights in *Jokes and Their Relationship to the Unconscious* on how certain species of the comic help to negotiate and make bearable extremely stressful or painful personal and group experiences. This suggests that the new, incompletely diasporicized community of re(dis)located African academics is beginning to acquire a collective unconscious in their North American location in conditions that are in certain respects "rehabilitative" and, in other respects profoundly stultifying. For this particular experience, Fanon's exhortations in *Black Skin, White Masks* on the nature of the "unconscious" are even more appropriate than Freud's: "In his [Jung's] view, in fact, the collective unconscious is bound up with the cerebral structure, the myths and archetypes are permanent engrams of the race. I hope I have shown that nothing of the sort is the case and that in fact the collective unconscious is *cultural*, which means acquired (1967 188; my emphasis).

It is, of course, too early to begin to map the contents and shapes of the newly "acquired" and growing collective unconscious of a community of academics that, as I have suggested, is still insufficiently diasporicized, still inchoate in the formation of critical self-awareness as a community. It is characteristic of Obiechina's work that his voice would be one of the very first to inaugurate this process, if only indirectly, in "The Dilemma of the African Intellectual." This, I think, explains the desperation, the directness, the bluntness even, with which in this article Obiechina attempts to restate the Fanonist tradition of scholarly commitment that has generally influenced his work and the works of many other prominent Third World postcolonial intellectuals of his generation. Most of the African and other Third World academics who are now located in North America are either increasingly indifferent to, or indeed actively waging textual battles of delegitimation against "commitment" as Fanon and Fanonists conceived of it in the twilight of colonialism and up to the first three decades of the postindependence period if we start with the independence of India in 1947. Achille Mbembe's *ex cathedra* assertions in his controversial article of 1992 (the same year that Obiechina published "The Dilemma of the African Intellectual,") "The Banality of Power and the Aesthetics of Vulgarity in the Postcolony," is characteristic of this latter group of textualist deconstructors of the Fanonist tradition of "commitment" among a new generation of Africanists based in North America:

The basic argument of this article is that, to account for both the imagery and efficacy of postcolonial relations of power, we must go beyond the binary categories used in standard interpretations of domination (resistance/passivity, subjection/autonomy, state/civil society, hegemony/counter hegemony, totalization/detotalization). These oppositions are unhelpful; rather, they cloud our understanding of postcolonial relations. The poverty of the hypotheses that guides a number of studies is, in this regard, telling in that the question posed by such research is limited to the problem of knowing whether the acts they describe and interpret are inscribed or not in a process of either resistance or accommodation to the established order; or "engagement" or "disengagement" with respect to the field of domination; or, more crudely, if such movements are "conservative" or "progressive." (3)

If Mbembe's exhortations and anathemas in this passage do not exactly seek to rise beyond good and evil, they certainly reflect the extreme relativism and the celebration of indeterminacy that characterize what I have elsewhere described as "the postmodern moment in Africanist scholarship," (1991) a moment that, I would suggest, Obiechina both intensely loathes and misrecognizes, at least as indicated in "The Dilemma of the African Intellectual." By this "postmodern moment" in Africanist scholarship is meant the decisive, if contradictory, influence on virtually all areas of Africanist scholarship, in the social sciences and the humanities, of both the methodologies and the idioms of poststructuralism and postmodernism as "cutting edge" disciplinary, textual and pedagogical practices and inscriptions. How is this inscribed in Africanist scholarship at the present time? I can only give rough approximations here: radical rejection of foundationalist representations of identity and community, with regard to Africa and the African diaspora; an emphasis on the "constructedness" or "inventedness" of all knowledges and modes of knowing that often entails violent belittlement of "traditional," "realist," or "dialectical" epistemologies; deconstructive dismantling or outright disavowal of all forms of totalizing, universalizing discourses and knowledges, with a corresponding shift to the microtextualities and micropolitics of local, specific, particular, and fragmentary knowledges. A recent brochure from Northwestern University's Institute for Advanced Study and Research in the African Humanities expresses this last point very well:

We are challenged to see how Africans work and rework routines and activities of everyday life through practices of representation. We are interested in how, within the lives of those we study, such representations are constructed and resisted and how they become commonsense knowledge. Africanists must test prevailing views that such "little practices of everyday life" are contained, and given shape and direction by global processes of colonialism alone. Africanists must examine how global processes and externalities, along with the dialectics of Africa and the West, fit among other forces, interests and experiences specific to individuals, small collectivities, sites and local contexts. ("Politics of Representation" 1992)

I would like to point out for especial notice here the way in which "global processes and externalities" are acknowledged, but only as one item in a field of heterogeneous, multiform articulations and identities. This dissolution of systemic processes into a play of diverse, heterogeneous, local and particular forces and representations in which no particular sites or forces are privileged is the mark of the extreme relativism and the ascendancy of epistemologies of dispersion that increasingly dominate Africanist scholarship, of the so-called "cutting edge" variety in North America today. Epistemologies of dispersion are of course as old as the beginning of mankind's systematization of knowledge and knowledge production into paradigms; what poststructuralism and postmodernism have done, as Jameson has suggested in a recent extended theoretical reflection, is to make these epistemologies the "cultural dominant" of late, postindustrial transnational capitalism.

I think Obiechina refuses to acknowledge this last point and therefore misrecognizes these epistemologies as just another variant of age-old Western inflation of individualism. Therefore, Obiechina loses sight of all of us, as part and parcel of the "dispersions" of late capitalism that these epistemologies, or the best expressions among them, are trying to make intelligible and commensurable. No particular area of the division of labor, and specifically, the internationalization or transnationalization of this, is as reflective of this "dispersion" as the world of professional academics. The long trend within late, transnational capitalism is for this new caste of "dispersed" academics not to "live in the same place" as its surrounding community and more to the point, to be "deterritorialized" even when they literally live in the same place with a community acknowledged as the complementary half of the traditional town-gown dialectic. Heroically, Obiechina rejects all this and even from the distance of a North American voluntary exile asks: "On whose side is the African intellectual?" The Dogon sage, Ogotemmeli, of Marcel Griaule's classic work, *Conversations with Ogotemmeli*, was perhaps more historically and institutionally placed to embody the organic solidarity between the intellectual and his/her community that Obiechina, in his constructions of an overly idealized imaginary of a centered modern African intellectualism, nostalgically yearns for. But needless to say, Ogotemmeli is not Abiola Irele, or Chikwenye Ogunyemi, or Emmanuel Obiechina himself; much has happened between the inception of colonial capitalism in French West Africa and the very last decades of this century, the period of an exceptional dispersal of African academics by transnational late capitalism into personal and collective experiences and encounters whose meanings they can as yet only very dimly fathom.

I mention Abiola Irele and Chikwenye Ogunyemi deliberately, for I could as well have mentioned many other prominent figures within the expanding community of relocated African academics in North America, say Isidore Okpewho, Abena Busia, Aliko Songolo, or Neil Lazarus. Abiola Irele and Chikwenye Ogunyemi serve merely metonymically as particularly trenchant critiques of Obiechina's totalizing nationalist discourse. Both of these scholars indeed share the deep awareness of a continental, racial destiny of Africa that marks Obiechina's nationalist orthodoxy, but both engage this orthodoxy at points of its ineffaceable fractures and gaps: Irele from the perspectives of a postindividualist interpellation of subjectivity and Ogunyemi from that of an excluded but reclaimed feminist subjectivity. Neither Irele nor Ogunyemi, I would imagine, would deny the need for "community," for the true inclusiveness of egalitarian social justice of Obiechina's vision.

But both would, again I expect, insist that discursive constructions of "community" must always be aware of the exclusions and elisions that always hover at the edge of such nationalist totalizing discourses. Only on the strength of such scruples, combined with a keen attentiveness to the dislocations endemic to late capitalism's transnationalization of (intellectual) labor, can the best of Obiechina's passionate plea for constructing true community between the intellectual and her/his community be realized.

## WORKS CITED

Appiah, Kwame Anthony. *In My Father's House: Africa in the Philosophy of Culture*. New York: Oxford University Press, 1992.

Armah, Ayi Kwei. *The Healers*. London: Heinemann, 1979.

———. *Two Thousand Seasons*. Nairobi: East African Publishing House, 1973.

Brink, Andre. *Writing in a State of Siege: Essays on Politics and Literature*. New York: Summit Books, 1983.

Cabral, Amilcar. *Unity and Struggle*. London: Heinemann, 1980.

Dhareshwar, Vivek (with James Clifford). *Traveling Theories, Traveling Theorists*. Santa Cruz: Center for Cultural Studies, 1989.

Du Bois, W.E.B. *The Souls of Black Folk*. New York: New American Library, 1965.

Fanon, Fratz. *Black Skin, White Masks*. New York: Grove Press, 1967.

———. *The Wretched of the Earth*. New York: Grove Press, 1968.

Freud, Sigmund. *Jokes and Their Relation to the Unconsciousness*. New York: Norton, 1963.

Griaule, Marcel. *Conversations with Ogotemmeli*. London: Oxford University Press, 1965.

Haraway, Donna. " 'Reading Buchi Emecheta': Contests for Women' s Experience in Women's Studies." *Inscriptions* 3–4 (1988).

Irele, Abiola. "African Letters: The Making of a Tradition." *Yale Journal of Criticism* V.1 (1991).

———. *In Praise of Alienation*. Privately published, 1987.

Jameson, Fredic. *Postmodernism; Or, The Cultural Logic of Late Capitalism*. Durham: Duke University Press, 1991.

Jeyifo, Biodun. "The Nature of Things: Arrested Decolonization and Critical Theory." *Research in African Literatures* XII.1 (Spring 1990): 33–48.

———. "Literary Theory and Theories of Decolonization." *Literary Theory and African Literature*. Eds. Josef Gugler, Hans-Jurgen Lusebrink, and Jurgen Martini. Hamburg: LIT Verlag, 1994.

———. "Africanist Scholarship and the Reconstruction of the Humanities Curriculum." Lecture. Ohio State University, Columbus, Ohio, 22 May 1991.

Macherey, Pierre. *A Theory of Literary Production*. London: Routledge, 1978.

Mbembe, Achille. "The Banality of Power and the Aesthetics of Vulgarity in the Postcolony." *Public Culture* IV.2 (Spring 1992).

Miller, J. Hillis. "Tradition and Difference." *Diacritics* (Winter 1972).

Mudimbe, V.Y. *The Invention of Africa: Gnosis, Philosophy and the Order of Knowledge*. Bloomington: Indiana University Press, 1988.

Ngugi wa, Thiong'o. *Devil on the Cross*. London: Heinemann, 1982.

Obiechina, Emmanuel. *Culture, Tradition and Society in the West African Novel*. Cambridge: Cambridge University Press, 1975.

————. "The Dilemma of the African Intellectual in the Modern World." *Liberal Education* 78.2 (March–April 1992).

————. *Literature for the Masses: An Analytical Study of Popular Pamphleteering in Nigeria*. Enugu: Nwanko-Ifejika Publishers, 1971.

————. *Language and Theme: Essays on African Literature*. Washington, DC: Howard University Press, 1990.

Ogunyemi, Chikwenye Okonjo. "Womanism: The Dynamics of the Contemporary Black Female Novel in English." *Signs: Journal of Women in Culture and Society* IX.11 (1985).

Omotoso, Kole. *Season of Migration to the South*. Cape Town, South Africa: Tafelberg Publishers, 1994.

"Politics of Representation: Struggles for the Control of Identity." Brochure. Institute for Advanced Study and Research in the African Humanities. Northwestern University, 1992.

Radin, Paul. *Primitive Man as Philosopher*. New York: Dover Publications, 1955.

Robbins, Bruce, ed. *Intellectuals: Aesthetics, Politics, Academics*. Minneapolis: University of Minnesota Press, 1990.

Sartre, Jean-Paul. *Between Existentialism and Marxism*. New York: Pantheon Books, 1974.

Sivanandan, A. *Communities of Resistance: Writings on Black Struggles for Socialism*. London: Verso, 1990.

Soyinka, Wole. *Myth, Literature and the African World*. Cambridge: Cambridge University Press, 1976.

————. *Art, Dialogue, and Outrage: Essays on Literature and Culture*. Ibadan: New Horn Press, 1988; London: Methuen, 1994.

# Select Bibliography

Achebe, Chinua. *Anthills of the Savannah*. New York: Anchor Press, 1988.

———. *Arrow of God*. London: Heinemann Educational Books, 1969.

———. *A Man of the People*. London: Heinemann, 1966.

———. *No Longer at Ease*. London: Heinemann, 1977.

———. *Things Fall Apart*. London: H.E.B., 1958.

———. "African Literature as Restoration of Celebration." *Chinua Achebe: A Celebration*. Eds. Kirsten Holst and Anna Rutherford. Oxford: H.E.B., 1990: 1–10.

———. "The African Writer and the English Language." *Morning Yet on Creation Day*. London: H.E.B., 1975: 55–62.

———. *Hopes and Impediments: Selected Essays*. New York: Doubleday, 1989.

———. *Morning Yet on Creation Day: Essays*. Garden City, NY: Anchor/Doubleday, 1975.

———. "The Novelist as Teacher." *Morning Yet on Creation* Day. London: H.E.B., 1975: 42–45.

Adams, Mohammed. "Nigeria–the Busted Boom." *International Perspectives* Jan.–Feb. 1987: 17–20.

Ade-Ajayi. *History and the Nation and Other Addresses*. Ibadan: Ibadan University Press, 1990.

Adedeji. J.A. "Oral Tradition and Contemporary Theatre in Nigeria." *Research in African Literature* 2.2 (Fall 1971).

Adeeko, Adeleke. "The Language of Head-Calling: A Review Essay on Yoruba Metalanguage." Ed. Iperi Yoruba. *Research in African Literatures* XXIII.1 (Spring 1992): 197–201.

Adelugba, Dapo. "Trance and Theatre: The Nigerian Experience." *Drama and Theatre in Nigeria: A Critical Source Book*. Ed. Yemi Ogunbiyi. Lagos: Nigeria Magazine, 1981: 203–218.

Aizenberg, Edna. "The Untruths of the Nation: *Petals of Blood* and Fuentes's *The Death of Artemio Cruz.*" *Research in African Literatures* XXX.I (Winter 1990): 58–103.

Alatas, Sayed. *Intellectuals in Developing Countries*. London: Frank Cass, 1977.

Albright, H.D., W.P. Halstead, and L. Mitchell. *Principles of Theatre Art*. 2nd ed. Boston: Houghton Mifflin, 1968.

Aluko, T.M. *Kinsman And Foreman*. London: Heinemann, 1966.

Amadiume, Ifi. *Male Daughters, Female Husbands*. London: Zed Book Ltd., 1987.

Amin, Samir. *Eurocentrism*. Trans. Russell Moore. New York: Monthly Press Review, 1989.

Amuta, Chidi. *Towards a Sociology of African Literature*. Oguta Zim, 1986.

Anderson, Benedict. *Imagined Communities: Reflections on the Origin and Spread of Nationalism*. London: Verso, 1983.

*Anglo-African*. 1862–65.

Appiah, Kwame Anthony. "Is the Post- in Postmodernism the Post-in Postcolonial?" *Critical Inquiry* XVII (Winter 1991): 336–357.

———. "The Postcolonial and the Postmodern." In *My Father's House: Africa in the Philosophy of Culture*. Oxford: Oxford University Press, 1992: 137–57.

Aristotle. *The Ethics of Aristotle*. Trans. J. Thomson. Harmondsworth: Penguin Books, 1970.

Armah, Ayi Kwei. *The Beautyful Ones Are Not Yet Born*. London: Heinemann, 1969.

———. *The Healers*. London: Heinemann, 1979.

———. *Two Thousand Seasons*. Nairobi: East African Publishing House, 1973.

Ashby, Eric. *University: British, Indian, African*. Cambridge: Cambridge University Press, 1966.

Ashcroft, Bill, Gareth Griffiths, and Helen Tiffin. *The Empire Writes Back: Theory and Practice in Post-Colonial Literatures*. London: Routledge, 1989.

Ayandele, E.A. "Africa: The Challenge of Higher Education." *Daedalus* (Spring 1982): 165–178.

———. *The Educated Elite in Nigerian Society*. Ibadan: Ibadan University Press, 1974.

Bakhtin, Mikhail. "Discourse Typology in Prose." *Readings in Russian Poetics: Formalist and Structuralist Views*. Eds. Ladislav Matejka and Krystyna Pomoroska. Cambridge, MA: MIT Press, 1971.

Bakhtin, M. M. & P. M. Medvedev. *The Formal Method in Literary Scholarship: A Critical Introduction to Sociological Poetics*. Trans. Albert J. Wehrle. Cambridge, MA: Harvard University Press, 1989.

Bamgbose, Ayo. "Deprived, Endangered, and Dying Languages." *Diogenes* 161, 41.1: 19–25.

Barbag-Stoll, Ann. *Social and Linguistic History of Nigerian Pidgin English*. Tubingen: Stalfenberg-Verlag, 1983.

Basden, G.T. *Among the Ibos of Nigeria*. London: Seeley, 1921.

Beier, Ulli. "Yoruba Theatre." *Introduction to African Literature*. London: Longman, 1967.

Bishop, Rand. *African Literature, African Critics*. Westport, CT:Greenwood, 1988.

Blyden, Edward W. "An Address before the Maine State Colonization Society, Portland, Maine, June 26th, 1862." In *Black Spokesman: Selected Published Writings of E. W. Blyden*. Ed. Hollis R. Lynch. Cass Library of African Studies: Africana Modern Library. London: Frank Cass & Co. Ltd., 1971.

———. *From West Africa to Palestine*. Freetown, Sierra Leone: T.J. Sawyer, 1973.

Booth, James. *Writers and Politics in Nigeria*. NewYork: Africana Publishing Company, 1981.

Boulton, Marjorie. *The Anatomy of Drama*. London: Routledge and Kegan Paul, 1960.

Brantlinger, Patrick. "Victorians and Africans: The Genealogy of the Myth of the Dark Continent." In *"Race,"Writing, and Difference*. Ed. Henry Louis Gates, Jr. Chicago: University of Chicago Press, 1986: 185–222.

Brink, Andre. *Writing in a State of Siege*: *Essays on Politics and Literature*. New York: Summit Books, 1983.

Cabral, Amilcar. *Unity and Struggle*. London: Heinemann, 1980.

Callaway, Helen. *Gender, Culture and Empire*: *European Woman in Colonial Nigeria*. Urbana: University of Illinois Press, 1987.

Campbell, Robert. "[Editorial]." *Anglo-African*, 12 September 1863.

Certeau, Michel de. *Heterologies*. Trans. Brian Massumi. Minneapolis: University of Minnesota Press, 1986.

———. *The Writing of History*. Trans. Tom Conley. "Translator's Introduction." New York: Columbia University Press, 1988.

Clausen, Christopher. "'National Literatures' in English: Toward a New Paradigm." *New Literary History* XXV.1 (Winter 1994): 61–72.

Clifford, James, and George Marcus. *Writing Culture*: *The Poetics andPolitics of Ethnography*. Berkeley: University of California Press, 1986.

Comas, James. "The Presence of Theory/Theorizing the Present." *Research in African Literatures* XXI.1 (Spring 1990): 5–31.

Craig, David, ed. *Marxists on Literature*. Harmondsworth: Penguin, 1975.

Culler, Jonathan. *On Deconstruction*: *Theory & Criticism after Structuralism*. Ithaca: Cornell University Press, 1982.

Curtin, Philip D. *Africa and the West*: *Intellectual Responses to European Culture*. Madison: University of Wisconsin Press, 1972.

Dabydeen, David and Nana Wilson-Tagoe. *A Reader's Guide to West Indian and Black Literature*. London: Hassib Publishing Limited, 1988.

Daiches, David. *Critical Approaches to Literature*. London: Longmans, 1969.

Darwin, Charles. *The Descent of Man and Selection in Relation to Sex*. 1st ed. London: John Murray, 1871.

Davies, Carol Boyce, ed. *Ngambika*: *Studies of Women in African Literature*. Trenton, NJ: Africa World Press, 1986.

DeGraff, Geoffrey and Hena Maes-Jelinek, eds. *Crisis and Creativity in the New Literatures in English*. Amsterdam: Rodopi, 1990.

Derrida, Jacques. *Margins of Philosophy*. Trans. Alan Bass. Chicago: University of Chicago Press, 1982.

Desai, Gaurav. "English as an African Language." *English Today* XXXIV.9 (April 1993): 4–11.

Dhareshwar, Vivek (with James Clifford). *Traveling Theories, Traveling Theorists*. Santa Cruz: Center for Cultural Studies, 1989.

Du Bois, W.E.B. *The Souls of Black Folk*. New York: New American Library, 1965.

Echeruo, Michael J.C. *Victorian Lagos*: *Aspects of Nineteenth Century Lagos Life*. London: Macmillan Education Ltd., 1977.

Egejuru, Phanuel. *Black Writers*: *White Audience*. Hicksville, NY: Exposition Press, 1978.

———. *The Seed Yams Have Been Eaten*. Ibadan: Heinemann (Nigeria), 1993.

———. *Towards African Literary Independence*. Westport, CT: Greenwood Press, 1980.

Egri, Lajos. *The Art of Dramatic Writing*. New York: Simon and Schuster, 1960.

Egudu, R.N. "Anglophone African Poetry and Vernacular Rhetoric: The Example of Christopher Okigbo." *Lagos Review of English Studies* I.1 (1979): 104–113.

———. "Social Values and Thought in Traditional Literature: The Case of Igbo Proverbs and Poetry." *Nigerian Libraries* VIII.2 (1972): 63–84.

Emenyonu, Ernest. *The Rise of the Igbo Novel*. Ibadan: Oxford University Press, 1978.

Emenyeonu, Ernest et al., eds. *Critical Theory & African Literature*. Ibadan: Heinemann, 1987.

Enekwe, O.O. *Igbo Masks: The Oneness of Ritual and Theatre*. Lagos: Nigeria Magazine, 1987.

Ewing, A.C. *Ethics*. London: The English Universities Press Ltd., 1973.

Fagunwa, D.O. *Ogboju Ode ninu Igbo Irunmale*. Edinburgh: Nelson, 1938. Trans. Wole Soyinka as *The Forest of a Thousand Daemons*. London: Nelson, 1968.

Fanon, Frantz. *Black Skin, White Masks*. New York: Grove Press, 1967.

―――. *A Dying Colonialism*. Trans. Haakon Chevalier. New York: Grove Weidenfeld, 1965.

―――. *The Wretched of the Earth*. New York: Grove Press, 1968.

Freud, Sigmund. *Jokes and Their Relation to the Unconsciousness*. New York: Norton, 1963.

Frow, John. *Marxism and Literary History*. Oxford: Blackwell, 1986.

Gakwandi, S.A. *The Novel and Contemporary Experience in Africa*. New York: Africana, 1977.

Gassner, John, ed. *A Treasury of the Theatre*. Vol. 1. New York: Simon and Schuster, 1967.

Gates, Henry Louis, Jr., ed. *Black Literature and Literary Theory*. New York: Methuen, 1984.

―――. *"Race," Writing and Difference*. Chicago: University of Chicago Press 1986.

Gella, Alexander, ed. *The Intelligentsia and the Intellectuals: Theory, Method and Case Study*. London: Sage, 1976.

Gerard, Albert. "Historiography of Black Africa: A Personal Testimony." *African Literature Association Bulletin* XIX.3 (Summer 1993): 24–32.

Gilman, Sander L. "Black Bodies, White Bodies: Toward an Iconography of Female Sexuality in Late Nineteenth-Century Art, Medicine, and Literature." In *"Race," Writing and Difference*. Ed. Henry Louis Gates, Jr. Chicago: University of Chicago Press, 1986: 223–261.

"GPD." "Who's a Third World Writer?" *The Economic & Political Weekly*. Bombay, India (November 22, 1986): 2022.

Greenblatt, Stephen. "Culture." *Critical Terms for Literary Study*. Eds. Frank Lentricchia and Thomas McLaughlin. Chicago: University of Chicago Press, 1990: 225–232.

Griaule, Marcel. *Conversations with Ogotemmeli*. London: Oxford University Press, 1965.

Gugelberger, George, ed. *Marxism and African Literature*. Trenton, NJ: Africa World Press, 1985.

Haraway, Donna. "'Reading Buchi Emecheta': Contests for Women' s Experience in Women's Studies." *Inscriptions* 3–4 (1988).

Harlow, Barbara. *Resistance Literature*. New York: Methuen, 1987.

Hopkins, Slade. "Dream on Monkey Mountain and the Popular Response." *Caribbean Quarterly* 23.2 (1977).

Horn, Andrew. "Ritual Drama and the Theatrical: The Case of Bori Spirit Mediumship." In *Drama and Theatre in Nigeria: A Critical Source Book*. Ed. Yemi Ogunbiyi. Lagos: Nigeria Magazine, 1981: 181–202.

Horton, Robin. "The Gods as Guests: An Aspect of Kalabari Religious Life." In *Drama and Theatre in Nigeria: A Critical Source Book*. Ed. Yemi Ogunbiyi. Lagos: Nigeria Magazine, 1981: 81–112.

―――. "Ikaki: the Tortoise Masquerade." In *Drama and Theatre in Nigeria: A Critical Source Book*. Ed. Yemi Ogunbiyi. Lagos: Nigeria Magazine, 1981: 481–94.

Hunt, Raymond. "The University Social Research Center: Its Role in the Knowledge Making Process." *Knowledge* 2–1 (September1980): 77–92.

Huszar, George B. de, ed. *The Intellectuals: A Controversial Portrait.* Glencoe, NJ: The Free Press, 1960.

Innes, C.L. *Chinua Achebe.* Cambridge: Cambridge University Press, 1990.

Innes, C.L. and Bernth Lindfors, eds. *Critical Perspectives on Chinua Achebe.* Washington, DC: Three Continents Press, 1978.

Irele, Abiola. *The African Experience in Literature & Ideology.* London: Heinemann, 1981.

———. "African Letters: the Making of a Tradition." *Yale Journal of Criticism* V.1 (1991).

———. "African Literature and the Language Question." *The African Experience in Literature and Ideology* (1981): 43–65.

———. "The African Imagination." *Research in African Literatures* XXI.1 (Spring 1990): 49–67.

———. "The Criticism of Modern African Literature." *The African Experience in Literature and Ideology.* Ibadan: H.E.B., 1981: 27–42.

———. *In Praise of Alienation.* Privately published, 1987.

Iyayi, Festus. *Heroes.* Harlow: Longman, 1986.

James, Louis. *The Islands in Between.* London: Oxford University Press, 1968.

Jameson, Fredic. *Postmodernism; Or, The Cultural Logic of Late Capitalism.* Durham: Duke University Press, 1991.

Jeyifo, Biodun. "The Nature of Things: Arrested Decolonization and Critical Theory." *Research in African Literatures* XXI.1 (Spring, 1990): 34–48.

———. "Literary Theory and Theories of Decolonization." *Literary Theory and African Literature.* Josef Gugler, Hans-Jurgen Lusebrink, and Jurgen, eds. Martini. Hamburg: LIT Verlag, 1994.

———. "Africanist Scholarship and the Reconstruction of the Humanities Curriculum." Lecture. Ohio State University, Columbus, Ohio, 22 May 1991.

Killam, G.D., ed. *African Writers on African Writing.* Evanston, IL: Northwestern University Press, 1973.

Kimbugwe, Henry. "Grace Ogot: The African Lady." *East African Journal* VI.4 (April 1969): 23.

Kincaid, Jamaica. *A Small Place.* New York: Farrar, Straus, Giroux, 1988.

Kopytoff, Jean Herskovits. *A Preface to Modern Nigeria: The "Sierra Leonians" in Yoruba, 1830–1890.* Madison: University of Wisconsin Press, 1965.

Kunene, Mazis. *Emperor Shaka the Great.* London: Heinemann, 1979.

Larson, Charles. *The Emergence of African Fiction.* Bloomington: Indiana University Press, 1972.

Levine, Philippa. " 'The Humanising Influences of Five O'clock Tea': Victorian Feminist Periodicals." *Victorian Studies* 33 (Winter 1990): 293–306.

Levi-Strauss, Claude. *Structural Anthropology.* Trans. Claire Jacobs and Brooke Grundfest. New York: Doubleday, 1967.

Lindfors, Bernth, ed. *Interviews with East African Writers, Publishers, Editors, and Scholars.* Athens, Ohio: Center for International Studies, African Program, 1980, 123–125.

Lloyd, David. *Nationalism and Minor Literature: James Clarence Mangan and the Emergence of Irish Cultural Nationalism.* Berkeley: University of California Press, 1987.

Longfellow, H.W. *Poems.* London: Dent, 1970.

Macherey, Pierre. *A Theory of Literary Production.* London: Routledge, 1978.

Machlup, Fritz. *Knowledge and Knowledge Production.* Princeton: Princeton University Press, 1980.

Martin, Wallace. *Recent Theories of Narrative*. Ithaca: Cornell University Press, 1986.

Mbembe, Achille. "The Banality of Power and the Aesthetics of Vulgarity in the Postcolony." *Public Culture* IV.2 (Spring 1992).

Mehta, Xerxes. "Performance Art: Problems of Description and Evaluation." *Journal of Dramatic Theory and Criticism* V.1 (Fall 1990).

Miller, Christopher L. "Theories of Africans: the Question of Literary Anthropology." *Critical Inquiry* XIII.1 (Autumn 1986): 120–139.

Miller, J. Hillis. "Tradition and Difference." *Diacritics* (Winter 1972).

Mlana, Penina Muhando. "Creating in the Mother-Tongue: The Challenges to the African Writer Today." *Research in African Literatures* XXI.4 (Winter 1990): 5–14.

Mofolo, Thomas. *Chaka*. Trans. D.P. Kunene. Oxford: Heinemann, 1981.

Moore, Gerald. *The Chosen Tongue*: *English Writing in the Tropical World*. London: Longmans, 1969.

Moyers, Bill. "The Fabric of Memory" (interview with Chinua Achebe). *Clinton Street Quarterly* XI.1 (Spring 1989): 8–12.

Mudimbe, V.Y. *The Invention of Africa*: *Gnosis, Philosophy and the Order of Knowledge*. Bloomington: Indiana University Press, 1988.

Mukherjee, Bharati. *The Holder of the World*. New York: Knopf, 1993.

Mutiso, G.C.M. *Socio-Political Thought in African Literature*. London: Macmillan, 1974.

Nazareth, Peter. "The Hospital." In *Two Radio Plays*. Nairobi: East African Literature Bureau, 1976.

———. "The Marvelous Latin American Reality of Gabriel Garcia Marquez." In *The Third World Writer*. Nairobi: Kenya Literature Bureau, 1978.

Nettler, G. "A Measure of Alienation." *American Sociological Reviews* XXII (December 1957).

Ngara, Emmanuel. *Art and Ideology in the African Novel*. London: Heinemann, 1985.

Ngugi, wa Thiong'o. *Decolonizing the Mind*: *The Politics of Language in African Literature*. London: James Currey Ltd., 1986.

———. *Devil on the Cross*. London: Heinemann, 1982.

———. *A Grain of Wheat*. London: Heinemann, 1967.

———. *Moving the Centre*: *The Struggle for Cultural Freedoms*. London: James Currey Ltd., 1993.

Njaka, E.N. *Igbo Political Culture*. Evanston, IL: Northwestern University Press, 1974.

Nwachukwu-Agbada, J.O.J. "Interview." *Commonwealth* XIII.1 (1990).

Nwankwo, Nkem. *A Song for Fela & Other Poems*. Nashville, TN: Nigerhouse, 1993.

Obiechina, Emmanuel. "Africa in the Soul of Dispersed Children: West African Literature from the Era of the Slave Trade." *Nsukka Studies in Africa in Literature* IV (January 1986): 101–160.

———. "Art and Artifice in Okara's *The Voice*," *Okike*: *An African Journal of New Writing* 3 (1972).

———. *Culture, Tradition and Society in the West African Novel*. Cambridge: Cambridge University Press, 1975.

———. "The Dilemma of the African Intellectual in the Modern World." *Liberal Education* 78.2 (March–April 1992).

———. *Language and Theme*: *Essays on African Literature*. Washington, DC: Howard University Press, 1990.

———. *Literature for the* Masses: An *Analytical Study of Popular Pamphleteering in Nigeria*. Enugu: Nwankwo-Ifejika Publishers, 1971.

Obienyem, J.C. "Oge," (poem), In *"Akpa Uche"*: *An Anthology of Modern Igbo Verse*. Ed. R.M. Ekechukwu. Ibadan: Oxford University Press, 1975.

Ogot, Grace. *The Graduate*. Nairobi: Uzima Press, 1980.

——. *Miaha*. Nairobi: Heinemann, 1983. Translated as *The Strange Bride*. Nairobi: Heinemann Kenya, 1989.

——. *The Other Woman*. Nairobi: Transafrica Publishers, 1976.

——. *The Promised Land*. Nairobi: East African Publishing House, 1966; 1974.

——. "Ward Nine." *Transitions* III.13 (March/April 1964): 41.

——. "The Year of Sacrifice." *Black Orpheus* XI (1963): 41–50.

Ogunba, Oyin. "Traditional African Festival Drama." In *Theatre in Africa*. Eds. Oyin Ogunba and Abiola Irele. Ibadan: Ibadan University Press, 1978.

——. "Traditional Content of the Plays of Wole Soyinka." *African Literature Today* 4 (1970).

Ogungbesan, Kola. "Wole Soyinka and the Novelist's Responsibility in Africa." In *New West African Literature*. Ed. Kola Ogungbesan. London: Heinemann, 1979.

Ogunbiyi, Yemi, ed. *Drama and Theatre in Nigeria: A Critical Source Book*. Lagos: Nigeria Magazine, 1981.

Ogunyemi, Chikwenye Okonjo. "Womanism: The Dynamics of the Contemporary Black Female Novel in English." *Signs: Journal of Women in Culture and Society* XI.11 (1985).

Okafor, Dubem. "The Cultural Validity of Soyinka's Plays." *Nsukka Studies in African Literature* I.2 (March 1979): 12–29.

——. *The Dance of Death: Nigerian History and Christopher Okigbo's Poetry*. Trenton, NJ: Africa World Press, 1998.

——. *Nationalism in Okigbo's Poetry*. Enugu, Nigeria: Fourth Dimension Publishers, 1980.

Okagbue, Osy. "Aspects of African and Caribbean Theatre: A Comparative Study." Unpublished Ph.D. dissertation, University of Leeds, 1990a.

——. "Identity, Exile and Migration: The Dialectics of Content and Form in West Indian Theatre" *New Literatures Review* 19 (Summer South): 1990b.

Okara, Gabriel. "African Speech . . . English Words." *Transition* IV.10.

——. *The Voice*. London: Heinemann, 1970.

Okeke-Ezigbo, Emeka. "The Role of the Nigerian Writer in a Carthaginian Society." *Okike* XXI (July 1982): 28–37.

——. "What Is a National Literature?" *Nigeria Magazine* 149 (1984): 1–13.

Okigbo, Pius N.C. *A History of Planning in Nigeria*. London: James Currey, 1987.

Okpaku, Joseph, ed. *New African Literature and Arts*. New York: Thomas Crowell Co., 1970.

Okpewho, Isidore. "Is There a Nigerian Literature?" *The Guardian* (Lagos) 6 October 1990: 18.

——. *Myth in Africa*. Cambridge: Cambridge University Press, 1983.

Omotoso, Kole. *Season of Migration to the South*. Cape Town, South Africa: Tafelberg Publishers, 1994.

Ondaatje, Michael. *Coming Through Slaughter*. New York: Penguin, 1976.

Onwuejeogwu, M.A. "An African Indigenous Ideology: Communal Individualism" (Inaugural Lecture). University of Benin, Nigeria, 1986.

——. *An Igbo Civilization*. London: Ethnographica, 1981.

Osofisan, Femi. "Enter the Carthaginian Critic . . . ? A Comment on Okeke-Ezigbo's 'The Role of the Writer in a Carthaginian Society.' " *Okike* XXI (July 1982): 38–44.

Osundare, Niyi. "African Literature and the Crisis of Post-Structuralist Theorizing," *Dialogue in African Philosophy Monographs Series*. Ibadan: Option Books and Information Services, 1993.

Ousmane, Sembene. *Xala*. London: Heinemann, 1975.

Palmer, Eustace. *An Introduction to the African Novel*. London: Heinemann, 1972.

Peterson, Kirsten Holst. *Criticism and Ideology*. Stockholm: Uppsala, 1988.

Plato. *The Collected Dialogues of Plato*. Eds. Edith Hamilton and Huntington Cairns. Princeton: Princeton University Press, 1963.

——— . *The Republic*. Trans. Benjamin Jowett. Cleveland: The World Publishing Company, 1946.

"Politics of Representation: Struggles for the Control of Identity." Brochure. Institute for Advanced Study and Research in the African Humanities. Northwestern University, 1992.

Popkin, Richard H. "The Philosophical Basis of Eighteenth-Century Racism." In *Studies in Eighteenth-Century Culture*: *Racism in the Eighteenth Century*. Ed. Harold E. Pagliaro. Cleveland: The Case Western Reserve University Press, 1973: 245–262.

Radin, Paul. *Primitive Man as Philosopher*. New York: Dover Publications, 1955.

*Research in African Literatures* XXIII.1 (Spring 1992). Special Issue: The Language Question.

Retamar. Roberto. *Caliban and Other Essays*. Minneapolis: University of Minnesota Press, 1989.

Robbins, Bruce, ed. *Intellectuals*: *Aesthetics, Politics, Academics*. Minneapolis: University of Minnesota Press, 1990.

Robson, Andrew E. "The Use of English in Achebe's *Anthills of Savannah*." *CLA Journal* 37.4 (June 1994): 365–76.

Roscoe, Adrian. *Mother Is Gold*: *A Study in West African Literature*. Cambridge: Cambridge University Press, 1971.

Sartre, Jean-Paul. *Between Existentialism and Marxism*. New York: Pantheon Books, 1974.

——— . *What Is Literature*? New York: Pantheon Books, 1949.

Schechner, R. *Performance Theory*. New York: Routledge, 1988.

Schiebinger, Londa. "The Anatomy of Difference: Race and Sex in Eighteenth Century Science." *Eighteenth-Century Studies* 23.4 (Summer 1990): 387–406.

Sidney, Philip. "An Apologie for Poetrie." *The Great Critics*. Eds. James Harry Smith and Ed Winfield. New York: W.W. Norton, 1951.

——— . "Astrophel and Stella." *The Norton Anthology of English Literature*, Vol. I. Eds. E. Talbot Donaldson et al. New York: W.W. Norton, 1968.

Sivanandan, A. *Communities of Resistance*: *Writings on Black Struggles for Socialism*. London: Verso, 1990.

Soyinka, Wole. *Art, Dialogue and Outrage*: *Essays on Literature and Culture*. Ibadan: New Horn Press (September 1963): 15–16.

——— . *The Interpreters*. London: Deutsch, 1965.

——— . *Myth, Literature and the African World*. Cambridge: Cambridge University Press, 1976.

Spitzer, Leo. *The Creoles of Sierra Leone*: *Responses to Colonialism, 1870–1945*. Madison: University of Wisconsin Press, 1974.

Stanislavsky, Konstantin. *Stanislavsky and the Art of the Stage*. Trans. David Magarshack. London: Faber and Faber, 1967.

Talbot, P. Amaury. *In the Shadow of the Bush*. London: Heinemann, 1912.

Tucker, Martin. *Africa in Modern Fiction*. New York: Frederick Ungar, 1967.

Tutuola, Amos. *The Palmwine Drinkard*. London: Faber and Faber, 1952.

Veeser, H. A., ed. *The New Historicism*. New York: Routledge, 1989.

Walcott, Derek. *Dream on Monkey Mountain and Other Plays*. London: Jonathan Cape, 1972.

——— . *The Joker of Seville and O Babylon!: Two Plays*. London: Jonathan Cape, 1979.

——— . "The Muse of History." *Critics on Caribbean Literature*. Ed. Edward Baugh. London: George Allen and Unwin, 1978.

——— . Interview. "Profile of a West Indian Writer." *The South Bank Show* (15 January 1989).

Wali, Obi. "The Dead End of African Literature." *Transition* IV.10 (September 1963): 13–15.

Wallace, Alfred Russell. *The Action of Natural Selection on Man*. University Series. 6. New Haven, CT: Charles C. Chatfield & Co., 1871.

White, Hayden. "The Politics of Historical Interpretation: Discipline and DeSublimation." In *The Content of the Form: Narrative Discourse and Historical Representation*. Baltimore: Johns Hopkins University Press, 1987: 58–82.

——— . "The Value of Narrativity in the Representation of Reality." In *The Content of the Form: Narrative Discourse and Historical Representation*. Baltimore: Johns Hopkins University Press, 1987: 1–25.

——— . "The Question of Narrative in Contemporary Historical Theory." In *The Content of the Form: Narrative Discourse and Historical Representation*. Baltimore: Johns Hopkins University Press, 1987: 26–57.

Wren, Robert. *Achebe's World: The Historical and Cultural Context of the Novels*. Washington, DC: Three Continents Press, 1980.

Zabus, Chantal. *The African Palimpsest: Indigenization of Language in the West African Europhone Novel*. Amsterdam: Rodopi, 1991.

——— . "The Logos-Eaters: The Igbo Ethno-Text." *China Achebe: A Celebration*. Portsmouth, NH: Heinemann, 1990: 19–30.

# Index

# About the Contributors

MICHAEL J.C. ECHERUO is William Safire Professor of Letters at Syracuse University. His publications include *Mortality, poems*; *Joyce Cary and the Novel of Africa*; *Victorian Lagos*; *The Conditioned Imagination: Studies in the Exo-Cultural Stereotype*; *The Dimension of Order*, and an edition of Shakespeare's *The Tempest*. He is currently working on a study of Chinua Achebe, having completed and published a comprehensive dictionary of Igbo language.

ROMANUS N. EGUDU is currently Professor of English at the University of Benin, Nigeria. Previously, he had served in a string of academic and administrative capacities, including Senior Lecturer in English, University of Nigeria, Nsukka; Professor of English and Director of Graduate Studies, University of Benin; Chairman, Anambra State Television Corporation; Provost, Eha-Amufu College of Education, Nigeria; and Director, Nigerian Universities Office, Washington, DC. He has written and published many books and several articles on African literature, comparative literature, and oral literature, as well as a book of his own poetry.

BIODUN JEYIFO is Professor of English at Cornell University. He taught previously at the universities of Ibadan and Ife in Nigeria, and at Oberlin College. He served in the early 1980s as National President of the Academic Staff Union of Nigerian Universities (ASUU) and as a member of the Central Working Committee of the Nigerian Labor Congress, the Central Federation of Nigeria's Trade Unions. Professor Jeyifo is the author of *The Truthful Lie, the Yoruba Popular Travelling Theatre of Nigeria,* and has written extensively on Marxist and postcolonial critical theory.

BERNTH LINDFORS is a Professor of English and African Literature at the University of Texas at Austin. He was the founding editor of *Research in African Literatures*, which he edited for about twenty years. He has written and edited many books, as well as numerous articles on anglophone African literature.

PETER NAZARETH is Professor of English and African-American World Studies at the University of Iowa. He was born in Uganda of Goan parents, his mother being born in Malaysia. Three of his plays were broadcast by the African Service of the BBC. He has published two novels and four books of literary criticism, including *In the Trickster Tradition: The Novels of Andrew Salkey, Francis Ebejer and Ishmael Reed*. He received the 1984 Distinguished Independent Study Course Award from the National University Continuing Education Association for his course and study guide, *Literatures of the African Peoples*.

CHIMALUM NWANKWO has taught at the University of Nigeria, Nsukka, and East Carolina University in Greenville. He is presently an Associate Professor in the English Department at North Carolina State University in Raleigh, where he teaches a broad range of courses that sometimes include American literature, world literature, African-American literature, and African literature. His diverse publications of critical essays, poems, and book reviews include a play, *The Trumpet Parable* (1985); two volumes of poetry, *Feet of the Limping Dancers* (1986), and the prize-winning *Toward the Aerial Zone* (1988); and a critical study, *The Works of Ngugi wa Thiong'o*. A reader and consultant to a handful of journals, Nwankwo's latest book of poems, *Voices from Deep Water*, is expected soon. Professor Nwankwo is still very active in the theater.

WOLE OGUNDELE was for many years Senior Lecturer in English at the Obafemi Awolowo University in Nigeria. He has written numerous essays on modern African Anglophone poetry and comparative ethnopoetics. He has held visiting fellowships at Corpus Christi College, Oxford, the University of Wisconsin at Parkside, and the University of Bayreuth, Germany. Dr. Ogundele is currently working on a book on the place of satire in the dramatic genius of Wole Soyinka.

DUBEM OKAFOR is a lover and teacher of poetry and literature. He was formerly Lecturer in English at the University of Nigeria, Nsukka; Reader and Chair of English, and Dean of Arts and Languages at Eha-Amufu College of Education; and quite recently, Associate Professor of English at Rockland Community College of the State University of New York. Dr. Okafor is presently in the English Department of Kutztown University of Pennsylvania, where he teaches world literature and African and postcolonial literatures. His publications include *The Dance of Death: Nigerian History and Christopher Okigbo's Poetry*; *Garlands of Anguish*; *My Testaments*; *Don't Let Him Die* (Memorial Anthology of Poems, edited with Chinua Achebe); *Jungle Muse* (edited poetry by several newer Nigerian Poets); *Nationalism in Okigbo's Poetry*; and essays and review essays in *Bim, Nsukka Studies in*

*African Literature, Ganga, Commonwealth Novel in English, Research in African Literatures*, and international fiction.

OSITA OKAGBUE is Senior Lecturer in Theater and Performance Studies at the University of Plymouth, Exmouth Campus. Formerly Assistant Lecturer in Drama/Literature at the University of Nigeria, Nsukka, Dr. Okagbue has published articles on contemporary African/Caribbean theater and African traditional theater in *Maske und Kothurn, New Literatures Review, Contemporary Dramatists, Contemporary American Dramatists, African Writers, Okike Educational Supplement*, and *Assaph.*

ISIDORE OKPEWHO is Professor of English, Comparative Literature, and Africana Studies and Chair of the Department of Africana Studies at Binghamton University. His scholarly publications include *The Epic in Africa*; *Myth in Africa: The Heritage of African Poetry*; *The Oral Performance in Africa*; and *African Oral Literature*. He has also published three novels: *The Victims*; *The Last Duty* (winner of the African Arts Prize); and *Tides* (winner of the Commonwealth Writers Prize for Africa).

CHARLIE SUGNET is Associate Professor of English and Director of the Creative Writing Program at the University of Minnesota. He has published widely in scholarly and literary journals.

SAM UKALA is Senior Lecturer in Theater Studies and Oral Literature at Edo State University, Ekpoma, Nigeria. He is a playwright, poet, prose fiction writer, theater director, and actor. His published plays include *The Slave Wife*; *The Log in Your Eye*; *The Trials of Obiamaka Elema*; *Break a Boil*; and *Akpakaland*, winner of the Association of Nigerian Authors and the British Council Prize for Drama, 1989. His short stories and poems have appeared in several anthologies, including *The Fate of Vultures* (BBC Prize-Winning Poetry). He is a keen researcher of folk theater, on which he draws to develop his theory of "folkism."